Politics and Suicide

Politics and Suicide argues that whilst the historical lineage of suicidal politics is recognised, the significance of autodestruction to the political remains under examined. It contends that practices like suicide-bombing do not simply embody a strange or abnormal 'suicidal' articulation of the political, but rather, that the existence of suicidal politics tells us something fundamental about the political as such.

Recent world events have emphatically shown our need for tools with which to develop better understandings of the politics of suicide. Through the exploration of several arresting case studies, including the 'Kamikaze' bombers of World War II, Jan Palach's self-immolation in 1969, Cold War nuclear deterrence, and the suicide-terrorist attacks of 9/11, Michelsen asks how we might talk of a political suicide in any of these contexts. The book charts how political processes 'go suicidal', and asks how we might still consider them to be political in such a case. It investigates how suicide can function as 'politics'.

A strong contribution to the fields of philosophy, particularly with reference to the writings of Gilles Deleuze and Felix Guattari, and international relations theory, this work will also be of interest to students and scholars of political theory and terrorism and political violence.

Nicholas Michelsen is Lecturer in International Relations Theory in the Department of War Studies at King's College London.

INTERVENTIONS

Edited by: Jenny Edkins, Aberystwyth University and
Nick Vaughan-Williams, University of Warwick

The Series provides a forum for innovative and interdisciplinary work that engages with alternative critical, post-structural, feminist, postcolonial, psychoanalytic and cultural approaches to international relations and global politics. In our first 5 years we have published 60 volumes.

We aim to advance understanding of the key areas in which scholars working within broad critical post-structural traditions have chosen to make their interventions, and to present innovative analyses of important topics. Titles in the series engage with critical thinkers in philosophy, sociology, politics and other disciplines and provide situated historical, empirical and textual studies in international politics.

We are very happy to discuss your ideas at any stage of the project: just contact us for advice or proposal guidelines. Proposals should be submitted directly to the Series Editors:

- Jenny Edkins (jennyedkins@hotmail.com) and
- Nick Vaughan-Williams (N.Vaughan-Williams@Warwick.ac.uk).

'As Michel Foucault has famously stated, "knowledge is not made for understanding; it is made for cutting" In this spirit The Edkins–Vaughan-Williams Interventions series solicits cutting edge, critical works that challenge mainstream understandings in international relations. It is the best place to contribute post disciplinary works that think rather than merely recognize and affirm the world recycled in IR's traditional geopolitical imaginary.'

Michael J. Shapiro, University of Hawai'i at Manoa, USA

Critical Theorists and International Relations
Edited by Jenny Edkins and Nick Vaughan-Williams

Ethics as Foreign Policy
Britain, the EU and the other
Dan Bulley

Universality, Ethics and International Relations
A grammatical reading
Véronique Pin-Fat

The Time of the City
Politics, philosophy, and genre
Michael J. Shapiro

Governing Sustainable Development
Partnership, protest and power at the world summit
Carl Death

Insuring Security
Biopolitics, security and risk
Luis Lobo-Guerrero

Foucault and International Relations
New critical engagements
Edited by Nicholas J. Kiersey and Doug Stokes

International Relations and Non-Western Thought
Imperialism, colonialism and investigations of global modernity
Edited by Robbie Shilliam

Autobiographical International Relations
I, IR
Edited by Naeem Inayatullah

War and Rape
Law, memory and justice
Nicola Henry

Madness in International Relations
Psychology, security and the global governance of mental health
Alison Howell

Spatiality, Sovereignty and Carl Schmitt
Geographies of the nomos
Edited by Stephen Legg

Politics of Urbanism
Seeing like a city
Warren Magnusson

Beyond Biopolitics
Theory, violence and horror in world politics
François Debrix and Alexander D. Barder

The Politics of Speed
Capitalism, the state and war in an accelerating world
Simon Glezos

Politics and the Art of Commemoration
Memorials to struggle in Latin America and Spain
Katherine Hite

Indian Foreign Policy
The politics of postcolonial identity
Priya Chacko

Politics of the Event
Time, movement, becoming
Tom Lundborg

Theorising Post-Conflict Reconciliation
Agonism, restitution and repair
Edited by Alexander Keller Hirsch

Europe's Encounter with Islam
The secular and the postsecular
Luca Mavelli

Re-Thinking International Relations Theory via Deconstruction
Badredine Arfi

The New Violent Cartography
Geo-analysis after the aesthetic turn
Edited by Sam Okoth Opondo and Michael J. Shapiro

Insuring War
Sovereignty, security and risk
Luis Lobo-Guerrero

International Relations, Meaning and Mimesis
Necati Polat

The Postcolonial Subject
Claiming politics/governing others in late modernity
Vivienne Jabri

Foucault and the Politics of Hearing
Lauri Siisiäinen

Volunteer Tourism in the Global South
Giving back in neoliberal times
Wanda Vrasti

Cosmopolitan Government in Europe
Citizens and entrepreneurs in postnational politics
Owen Parker

Studies in the Trans-Disciplinary Method
After the aesthetic turn
Michael J. Shapiro

Alternative Accountabilities in Global Politics
The scars of violence
Brent J. Steele

Celebrity Humanitarianism
The ideology of global charity
Ilan Kapoor

Deconstructing International Politics
Michael Dillon

The Politics of Exile
Elizabeth Dauphinee

Democratic Futures
Revisioning democracy promotion
Milja Kurki

Postcolonial Theory
A critical introduction
Edited by Sanjay Seth

More than Just War
Narratives of the just war and military life
Charles A. Jones

Deleuze & Fascism
Security: war: aesthetics
Edited by Brad Evans & Julian Reid

Feminist International Relations
'Exquisite Corpse'
Marysia Zalewski

The Persistence of Nationalism
From imagined communities to urban encounters
Angharad Closs Stephens

Interpretive Approaches to Global Climate Governance
Reconstructing the greenhouse
Edited by Chris Methmann, Delf Rothe & Benjamin Stephan

Postcolonial Encounters in International Relations
The Politics of Transgression in the Maghred
Alina Sajed

Post-Tsunami Reconstruction in Indonesia
Negotiating normativity through gender mainstreaming initiatives in Aceh
Marjaana Jauhola

Leo Strauss and the Invasion of Iraq
Encountering the Abyss
Aggie Hirst

Production of Postcolonial India and Pakistan
Meanings of partition
Ted Svensson

War, Identity and the Liberal State
Everyday experiences of the geopolitical in the armed forces
Victoria M. Basham

Writing Global Trade Governance
Discourse and the WTO
Michael Strange

Politics of Violence
Militancy, International Politics, Killing in the name
Charlotte Heath-Kelly

Ontology and World Politics
Void Universalism I
Sergei Prozorov

Theory of the Political Subject
Void Universalism II
Sergei Prozorov

Visual Politics and North Korea
Seeing is Believing
David Shim

Globalization, Difference and Human Security
Edited by Mustapha Kamal Pasha

Imagining World Politics
Sihar & Shenya, A Fable for Our Times
L.H.M Ling

International Politics and Performance
Critical Aesthetics and Creative Practice
Edited by Jenny Edkins and Adrian Kear

Memory and Trauma in International Relations
Theories, Cases, and Debates
Edited by Erica Resende and Dovile Budryte

Critical Environmental Politics
Edited by Carl Death

Democracy Promotion
A Critical Introduction
Jeff Bridoux and Milja Kurki

International Intervention in a Secular Age
Re-enchanting Humanity?
Audra Mitchell

The Politics of Haunting and Memory in International Relations
Jessica Auchter

European-East Asian Borders in Translation
Edited by Joyce C.H. Liu and Nick Vaughan-Williams

Genre and the (Post)Communist Woman
Analyzing Transformations of the Central and Eastern European Female Ideal
Edited by Florentina C. Andreescu and Michael Shapiro

Studying the Agency of being Governed
Edited by Stina Hansson, Sofie Hellberg Maria Stern

Politics of Emotion
The Song of Telangana
Himadeep Muppidi

Ruling the Margins
Colonial Power and Administrative Rule in the Past and Present
Prem Kumar Rajaram

Race and Racism in International Relations
Confronting the Global Colour Line
Alexander Anievas, Nivi Manchanda and Robbie Shilliam

The Grammar of Politics and Performance
Edited by Shirin M. Rai and Janelle Reinelt

War, Police and Assemblages of Intervention
Edited by Jan Bachman, Colleen Bell and Caroline Holmqvist

Re-Imagining North Korea in International Politics
Problematizations and Alternatives
Shine Choi

On Schmitt and Space
Claudio Minca and Rory Rowan

Face Politics
Jenny Edkins

Empire Within
International Hierarchy and its Imperial Laboratories of Governance
Alexander D. Barder

Sexual Politics and International Relations
How LGBTQ claims shape International Relations
Edited by Manuela Lavinas Picq and Markus Thiel

Emotions, Politics and War
Edited by Linda Åhäll and Thomas Gregory

Jacques Lacan: Between Psychoanalysis and Politics
Edited by Samo Tomšič and Andreja Zevnik

The Value of Resilience: Securing Life in the 21st Century
Chris Zebrowski

Political Aesthetics: Culture, Critique and the Everyday
Arundhati Virmani

Walzer, Just War and Iraq: Ethics as Response
Ronan O'Callaghan

Politics and Suicide
The Philosophy of Political Self-destruction
Nicholas Michelsen

Late Modern Palestine
The subject and representation of the second intifada
Junka-Aikio

Negotiating Corruption
NGOs, Governance and Hybridity in West Africa
Laura Routley

The Biopolitics of Lifestyle
Foucault, Ethics and Healthy Choices
Christopher Mayes

Critical Imaginations in International Relations
Aoileann Ní Mhurchú and Reiko Shindo

Time, Temporality and Violence in International Relations
(De) Fatalizing the Present, Forging Radical Alternatives
Anna M. Agathangelou and Kyle Killian

Politics and Suicide
The philosophy of political self-destruction

Nicholas Michelsen

LONDON AND NEW YORK

First published 2016 by Routledge

2 Park Square, Milton Park, Abingdon, Oxfordshire OX14 4RN
711 Third Avenue, New York, NY 10017

Routledge is an imprint of the Taylor & Francis Group, an informa business

First issued in paperback 2017

Copyright © 2016 Nicholas Michelsen

The right of Nicholas Michelsen to be identified as author of this work has been asserted by him in accordance with sections 77 and 78 of the Copyright, Designs and Patents Act 1988.

All rights reserved. No part of this book may be reprinted or reproduced or utilised in any form or by any electronic, mechanical, or other means, now known or hereafter invented, including photocopying and recording, or in any information storage or retrieval system, without permission in writing from the publishers.

Notice:
Product or corporate names may be trademarks or registered trademarks, and are used only for identification and explanation without intent to infringe.

British Library Cataloguing in Publication Data
A catalogue record for this book is available from the British Library

Library of Congress Cataloging-in-Publication Data
Michelsen, Nicholas.
   Politics and suicide : the philosophy of political self-destruction / Nicholas Michelsen.
      pages cm. — (Interventions)
   1. Suicide—Political aspects. 2. Self-immolation. 3. Hunger strikes. 4. Suicide bombings. 5. Mass suicide. 6. Political violence—Philosophy. I. Title.
   HV6545.M45 2016
   303.601—dc23
   2015018919

ISBN: 978-1-138-94210-3 (hbk)
ISBN: 978-0-8153-7753-5 (pbk)

Typeset in Times New Roman
by Apex CoVantage, LLC

This book would not have been possible without the inspiration, generosity, advice or patient reading of Victoria Michelsen, Vivienne Jabri, Claudia Aradau, Julian Reid, and Michael Dillon.

Contents

Introduction   1

1   Kamikaze   15

State suicide   15
Politics, the assemblage of desire   18
The fascist assemblage   23
Revolution and annihilation   32
Mishima's revolution   40

2   Self-burning   57

Immolāre   57
Death and desire   66
Events and death   70
Palach's revolution   76
On suicide machines   82

3   Hunger striking   99

Crossing the threshold   99
Bodily inscription   102
Decoding death   106
Exchange   107
Terror and production   112

4   Terror   126

Human bomb   126
The despot   130
Liberal suicides   134
Terror and liberalism   141
A politics from the outside   147

xiv Contents

5 Cult and revolution **163**

Revolutionary suicide 163
Jonestown 166
Millenarianism 171
Dying well 176
Afterword: on machines 178

Index 189

Introduction

The act of self-annihilation has, in one form or other, marked saints and secularists, monarchists and democrats, revolutionaries and fascists. It has been understood in terms of heroism and villainy, grace and profanity, vision and parochialism, ardour and acquiescence, dignity and debasement. Its history has borne witness to celebration and denigration; a sense of indignation and inevitability, shock and expectation, poignancy and horror. Such redolence begs for scholarly attention, yet there have been remarkably few attempts to identify *a politics* residing in our potential for deliberate self-destruction. Indeed, to be identified as a suicide is generally to be stripped of political content. In an act of suicide everything the actor has including the potential for experience is autonomously placed in question. Thus a political suicide implies a politics residing in the departure from authorship, and so from the power to determine a sovereign meaning. The thought of politics *and* suicide is one that we do not yet have the tools to sustain; accordingly, the practice of political suicide is invariably degraded or denied in the light of an assumption of its impossibility.

Recent events have emphatically shown our need for tools with which to develop better understandings of the politics of suicide. In Tunisia, Mohamed Bouazizi's very public suicide provided the spark for the events now termed collectively as the Arab Spring. In China, Buddhist monks are currently conducting an extensive campaign of self-incinerations, protesting the encroachment of the state. The contemporary practice of hunger striking is fully globalised, appearing across states in the developed and the developing world. Suicide bombing, by transnationally networked terrorist groups and as an increasingly normalised insurgent tactic in, for example, Syria and Iraq, seems to have become part and parcel of our international politics. In relation to all the above, we are called to the thought of politics and suicide, since all imply the embodiment of a passionate commitment so absolute that the individual in question is willing to die. Excessive politics are clearly not a recent phenomenon, but rather, as old as the political itself, and can emerge in relation to any particular ideational structure or cultural ethos. The politics of suicide, in this sense, goes well beyond an individual capacity. Nazi Germany, in its frenzied liquidation of its own population, and rabid rush to total war, seemed to thinkers that will figure importantly in this book to define a suicidal state in this sense.[1] Similarly, the adoption of mutually assured destruction (MAD) as a strategy of nuclear deterrence in the Cold War suggested that an autodestructive or suicidal bent had subsumed interstate politics. Today global politics continues to tarry with innumerable alleged to be suicidal dynamics, as eschatological discourses on the ever-increasing likelihood of collective catastrophe pervade the contemporary era.

Political modernity constitutively seeks its inoculation from the possibility for suicide in its name. The pursuit of a political project up to the point of death is seen simply to expose a practice as tainted by an archaic religiosity. Authors writing about political self-destruction in the afterglow of 9/11 have seen no reason to question this imputation of archaism. The global dissemination of the practice of suicide bombing has, after all, been seen as the defining characteristic of self-identified Islamist movements, for whom politics is indissociable from faith. From Hezbollah to Hamas, Islamic Jihad, Al Qaeda, the Taliban or Islamic State, a shared deployment of self-destruction allows a frustrating complexity of sociopolitical formations and milieus to be conceptually organised around an unlimited commitment to execute divine law. Of course, the practice of suicide bombing is recognised to have been adopted by a much wider range of faith and secular groups, from Tamil separatists in Sri Lanka to the Kurds in Turkey. This, and the fact that it shares its self-destructive ontology with such a multiplicity of contemporary political practices, including hunger striking and collective suicide or self-incineration in political protest, has simply been read to prove that the distribution of zealotry, understood as an urge to interrupt the inexorable progress of modernisation, is wider than we might have hoped in the globalised twenty-first century. Self-annihilation is the defining marker of an urge to transcendence which modern political reason is supposed to render passé.

Critics of modern historization have often accepted its claim that premodernity was defined by divine sovereignty over death, as consequent to God's exclusive offer of entry into immortality; they simply dispute the passé character of this problematic.[2] Whilst suicide, inasmuch as it implied an individual escape from the God's authority over death, was explicitly proscribed in premodernity, religious order encouraged self-destruction qua martyrdom as the corporeal affirmation of God's sovereignty.[3] Following political theologians like Ernst Kantorowicz,[4] critics of modernist teleology argue that the emergence of the concept of sovereignty in Europe simply reorientated premodern uses for suicide in this context, exposing, in the process, the religious roots of modern politics.[5] In the offer of membership of an idealised mass-self, nation or community, the attempt to transcend the consciousness of death is seen as reinstituted under secular authority. Through heroic self-sacrifice for the community, put simply, modern afterlives were instituted to replace the old ones. Read as the secularisation of sacrificial exchanges, contemporary practices like the human bomb, self-immolation, hunger strike, or cult suicide, are folded into the fabric of the modern as the indelible trace of its prehistory.[6] Political self-sacrifice provides proof that the fear of death continues to be the constitutive force in modernity, as it was in premodernity, all modern political praxis being a continuing attempt to construct the illusion of permanence and stability now that the 'religious antidote' to death has become problematic.[7]

Thus, the popular heroes of 9/11, those passengers who brought down Flight 91 and the firemen who risked life in the collapsing World Trade Center have a modern political sense inasmuch as they died on behalf of values that are literally foundational for our societies.[8] Inasmuch as an architecture of ideals still defines modern politics, genealogies of political self-sacrifice demolish the assumption of our ontological integrity from self-destructive acts.

Under this critique, still, a political suicide cannot take place. What is political in self-sacrifice is that which confronts and opposes our mortal limits. The desire for an afterlife, personal, symbolic or communal, is what explains self-sacrificial political practices. The political in self-sacrifice is not death, but the sublimation of mortality through ritual praxis. Politics, writ now as a modernised theology, is the continued attempt to transcend individual death. This is to see any potential trace of politicality in self-incinerations, suicide bombings, hunger strikes or mass suicides, as located only in their ciphered denial of death. Following this rationale, the self-sacrifice does not commit suicide; she seeks to live forever.[9] Critics of modernity's claim to have surpassed faith thus preclude politicality in the wilful departure from semiosis, and can offer no tools which might grasp a desire which could take the actor over the threshold of their annihilation. Such a movement can only be understood as the output of delusion, a reach for sovereignty precisely where such meaning cannot be found. A political desire that reaches all the way to self-abolition must be a contradiction in terms. Politics implies territories of being and signification, whether individual or collective, whereas death is simply the ultimate abolition of meaning.[10] Indeed, the account of politics as resting on the creation of collective meaning may be seen as constitutively linked to the consciousness of the possibility of its lack, and thus to the fear of individual death. It renders impossible, even unconscionable, the thought of politics in death. What cannot be thought with a conceptual toolbox concerned with identifying in politics the continuity of theological forms is precisely that which appears constitutive in events like the Kamikaze pilots of World War II, hunger strikes, self-immolations, suicide bombings, or cult suicides; a political desire that is only such because it reaches all the way to self-destruction. The modern political tradition and its erstwhile critics share the assumption that death carries no political potency or fertility unless it communicates transcendent content.

To think politics and suicide requires we think much more fundamentally against the grain. The philosophers Gilles Deleuze and Felix Guattari's contention that politics is neither a question of modern rationality nor heroic meaning may be interjected here. The political, they suggest, is a field of assemblage for desires that open, expand, explode, break and create, and those which enclose, form, code and stabilise. Politics is precisely not, in this sense, a meaning or even set of meanings; it is an immanent quality of embodied existence and not its interpretation. This claim, evocatively, leads Deleuze and Guattari to venture an even more unsettling contention, which forms the central problem of this book. Inasmuch as they must break us, they argued, political desires are integrally prone to turning 'into lines of abolition, of destruction, of others and of oneself. A passion for abolition. . . . When they end up with death, this is a function of a danger which is proper to them.'[11] Politics, is not only open to self-destruction, but constitutively so. To build creative political (revolutionary) lines, in particular, they argue, is to flirt with personal or collective suicide. This is not a claim made in passing or offhandedly. Here an entire political philosophy seems to hinge on the positing of the immanence of politics and suicide. Deleuze puts this most clearly when he writes that the fundamental organising question of a creative political life, as he understands it, is 'how can one trace out the line of flight in spite of knowing that it leads us to abolition.'[12] Deleuze and Guattari explicitly place the figure of the political suicide at the constitutive limit of the thought of the political. The theoretical excavation and examination of this assertion will be the central aim of this book. In this sense, the following chapters form a philosophical exegesis of the work of these philosophers, alongside and in communication with those engaged in similar or related projects, in particular Michel Foucault, Jean Baudrillard, Paul Virilio and Alain Badiou, so as to allow us think past and beyond the dominant placement of self-destruction in modern and postmodern political imaginaries. The need to locate and excavate new tools by which to think politics and suicide derives from the fact that, in doing so, we must take flight from the dominant tragic vernacular of political thought. From the account of politics as a techne predicated on the institution of a social contract, best exemplified by Thomas Hobbes, to Aristotelian visions of politics as praxis, taking various forms, characterised by G.W.F. Hegel, Hannah Arendt and Martin Heidegger, the relationship between the political and death precludes the thought of politics and suicide. The brief survey of the political theoretical tradition, in these representative forms, which follows aims to illustrate why the experimental or exploratory approach taken in this book is necessary.

The father of social contract theory, Thomas Hobbes, is often deemed to have articulated the definitive theory of death and the political. His premise continues to be determinant, that death is that which is feared and avoided above all. Horror of death pervades *Leviathan*. It is the fear of death in the state of nature which drives men to establish the social contract. Of all the 'passions that encline men to Peace', first is 'Feare of Death'.[13] Similarly, it is fear of death which drives men to continue to obey the sovereign. Hobbes' account of the political is Platonic inasmuch as he sees it as a work of craft or techne, a constructed or instituted object.[14] It is fear of death which essentially underpins the work of making-political. As Seery points out, Hobbes's account of death is more 'exhortative than descriptive'.[15] In response to 'the miseries, and horrible calamities, that accompany a Civill Warre' according to 'that dissolute condition of masterlesse men' who might risk death in challenging their sovereign, Hobbes sought to 'convince his fellows that death was ever to be eschewed'.[16] Civil order, for Hobbes, requires the demolition of any register (in particular, of course, Christianity) which might establish a basis for risking death.[17] Hobbes articulation of death is 'qualified'; most importantly, what is 'worst of all, [is]continuall feare, and danger of violent death', not death as such.[18] As such, 'a covenant not to defend my selfe from force, by force, is always voyd'; in the face of certain violent death at the hands of the state, man will inevitably choose the 'lesser evill' of departing the social contract and in doing so resubject himself to the state of nature.[19] Of course, Hobbes argued that whilst civil peace is achievable through the social contract, a state of war or international state of nature persists.[20] As a consequence, Leviathan must be defended from death at the hands of other Leviathans, or disintegration into a state of nature.[21] This, he argued, occasionally requires the death of citizens, and Hobbes states categorically there is no 'Liberty to refuse' such death when 'our refusal to obey, frustrates the End for which the sovereignty was ordained'.[22] Man may be forced to submit to death when the commonwealth is existentially threatened. Civil order deters death, keeping at bay the horrors of mortality, and it does so by occasionally demanding the sacrifice of its citizens. A politics of death, involving articulations of the political which require individual deaths in war, is the paradoxical and thus tragic guarantee of the political understood as a construction to counter death.

Death plays a no less organising role in the work of G.W.F. Hegel; it is the 'the absolute master'. We cannot deny, circumvent or counter death because it is a 'natural negation' of consciousness. Because we are inevitably 'subject to natural corruption', and we can do nothing to negate that bodily corruption, 'the only thing I can do is embody negativity.'[23] The progressive embodiment of natural negation constitutes the life of spirit, as the praxis by which man engages in an active relationship with his mortality.[24] For Hegel, then, death is continually transformed in relationship to progressive sociohistorical embodiments of negation. As Adkins points out, this means that death itself is determined by the 'type of community it encounters'.[25] Hegel charts various ways in which the embodiment of negation is effected: first through the struggle for recognition in conflict by which individual consciousness seeks to posit itself as a subject independent of brute animality and its natural negation.[26] In the celebrated master-slave dialectic, Hegel posits that it is precisely an 'unwillingness to risk life' on the part of the slave, to meet annihilation head-on, which determines the respective position of the master, and ensures that that master is now set in a relation of dependency on the slave for his subjective independence from natural negation.[27] The political is the coming to fruition of reason by which a subject is able to comprehend itself as such by embodying natural negation in a community. As for Hobbes, a martial death to ensure the survival of the nation-state is written into the very fabric of the political as such. For Hegel, 'to be a citizen . . . is to be wholly bound to [the state]. One's identity is found only in relation to the state. As a result one willingly risks death in order to preserve the state.' In this way, the community "introjects" negation.[28] For Hegel, death in war is the constitutive mechanism of political communality: in the Greek states it was precisely 'through the death of those who die in battle, [that] the community as a whole was preserved'.[29] Military death is the very essence of citizen-subjectivity as the collective embodiment of natural negation. That collective embodiment of negation reaches its political limit in the Terror of the French Revolution, where death was upheld by and for the community. The murderous abstract liberty of the French Revolution was the collective political embodiment of the work of negation: 'Insofar as the individual will appears to the community of the Terror as at odds with the universal will, it must be eliminated.'[30] It is precisely in man's confrontation with death, by which he upholds the negative, that he pursues the life of spirit. Broadly speaking, Hegel's account establishes man as becoming a political subject only via his active embodiment of death. As Achille Mbembe eloquently put it, for Hegel 'politics is death that lives a human life.'[31] The political, for Hegel, is the definitive field for the necessary sublimation of death via its violent embodiment in history.

Hannah Arendt understood the political in similarly Aristotelian terms to Hegel, as a praxis (rather than Platonic techne), but her political thought resists Hegelian systematisation.[32] Furthermore, inasmuch as a core concept of the political exists for Arendt, she expressly understands it as a struggle to defy, rather than embody, mortality.[33] Arendt states explicitly in *The Human Condition* that her political thought is centred around natality, and as such, that it is diametrically opposed to any metaphysics of death which inevitably leads, she argued, to political passivity. Politics is defined as the force of natality embedded in 'labour, work and political action'. It is that which makes us human rather than animal, the natural world being dominated by death and cyclicality.[34] In this way, politics is a work against death, whereby through 'word and deed' we rebirth ourselves and 'insert ourselves into the human world' of the immortal polis.[35] Political 'communities can and must defy the natural fact of human mortality,' combating death directly through natal practices which construct memory and spatiotemporal permanence.[36] Politics is essentially a matter of remembrance and storytelling, by which we defy the natural. As Kateb, and Seery following him, notes, despite establishing death as in direct opposition to politics, Arendt, like Hobbes, must then "smuggle" it back in.[37] The necessity of a political encounter with death thus lurks constantly 'in the background of Arendt's theory'.[38] Whilst in Hobbes' case, the sacrifice of individual citizens was required to defend the Leviathan against death at the hands of other leviathans, and in Hegel's case, affirms the very nature of political subjectivity as an embodiment of natural negation, for Arendt, the active risk of death is simply a consequence of the pursuit of the immortalising or memorialising projects which define the political as such.[39] As such, her vision of the natal is thus unable to avoid a 'parasitic commitment to the politics of deathliness'.[40] Arendt's conception of political freedom insists on the creation of 'entirely new possibilities'.[41] This injunction to pure natality cannot but face death; 'Arendtian actors must fight to the death, paradoxically, in order to defy death.'[42] In this sense, Seery's conclusion seems undeniable, that Arendt's 'necessary and too adamant separation of politics and death' seems to contain 'the seeds of its own theoretical demise'.[43] A politics of death is the tragically unavoidable consequence of the political being defined as purely natal praxis.

Martin Heidegger was, of course, as much the target of Arendt's critique of political morbidism as Hegel. Heidegger subjects death to phenomenological analysis, a mode of engagement that contrasts explicitly with the Hegelian dialectic. For Heidegger, the historically shifting ways in which we deal with death in the everyday only operate at the ontic level of semblance. Death itself cannot have a history; rather, a phenomenological analysis of the way in which we relate to death in everyday life unconceals the ontological significance of death to human being (Dasein) as defined by its finitude.[44] Heidegger argues, in contrast to Hobbes, that fear of death is always misplaced.[45] Ontologically speaking, death is definitively a source of anxiety as Dasein's most essential and ownmost possibility. Death is not our fulfilment, ending or disappearance; rather, Dasein's being is defined by its essential finitude, its trajectory towards death.[46] We are, in a sense, always dying, reaching towards the unsurpassable limit of our being-in-the-world. Our anticipation of that limit defines us as free to pursue our possibilities.[47] Facing our finitude underpins our capacity for authenticity; as freedom for our factical possibilities. In this way, Dasein's mode of being, defined by a care which stretches beyond itself into the world, is only on account of the essential uncanniness of Dasein's being as finite. It is precisely because Dasein is an anxious being-towards-death that it is able to stand outside itself – and be ever directed towards its possibilities: 'Being-towards death, as anticipation of possibility, is what makes this possibility possible, as sets it free as possibility.'[48] Freedom is freedom towards death.[49] Heidegger 'the Nazi' is rarely seen as a comfortable resource for political theory. Heidegger rarely talks explicitly of politics, but where he does his reflections are 'entangled in some manner with the most monstrous politics of the twentieth century'.[50] The political is the site of what Michael Dillon termed an 'enormous lacuna in Heidegger's thought'.[51] In *Being and Time* Heidegger is attempting to ground spatiality on temporality, and this clearly makes thinking the political (a spatial field of being-with-others) awkward.[52] Dillon responds to this problem by theorising the political in Heidegger as a topos for the shared encounter with finitude.[53] Being-with-others is determined by our collective openness, the transcendence of ourselves which is the very fundamental character of being-towards-death.[54] The obligatory freedom of the human is essentially shared; finitude constitutes a topos for (linguistically mediated) free encounters. Dillon reads Heidegger's ontology of death as suggesting that the political is thus essentially tragic: 'Tragic is the word which best describes Heidegger's understanding of the "essence" of human being ... as a mode of being, [which] is actually constituted by, and continuously, therefore, exhibits, a complex lack or absence.'[55] This indicates not the inevitability of misery, but the simple fact that 'being temporal we live by virtue of death and are consequently always already differentiated, open and excessive creatures indebted to an excess that we can never master.'[56] In this way, '(in)security, namely the obligatory freedom of human being itself, is the opening which calls forth the prospect of a political life'; this stands in explicit opposition to the Hobbesian assumption of security as the foundation of politics, but it shares a refusal to see a politics in death.[57]

The political here is not opposed to death, as defined by an urge to ontological security in its shadow, but is itself called into being by mortal freedom. Appreciation of mortality makes politics 'capable of effecting a transformation of human being'.[58] The topos of encounter with obligatory freedom, i.e. politics, is therefore, for Dillon, integrally comported towards questions of justice. Taking a stand on a matter of justice 'is where the risk – the radical (in)security – of human being is decided daily'. Also integral to this tragic 'politics of freedom' is the possibility of violence. Political being-in-common is as constitutively prone to autodissolution as it is comported toward justice.⁵⁹ Violence is the specific conundrum of being-in-common: 'the political arises precisely because we are condemned by our mortal life to be free,' yet that mortal freedom ineluctably entails violence as a possibility 'by virtue of the free differential composition of being'.⁶⁰ As Peg Birmingham pointed out, Heidegger's political space intrinsically ties together the possibility of terror and openness to the new.⁶¹ For Dillon, tragedy in its theatrical form is the democratic response to this potentiality, which by 'continuously holding open the question of violence entailed in the metaphysical means of trying to secure ourselves from it' educates us in what it means to be political, and allowing us to comprehend the free political subject as invariably 'prone to excess'.⁶² The liminal status of death in Heidegger's philosophy seems to suggest that it may constitute the political, but at the same time insists that it can never be a part of it. For Heidegger, suicide is the excessive act which intrinsically betrays our mortal (political) freedom: 'Through suicide . . . I precisely relinquish the possibility as possibility.'⁶³ In 'bringing about one's own demise' one deprives Dasein of its grounds for authentic existence as 'being toward death'.⁶⁴ The violence which constantly threatens the self-destruction of being-in-common is the excess of the political: political possibility betrayed. The political calls up death (as its constitutive excess) but there can be no politics in dying.

Georges Bataille is perhaps the first to suggest means to conceptualise the politicality of morbid excess beyond the analytic of an integral tragedy. Bataille's work hinges on a radically novel conceptualisation of death as superabundance. Death is not, in this sense, a symptom of organismic decline, nor, crucially, is it a matter of ontological lack. For Bataille death is never simply a negation, it is the 'profound truth of that movement of which life is the manifestation'.⁶⁵ Death is life's natural excess or superabundance. As Mbembe puts it:

> For Bataille . . . [l]ife itself exists only in bursts and in exchange with death. He argues that death is the putrefaction of life, the stench that is at once the source and the repulsive condition of life. Therefore, although it destroys what was to be, obliterates what was supposed to continue being, and reduces to nothing the individual who takes it, death does not come down to the pure annihilation of being. Rather, it is essentially self-consciousness; moreover, it is the most luxurious form of life, that is, of effusion and exuberance: a power of proliferation.⁶⁶

Bataille understood all societies as defined by the surplus energy they must expend. This is in accordance to his concept of general economy, which determines that 'there is generally no growth but only a luxurious squandering of energy in every form.'⁶⁷ Societies are defined by their respective relationships to 'the senseless luxury and excess of death'.⁶⁸ For Bataille, as opposed to Hegel, therefore, political sovereignty is universally defined by the manner in which the absolute expenditure of excess energy – what he terms the 'accursed share' – is operationalised. Political sovereignty finds manifestation not in utilitarian regulation but in the absolute manner in which the excess is consumed as such. In this way, politics is characterised by radical transgression, an excession of meaning in general, but particularly of taboos surrounding death.[69] Such transgressions exceed the limits of the profane (political) world, but precisely do not destroy it.[70] Rather, the political is definitively a field in which such limits occasionally do not apply. Politics like eroticism and religion is a fractal of the sublime realm in which death is always in question. This leaves open a hint of possibility that the embrace of suicidal death might not only be viewed as political, but as a politics.

Bataille implies that at stake in the extradition of suicide from political theory is not simply the censoring of our understanding of political events in the constitutive passing of which agents choose to die,[71] but precisely the capacity to recognise a politics immanent to the desire for self-excess. Despite the variance in historical and cultural contexts for suicide bombings, self-burnings in protest, mass suicides, hunger strikes, apocalyptic warfare or collective suicide, a disturbing continuity is certainly implied, in this sense, which reflects the presence of a constitutive movement out and beyond the self. In such acts we see the rejection of sovereign ipseity, in their immanent problematization of any and all appeals to transcendence. These agents embody their own departure, through a will that effaces its powers of authorship and all claims to a transcendent semiosis. Self-destruction thus precisely implies a passionate excess, beyond rationality, structure, law, myth or identity. This nonsovereign politics is what cannot be countenanced by modern or even most postmodern political imaginations: a politics beyond rationalisation or even signification, an excess as such.

Into the space evoked by Bataille, calling us to the political theorisation of excess as such, Deleuze and Guattari introduce their thought of a suicidal political desire. I will argue in the chapters that follow that their two-volume philosophical magnum opus *Capitalism and Schizophrenia* literally hinges on their claim that there is nothing more vital to political creativity than the potential for its absolutization in a passion going so far as death. Their thought is orientated by the claim that all creative, qua revolutionary, politics necessarily works with a dangerous and destructive suicidal potentiality. Indeed, they claim that every artist, just as every revolutionary, knows this to be the case: To bring the new into the world is always to break oneself in its delivery. Any institution of the new, in this vision, carries formidable risks. The disastrousness in their political thought should impact upon the growing field of study that asserts Deleuze and Guattari's value and significance as thinkers, but it largely has not done so up to this point. Partly this is because the problematic of the destructiveness of political creation and, indeed, the creativeness of political destruction, is not theirs alone. The thought of the catastrophe integral to politics is central to many of the philosophers Deleuze and Guattari were closely engaged with, borrowed from and debated with. This book maps these conversations and transmissions with contemporaries and critics so as to delineate the space for the thought of a suicidal politics. In this regard, the book seeks to think beyond the limits in political theory by showing how the space for the thought of politics and suicide is carved out and disputed in and beyond Deleuze and Guattari's work.

The preceding discussion of the place of death in the major political theoretical tradition, both in its Platonic and Aristotelian forms, simply aimed to expose how underdeveloped the thought of politics and suicide is as a problem. The space within which politics and suicide may be thought could not be mapped or explored in these, or their succeeding literatures, because they invented no concepts with which to do so. Only by excavating Deleuze and Guattari's toolbox of concepts, along with those of philosophical contemporaries who move in this space, we can begin to think about events such as the Kamikaze, hunger strikes, self-incinerations, mass suicides or suicide bombings, along with the state and international practices that constitutively operationalise self-destruction. Here philosophy serves the purpose to which Deleuze and Guattari dedicated it when they claimed that 'philosophy is not communicative, any more than it is contemplative and reflective: it is creative or even revolutionary, by nature,' to the extent that concepts it invents respond to 'real problems'.[72]

Turning now to the structure of the book: Chapter 1 is rooted in the observation that it is already long past time to reconsider the assumption that politics and suicide have no seat together at the feast of modernity. With the fascist states of the 1940s, a self-destructive politics was manifestly realised on an industrial scale, with entire societies setting out on apocalyptic paths. The Japanese Kamikaze bombers which, towards the close of World War II in the Pacific, confounded and terrified American seamen by using their aircraft as guided missiles, exemplify the administered suicidalism that distinguished these political formations. Like Nazi Germany in its rush to total war and simultaneous pursuit of self-liquidation, in the Meiji state the will to carve out a new world could countenance no limits, and dragged with it into the abyss the crème de la crème of the next generation of a society's intellectual and cultural elite. Chapter 1 examines the event of fascism, and the broader theory of the suicide state – its conceptualisation that Deleuze and Guattari borrowed from Paul Virilio. The chapter identifies and explores the troubling relationship between fascist suicide and revolutionary politics posited here, as well as in the work of Deleuze and Guattari's principle critic, Alain Badiou, though a reading of the postwar Japanese novelist Yukio Mishima's suicide.

Chapter 2 turns to the practice of self-incineration in political protest, from Thich Quang Duc in Vietnam in 1963 to Jan Palach in Czechoslovakia in 1968 and Mohamed Bouazizi in Tunisia in 2010. Individuals have set themselves alight, to wildly varying effect, across a vast range of cultural, ideological, religious and geographical locales, with particularly significant numbers of cases in countries as dispersed as Vietnam, America, Europe, Soviet Russia, South Korea, India, Turkey, Romania, China and Pakistan, for a wide range of political aims and intentions. The chapter argues that immanent to the act of self-incineration is the manner in which the actor's hopes and expectations immediately become inaccessible, evacuated by the event itself. Consequences and intentionality are severed. Here, to conceptualise the politics of self-incineration without recognising the immanent qualities of a self-destructive departure is to obviate the act, and to preclude any grasp of its capacity to insert a creative rupture into political order. This chapter excavates Deleuze and Guattari's distinctive account of creative event though Deleuze's engagement with Maurice Blanchot on suicide, and then draws on this toolbox to theorise the self-incineration of Jan Palach in Prague in 1969. Binding Jan Palach's event to the period in which he died, the chapter concludes by engaging Derrida's observation that the Cold War, or postfascist order, would inevitably be defined by suicidal autoimmunitary logics.

Chapter 3 examines the hunger strike or death fast, locating its practice in relation to the War on Terror launched after 9/11. The hunger strike appears to contrast fundamentally to that of self-burning in protest, or indeed, the human bomb, inasmuch as it is defined by a slow withdrawal rather than a sudden and explosive rupture. The chapter argues that the will to go to the threshold of death and pass over is, however, no less integral to its practice. This account of the politics of hunger striking, illuminating its particular relevance today as a politics of suicide, is developed by way of a theoretical exchange between Jean Baudrillard and Deleuze and Guattari. Baudrillard was principally concerned, in a number of works, with the symbolic function of self-sacrifice. The role of death in the contrasting Universal Histories developed by these thinkers suggests two quite different analyses of the politics of suicide today.

Chapter 4 turns to the contemporary phenomenon of the terroristic human bomb, particularly in its relationship to the liberal state. Focussing on recent analytical engagements drawing on the concepts of bio- and thanato-politics, this chapter critically examines political theorisations of suicide-bombing in all its forms, following Michel Foucault and Giorgio Agamben. Bringing Foucault into closer dialogue with Deleuze, the chapter continues the elaboration of Universal History in Deleuze and Guattari. It concludes by examining Foucault's writings on Blanchot's concept of the Outside, which play a central role in Deleuze's activist reading of his work into a vitalist politics of desire.

In chapter 5, the phenomenon of collective suicide, as displayed in the Jonestown cult mass suicides, and its relationship to the broader problematic of revolutionary politics, is examined. This concluding chapter is concerned to elaborate the dangers associated the thought of politics and suicide, as articulated by Paul Virilio, whose work, in this regard, may be read as a direct response to Deleuze and Guattari's claims regarding the integral disastrousness of creativity. In this sense, Deleuze and Guattari's account of political life as a question of desires and passions rather than meaning and semiosis is brought into focus by the extraordinary horror of the Jonestown event, alongside the broader question of why politics and suicide must be thought, and the potentially fatal, real and intellectual, consequences of doing so. In thinking politics and suicide, the following chapters seek to think with Deleuze and Guattari by subjecting them to the challenges of their own philosophy. This is, after all, precisely what they demanded of us.

Notes

1. P. Virilio, "The Suicidal State," in *The Virilio Reader*, ed. J. DerDerian (Oxford: Blackwell, 1998), pp. 29–45; M. Foucault et al., *Society Must Be Defended: Lectures at the Collège de France, 1975–1976*, Vol. 1 (Basingstoke: Palgrave Macmillan, 2003);

12   *Introduction*

   G. Deleuze and F. Guattari, *A Thousand Plateaus: Capitalism and Schizophrenia* (London: Continuum, 2004b).
2. T. Asad, *On Suicide Bombing* (New York: Columbia University Press, 2007), p. 78.
3. Z. Bauman, *Liquid Life* (Cambridge: Polity Press, 2005), p. 44.
4. Kantorowicz's 1951 work charts the emergence of the concept of heroic death for one's country (*pro patria mori*), 'within the political concepts of the medieval Christian world'. In the political discourse of medieval Europe, death for the heavenly Jerusalem originally took precedence over earthly cities, but as the corpus mysticum of Christianity gradually came to be bound to the social body itself, the idea of charity or caritas for which Christian martyrs died came to be identified with love of country or *amor patriae*. This secularisation of the sacrificial corpus mysticum allowed 'the state as an abstract notion or the state as a juristic person' to achieve 'a semi-religious or natural-religious exultation'. E. H. Kantorowicz, "Pro Patria Mori in Medieval Political Thought," *American Historical Review* 56, no. 3 (1951): 472–492.
5. Kantorowicz 1951; Asad 2007; Z. Bauman, *Mortality, Immortality and Other Life Strategies* (Cambridge: Polity, 1992).
6. Asad 2007, p. 88.
7. Bauman 2005, p. 44. See also Bauman 1992, pp. 50, 91. In this sense, Bauman (1992) follows Phillip Aries closely in assuming that death is radical reproblematised at various cultural locations. Modernity is defined by the fact that mortality is no longer kept close and familiar, as a daily companion, comprehensible through religious discourses of absurdity (the danse macabre in Christian traditions) and communal equanimity. With the modern weakening of communal ties, for Bauman, deterring death emerges as the central project that a politics must address.
8. G. Hage, "'Comes a Time We Are All Enthusiasm': Understanding Palestinian Suicide Bombers in Times of Exighophobia," *Public Culture* 15, no. 1 (2003): 65–89; T. Barkawi, "On the Pedagogy of 'Small Wars,'" *International Affairs* 80, no. 1 (2004): 19–37, 28.
9. Asad 2007; Bauman 2005; Kantorowicz 1951.
10. As Bauman (1992) puts it:

   There is hardly a thought more offensive than that of death; or, rather, of the inevitability of dying; of the transience of our being-in-the-world . . . Death is the ultimate defeat of reason, since reason cannot think death . . . the horror of death is the horror of void, of the ultimate absence, of non-being. The conscience of death is, and is bound to remain, traumatic. (p. 13)

11. G. Deleuze and C. Parnet, "Many Politics," in *Dialogues II* (London: Continuum, 2002), pp. 141–142.
12. Deleuze and Parnet 2002.
13. T. Hobbes, *Leviathan* (New York: Dover, 2006), p. 72.
14. M. Dillon, *Politics of Security: Towards a Political Philosophy of Continental Thought* (London: Routledge, 1996), p. 54.
15. J.E. Seery, *Political Theory for Mortals: Shades of Justice, Images of Death* (Ithaca, NY: Cornell University Press, 1996), p. 8.
16. Hobbes 2006, p. 102, in Seery 1996, p. 8.
17. Hobbes 2006, pp. 68, 181–187.
18. Ibid., p. 70; see also Seery 1996, p. 8.
19. Hobbes 2006, p. 78.
20. Ibid., p. 71.
21. Ibid., p. 179.
22. Ibid., p. 122.
23. S. Zizek, *The Ticklish Subject: The Absent Centre of Political Ontology* (London: Verso, 2008), p. 124.

24. G. W. F. Hegel, A. V. Miller et al., *Phenomenology of Spirit* (Oxford: Clarendon Press, 1979); B. Adkins, *Death and Desire in Hegel, Heidegger and Deleuze* (Edinburgh: Edinburgh University Press, 2007).
25. Adkins 2007, p. 75.
26. J.-A. Mbembe, "Necropolitics," *Public Culture* 15, no. 1 (2003): 11–40, 14; Adkins 2007, p. 79.
27. Adkins 2007, p. 83.
28. Ibid., p. 89.
29. Ibid., p. 91; see also Bauman 1992.
30. Adkins 2007, pp. 101–102. Mastering death cannot be fulfilled politically; it is in religious community that we find the 'completion of Hegel's project' (p. 111).
31. Mbembe 2003, p. 14.
32. E. Vollrath, "Hannah Arendt and the Method of Political Thinking," in *Hannah Arendt: Critical Assessments of Leading Philosophers*, Vol. 1, ed. G. Williams (London: Routledge, 2006), pp. 289–305, 261.
33. G. Kateb, "Death and Politics: Hannah Arendt's Reflections on the American Constitution," *Social Research* 54, no. 3 (1987). See also Seery 1996, p. 13.
34. Seery 1996, p. 13.
35. Hannah Arendt, quoted in Birmingham, Peg. "Heidegger and Arendt: The Birth of Political Action and Speech." *Heidegger and Practical Philosophy* (2002): 191–218, p. 192.
36. Seery 1996, p. 14.
37. Kateb 1987; Seery 1996, p. 16.
38. Seery 1996, p. 16.
39. See Kateb 1987.
40. Seery 1996, p. 15.
41. Dillon 1996, p. 31.
42. Seery 1996, p. 17.
43. Ibid.
44. For Adkins (2007), death is, regardless of Heidegger's claims, the transcendent concept in *Being and Time*.
45. M. Heidegger, *Being and Time* (Oxford: Blackwell, 1962), p. 298.
46. Ibid., p. 304.
47. Ibid., p. 308.
48. Ibid., p. 307.
49. Ibid., p. 311.
50. D. J. Schmidt, "The Baby and the Bath Water: On Heidegger and Political Life," in *Heidegger and Practical Philosophy*, ed. F. Raffoul and D. Pettigrew (Albany: State University of New York Press, 2002), p. 159.
51. Dillon 1996, p. 100.
52. As Adkins (2007, p. 70) points out, Heidegger would later admit that it was an 'untenable' to base spatiality on temporality.
53. Dillon 1996, p. 100.
54. See also Birmingham 2002.
55. Dillon 1996, p. 65.
56. Ibid., p. 141.
57. Ibid., p. 128.
58. Ibid., p. 129.
59. Ibid., p. 156.
60. Ibid., p. 151.
61. Birmingham 2002, p. 198.
62. Dillon 1996, p. 151.
63. Heidegger in ibid., p. 60.
64. Heidegger 1962, p. 305.

65. G. Bataille, *The Accursed Share: An Essay on General Economy* (New York: Zone, 1991), p. 35.
66. Mbembe 2003, p. 15.
67. Bataille 1991, p. 33.
68. Ibid., p. 35.
69. G. Bataille, *Erotism: Death and Sensuality* (San Francisco: City Lights Books, 1986), pp. 40–48; see also Mbembe 2003.
70. Bataille 1986, p. 67.
71. As Hage (2003, p. 67) points out regarding Palestinian suicide bombings.
72. G. Deleuze, F. Guattari et al., *What Is Philosophy?* (London: Verso, 1994), p. 136.

1 Kamikaze

State suicide

Historical experience suggests that, given the right conditions, states can go suicidal. Such suicide states are often symptomatic of a totalitarian nationalism, but this does not bring us to the crux of the matter. The postwar Japanese novelist Yukio Mishima claimed that 'nineteenth century Asia had only these alternatives: to accept the West and to survive after complete surrender to Westernisation; or to resist and perish.'[1] The Meiji constitution was viewed precisely in terms of surrender by the deposed military class. As Mishima liked to recall, in 1877, one hundred samurai launched an uprising against that surrender, meeting the regimes modern weaponry with swords, and committing suicide when the inevitable defeat occurred. Mishima saw in this act of collective suicide a compressed illustration of the loss inherent in the process of Japan's modernisation, which had resulted, he argued, in the progressive extradition of death from culture and society.[2] This assignment of a vital political function to self-destruction is the marker of Mishima's distinctive fascism, and would determine his reading of the disastrous progression of the Meiji regime during World War II as the last ember of Japan's creative potential.

The catastrophic telos of modern mechanised warfare seems to have been recognised by Japan's naval leaders. Japan's 'inevitable' entry to the conflict coincided with an explicit assessment within the hierarchy that the war would be absolutely disastrous.[3] In this sense, we can see traces of apocalypticism written into the war-project from the start. The sense that the war involved a collective desire for death was a recurrent theme in immediate postwar literatures.[4] Certainly by 1944, the Japanese military apparatus could not have failed to recognise that extinction, in military, if not yet biological, terms, was on offer. In this millenarian climate, Vice Admiral Onishi established the 'special attack' corps, now more commonly recognised under the idiom of the kamikaze.[5] Initially comprised of highly expert airmen who had spectacular success in guiding their bomb-laden planes onto their targets, the quality and length of training of special attack pilots would decrease to a nominal period by the end of the war, and their tactical effectiveness correspondingly declined. By the close of action in the Pacific, four thousand young men, around three-quarters drawn from high schools and the remainder from the top universities, received brief and basic flight training before being sent immediately to death. There was apparently little illusion, within the state bureaucracy, that the war could be won with suicidal methods, but it certainly convinced the Americans that Japan would remain fully committed under almost any conditions. This was supported by the fact that the kamikaze did not appear ex nihilo, but joined an extant array of other suicidal attack methods including explosive speedboats, which deployed even younger men of 15 or 16, and experiments with manned torpedoes or *kaiten*. More successful, and infamous amongst American soldiers, were *banzai* infantry special attacks, either with sword, antitank lunge mines – which were cone-shaped explosive charges attached to a six-foot pole which fired on impact – or satchel bombs in the Philippines and Okinawa. Indeed, prior to 1944 it was already tacit convention that Japanese pilots for whom escape was impossible, due to aircraft fault or damage, would seek to crash, if in as militarily useful a manner as possible. The context in which the kamikaze emerged was thus richly steeped with autodestructive activity. The apparently systemic and generalised quality of these practices suggests that the kamikaze programme cannot be explained solely through tactical or strategic rationalisation.[6] The entire Japanese state appeared, to its US opponent, to have gone suicidal.

The kamikaze pilots have often been viewed as a unique cultural artefact.[7] Indeed, the sentiment that they were 'the culmination of centuries of tradition' is found in most of the literatures that have emerged following the war.[8] Clearly there is specificity with respect to any cultural milieu, and suicide had a distinct set of meanings in Japan. Japanese literature contains innumerable examples of honourable or valorised death taking place on the field of battle or in defence of honour.[9] In this vein, the kamikaze may be, and this was an interpretation encouraged by the Meiji regime itself, seen as the continuation of the ethos of the samurai class that had ruled Japan until the Meiji restoration. As laid out in texts such as the *Hagakure*, the martial ethos of the Samurai class emphasised frugality, stoicism, honour, obedience, a sense of duty, a warlike spirit, loyalty and courage, grounded in self-discipline unto death.[10] The kamikaze were commonly read as revealing how this ethos had 'filtered down to lower classes and became a common value system among the Japanese'.[11] Ruth Benedict famously viewed the Japanese cultural milieu as suspended between aesthetics and militarism, the two coming together in the kamikaze to make sense of martial death as paradigmatically sublime in the Japanese context. In this reading, the kamikaze emerge from a distinctly Japanese sensibility: the construction of a culture that viewed death as a route to symbolic value.[12]

The problem here is that a clear break from the historical lineage of martial suicide in Japanese culture is precisely established by the state-planned character of the kamikaze. The very modernity of the kamikaze suggests the appeal to cultural endogeneity lack sufficiency. The Meiji state was highly active in militarising Japanese society in the period leading up the War, and drew explicitly on the tropes and movements of European fascism in doing so. Centralised army training aspired to mirror, but in the process radically transformed the *bushido* chivalric code, so as to fit it around a state-nationalist diagram alien to it. The response is to view the practices as the output precisely of an overly successful dissemination of totalitarian state ideology. There was certainly a powerful state-led rejection of the gangrene of the past, and an emphasis on palingenesis or a need to rebirth Japanese society, so that the prior humiliations by the Western agents of modernity could be reversed. The education system had been so militarised that by 1925 military officers were being placed in every school, with hours of military drilling, including instructions in bayonet fighting, now part of the daily routine. The educational system instituted by the Meiji restoration entrenched martial themes bound to responsibility to the sacralised figure of the emperor. Shooting ranges and other martial practices would, by 1943, include teaching students suicidal methods.[13] Schools become channels for the state ideology, and would be prime locations for the recruitment of kamikaze pilots.[14] Ideology thus appears, to many historians, the prime mover of state suicide. Under the formal ideology, death was explicitly framed as conferring nationalised immortality at the Yasukuni shrine, much like Munich's Tomb of Martyrs.[15]

A totalitarian fidelity to the emperor is noted in some of the diaries and last letters of individual pilots, revealing notes of devotion to 'a life of resignation and self-denial . . . a chance to die for my country', as one ensign put it, or for the 'Japanese way of life'. Recent collections of pilot diaries have, however, cast doubt upon the ease with which the articulation of the kamikaze as revealing the ideological co-option of individuals or simply expressing long-running Japanese cultural forms of 'life through death'.[16] The danger is that of radically oversimplifying pilots' own interpretations of their act, which vastly exceeded the state narrative. Many did not embrace, and indeed, were often critical of the imperial ideology.[17] These were not 'men experiencing the bitterness of defeat and unwilling to accept reality',[18] but neither were they convinced by the promise of transcendence offered by the state ideology.[19] Each pilot found their own, remarkably diverse, ways of resigning themselves an action that they had little real choice in.[20] Making sense of individual participation through a theory of semiotic interruption, Ohnuki-Tierney argues that these young men were defined precisely by that which they lacked in understanding of the state-nationalist project. They sought to rationalise their deaths with meanings of diverse kinds because they did not recognise the state for what it was. The implication here is that what the pilots desired was not what the totalitarian state desired.[21] If the pilots clearly were caught up, and thus had to come to terms with a suicide already decided for them, how did such a curious urge come to so completely capture the life of the state?

The philosophers that the student pilots read were no less subject to the inexorable movement of a seemingly suicidal state desire. Tanabe Hajime, a member of the Kyoto School which had so profoundly influenced the work of Martin Heidegger, gave lectures to students about to be deployed as kamikaze. He would, in the aftermath of the war, develop a philosophy of self-transcendence as opening only from an active participation in catastrophe.[22] In developing this philosophy, Hajime explicitly sought to give a repentant sense to the apocalyptic passion which he perceived to have captured him along with the entire societal formation.[23] Neither Japanese culture nor the signifying regime of the state can explain how a state suicidalism emerged, he implied. The war had assumed its own dynamic trajectory, pulling in everything around it. The implication here is that the totalitarian bureaucracy was, like the pilots, captured to the death-project. Certainly, the special attack concept was developed within the military hierarchy, which then presented it to the state, where it was initially received with considerable suspicion.[24] That suspicion is not surprising; with the kamikaze the very vital function of the totalitarian state, its containment of the life of the totality, was placed in service to a specifically military formation of desire: triumph in death.

For Deleuze and Guattari, the integral nature of all fascist projects, as distinct from totalitarian ones, is exposed here. They argue that the secret of fascism is the presence, within the state, of a military line that captures the whole and sets it to an entirely morbid task. That suicidal vocation belongs to a war machine and not to totalitarian bureaucracy; indeed it is the pure expression of the unlimited essence of war. Fascism is defined by its destructive excess, not the totalitarian desire for order and ontological security. Thus for Deleuze and Guattari, it was necessarily Japan's military, not its bureaucrats, that were the pastors of the suicidal line. In keeping with the dictate to excess, at the end of the war, many of those pastors, including Admiral Ohnishi, would die via seppuku – the traditional method of self-disembowelment – rather than return to a shamed order.[25] Following the emperor's declaration of defeat in the aftermath of the bombing of Hiroshima and Nagasaki, Vice Admiral Ugaki, one of the founders of the kamikaze programme, would commandeer a D4Y Suisei dive-bomber and set its flight into a mountain side.[26] Here the suicidal war machine that subsists within every fascist body is revealed as defined by an unlimited urge to flight.

Politics, the assemblage of desire

Only the creation of concepts makes it possible to think and act. Philosophy, the singular function of which is the creation of concepts, is what allows us to become political, whether we become revolutionaries or fascists. All philosophy, in this sense, is political philosophy. We can only assess concepts by reference to how they relate to problems and how they open up our capacity to respond to them. Deleuze and Guattari's concept of the desiring-political carries their central indictment of Freud, that he puts death in desire and in doing so mortifies life by measuring it against death.[27] Psychoanalysis is resignation to our fate.[28] Its intellectual legacy is a tragic dogma that has much to answer for with respect to the political failure of emancipatory projects in the last half century. The problem is not Freud's recognition of the effects of the familial structure, but his representation of that structure as expressing fundamental truths about the nature of desire.[29] His 'ridiculous' concept of the 'death instinct'[30] traps us into a vision of ourselves by which our self-repression is not only natural, but desirable.[31] Freud leaves us only two options: to desire our own repression, and as such 'remain desire', or revolt, in a descent into psychosis, and 'lose itself as desire'.[32] This is, clearly, no choice at all. The priest-kings of psychoanalysis offer us only 'bad conscience'.[33] We need to be cured of their insistence that we must assume the status of tragic figures.[34] Unlike Marcuse,[35] Deleuze and Guattari set out in pursuit of a full reconstruction of the theory of the unconscious, and with it the energetics of critique.[36]

Lacan's reworking of Freud's death instinct as integral lack sustained its repressive political function, even if his 'ontological thesis about subjectivity' is quite different from Freud's.[37] The unity of the ego becomes, for Lacan, a fiction underpinned by our consciousness of mortality.[38] Inasmuch as it institutes a foundational void at the heart of the symbolic structure, mortality provides the basis for the *defensive becoming* of a fractured subjectivity. There are clearly interesting parallels here to Heidegger's concept of anxiety, as well as Hegel's introjection of the negative.[39] For Lacan the myth of the unified self is a pragmatic response to our absent centre. Lack (consciousness of human mortality) is the abhorrent source of fractured subjectivity that must be constantly effaced (through ego-construction).[40] Deleuze and Guattari accepted Lacan's insights about the inherently fractured nature of the self,[41] but rejected his Freudian reintroduction of death into the structure of desire. Life lived in bondage to death always falls short of its radical capacities.[42] By putting death in desire once more, through the theatre of lack, Lacan blockaded the integrally revolutionary politics of the fractured unconscious.[43] This radical claim is reached subtractively, from a critique of the metaphysic of lack, followed by a speculative or intuitive leap into a radical philosophy of difference. Repudiating the 'lack-centred' unconscious, Deleuze and Guattari posit an unconscious that bursts at the seams. This allows Deleuze and Guattari to think of the unconscious as an immanently political field. By putting a philosophy of difference to work, Deleuze and Guattari establish the epistemological legitimacy for their theory. Here politics is explicitly positioned prior to epistemology.

For Deleuze and Guattari, the unconscious is the factory or locus for the processing of a fully unstructured desiring-flow which originates outside us, in our families or workspaces (social forms), in transversal spaces between us and our fellows (loves, friendships), as well as emerging dynamically within the topology of the unconscious itself (habits). The Lacanian metaphysic of lack precludes our grasp of the unconscious as already a field of political struggle with respect to the relative freedom of desire to flow. The unconscious is simply the field for desire's assemblage, which flows beyond us as individuals; it connects us to the world through writing machines, drinking machines, loving machines, fearing machines, friendship machines, attraction machines, compulsive machines, creative machines, destructive machines. The unconscious is, in other words, a complex machine of machines for the assemblage with alterity. Psychoanalysis mistakes these machines for permanent structures in the unconscious, where they are simply functions of assemblage with contingent social norms, like the nuclear family.[44] Subjectivity does not lack; it is filled with partial escapes and reformations, partial objects and partial selves.[45] The claim here is that selfhood is exuberantly full: an endless process of combination, deviation and reassociation, a dynamic emergent assemblage of assemblages. We are always more than the sum of our parts. We *are* their overflow, part-assembling and then taking flight from our constituent assemblages. We are rendered different by our different overlapping milieus. There is no essential or structural restraint on our becomings. Even if we are organised by habitual formations, our basic state is one of untrammelled experimentation.[46]

The natural state is one of passing through, reassembling, moving from place to place in a state of flux, but its observable manifestations are highly territorialised, often around discrete objects. Desire is trapped and organised.[47] Such reterritorialisations are indicative not of underlying or foundational structures, but a polarity of process to which desire is continually subjected. Desire is deterritorialised and deterritorialising in its natural state, that is to say, free of structural predeterminants or objective formations. Reterritorialisation marks a process which draws desire into determinate structures, folds it into closed cycles; deterritorialisation unfolds structures, allowing us to reassemble, transform, or become different. Particular assemblages always integrate both processes.[48] The unconscious field is integrally political inasmuch as it is defined by the perpetual interaction of these two movements. To claim deterritorialisation always has primacy, as Deleuze and Guattari do, is to challenge any assumption that creativity occurs when things are appropriately organised or territorialised. Creativity occurs when a form is departed from. Reformation tastes of sorrow.[49] Freud's concept of the ego constructing 'flight' from the instincts takes on a new connotation in this context. When desire deterritorialises it builds 'lines of flight'. Creative subjects are made in flight from structure, in the deterritorialisation of the ego.

The dogma of lack is not simply an error; it standardises the unconscious to harness desire's integral productivity to serve existing social relations and consumer regimes of accumulation.[50] Lack is thus a wholly reactionary concept. Revolutionary politics involves tapping into the escapes integral to the extant regime and diverting them away from the reactive territorialities by plugging them into a revolutionary plateau.[51] Revolutionary politics is a matter of accelerating the contemporary formation to beyond its immanent limits.[52] A traditional revolutionary politics based on large-scale mass mobilisations invariably produces 'mass machines [that] refuse to liberate revolutionary energy'. Instead Deleuze and Guattari call for a politics based on the maximum possible decoding. This is a matter of distinguishing two opposed sociopolitical modes of critique: the political programme versus the permanent deterritorialisation of desiring-flows.[53] This is a move away from visions that seek signposts to a stable revolutionary identity or faithful activist milieu, towards the pursuit of a permanent condition of transformation,[54] moving ever closer and closer to a great rip in the social fabric.[55]

Deleuze and Guattari's conceptual grammar of politics posits that the relative deterritorialisation or reterritorialisation of desire within any assemblage determines its politics. A political field is striated by lines of territorialised desire. Such striation can be molar or molecular, that is to say territorialised in rigid or supple segments, which are relatively impermeable or permeable. The opposite topographical state for the field of desire is smooth, that is to say a state in which desire flows freely, fully deterritorialised. Revolutionary events are lines of flight which smooth the order of striation. Accepting that there are differences in emphasis between the first and second volumes of *Capitalism and Schizophrenia* should not mislead us into assuming that there is a break in approach.[56] The field of the political is the tangled assemblage of both polarities of desiring-process. Reterritorialisations striate and hierarchically structure desire. When assembled with a molar line, desire is organised in highly determined and stable formations. By contrast, relative degrees of deterritorialisation pervade molecular formations. Drawing a molecular line leaves open the possibility for relative shifts or movements; thresholds of becoming are assumed. Molecularizations herald deterritorialising lines of flight which reorientate an entire assemblage. Individuals are made up of diverse psychical formations, which draw us in various directions or pull us into habitual behaviours. Such machines, habitual or otherwise, will have various (molar, molecular, flight) lines to them, such that obsessive behaviour may be useful in some scenarios and deleterious in others. Psychical assemblages always have limits or horizons upon which lines of flight may be built into entirely new assemblages, as a when a heavy drinker turns into an alcoholic, or a compulsive neurotic into an obsessive psychotic. Such is also the case in the field of social organisation. Desiring-machines are never simply molar, or molecular, or revolutionary, but tend towards the pole of reterritorialisation or deterritorialisation in accordance with their assemblage of lines. A party, for example, will form a complex assemblage of such lines. Regardless of its ideological content, a political party will involve molar reterritorialisations around charismatic leaders, key ideas and interpretations of historical events, institutional bodies, administrative processes, class associations, funding sources and so forth. It will also entail molecular lines of relative deterritorialisation and reterritorialisation: complex intraparty tensions and competitions between different bureaucratic bodies within the apparatus, backbench associations, grass-roots movements, or particular think tanks. Finally a party will possess directionalities or intensive trajectories which emerge out of these internal inconsistencies, where new concepts or problems emerging from the outside, such as electoral success, force the party assemblage as a whole to shift and change function entirely.

The lines allow for the invention of a political diagrammatics. Diagrams are rules of thumb for workable mass arrangements of desire; they are thus real but virtual, actualised with only varying degrees of purity, and so map the conditions of possibility immanent to the social field. Deleuze and Guattari's Universal History charts a number of 'virtual' models for the organisation of human societies.[57] *Anti-Oedipus* maps three of these diagrams: the primitive, despotic and capitalist regimes. Their Universal History is not teleological in the Hegelian sense. Capitalism has an organising position because, as a virtual diagram, it constitutively approaches the maximal degree of deterritorialisation and decoding that a social field can achieve.[58] Primitive or prestate regimes are defined by their molecularity, a supple striation which ensures that coded desires circulate within societally designated bounds. The despotic or sovereign diagram, by contrast, establishes a hierarchical molar organisation, defined by centralisation and rigid caste systems, accompanied by an absolute decisional power over the life and death of the citizenry. Here everything is done to ensure the codes are rendered immobile. The rigid molarity of despotic regimes contrasts explicitly with the supple molecularity of primitive regimes, as well as the radical decoding of capitalist commercialism.

A Thousand Plateaus introduces a fourth diagram to the Universal History, which lives alongside the primitive regime, the despotic state and capitalism; that of the war machine. The war machine is defined by its active construction of smooth space for the circulation of deterritorialised desire. It is swept by a line of flight. Its paradigmatic actual articulation was the nomadic hordes of ancient horsemen which swept large sections of central Eurasia. Despotic state apparatus are distinguished fundamentally from war machines in *A Thousand Plateaus*.[59] States striate space, constructing a machine to territorially overcode desiring-flows. War machines, by contrast, are a 'machine of mutation' that releases ever more disordered and deterritorialising flows. The war machine is the diagram underpinning any and every function which actualises a machine for mutation and transformation. As a consequence it is intrinsically linked to creativity and death. Any assemblage which emits lines of flight, 'quanta of deterritorialisation' or 'mutant flows', whether social, cultural, aesthetic, political and/or economic, has built a war machine to smooth space.[60] War machines maximise fluxion by occupying geographies (whether physical or intellectual) without building interiorised territories upon them – they smooth spaces. Unsurprisingly, Deleuze and Guattari ascribe the invention of the war machine to nomadic social systems. This is not to imply that war machines are only built by nomadic societies. When any practice is productive of new flows it has smoothed space, and so employs a war machine. For this reason, writing and music can be understood as war machines. Actual war is the means by which nomadic orders build and defend smooth spaces (deserts, oceans) against territorial state apparatus. Actualisations of the war machine, such as the nomadic tribes of the steppe, assembled various molar and molecular lines to constitute their social orders, so organising actual nomadic societies around lineal rulers or ancestral regimes.

The concept of the war machine exposes the catastrophe integral to politics. Nomadic war machines can, and often have, turned into despotic states in the course of their passage through history.[61] War machines are clearly also harnessed by both despotic states and capitalist states. This is critical for the conceptualisation of fascism, and in turn, the suicidal trajectory of the Meiji fascist regime. Fascism, Deleuze and Guattari argue, appears when war machines are combined with state apparatuses in particular ways. The state must invariably overcode the war machine with its destructive function. Once overcoded by the state, a war machine is prone to an excessive embrace of that destructive supplement. The state apparatus, at the same time, is rendered vulnerable to a counter-coup.[62] Harnessing war as a means to a state end always entails the supplemental risk of the war machine swallowing the state whole and then sending it in pursuit of a purified function. In pure or total war, the war machine's power of metamorphosis returns as a perverse monstrosity, an overwhelming urge to abolition which co-opts the state and sets it upon an apocalyptic trajectory: The unlimited essence of war as an act of force that Clausewitz identified is given free rein.[63] This dynamic interaction is the source of the suicide state.

The fascist assemblage

The account of the suicide state in *A Thousand Plateaus* illustrates the real utility of desiring-political cartography, but it also presents challenges to the claim to a revolutionary intellectual project pronounced in *Anti-Oedipus*. In *Anti-Oedipus*, fascism is articulated as lying at one pole of the fundamental political dichotomy between paranoia and schizophrenia that structures the work.[64] Fascism names the seductions of paranoiac sensibility – from the reactionary lure of political identity to the overcodings affected by the family unit on the individual psyche;[65] the general tendency towards paranoiac enclosure.[66] Fascism appears as the paranoiac adversary of schizoanalysis, which enjoins us to pursue with abandon our deterritorialisation as revolutionary praxis. In *A Thousand Plateaus*, fascism is no longer a 'general category'.[67] Rather, fascism is mapped via its specific historical articulation in German National Socialism.[68] Fascism is no longer treated as a virtual concept or diagram, but an actual historical assemblage of desire. Now, only its suicidal lines of flight, its commitment to acceleration, distinguished fascism from everyday totalitarianism. As Paul Virilio made explicit, the implication here is that Nazism's closest relative was not amongst its contemporaries in Europe, despite resonances with Marinetti and the Italian futurists,[69] but rather in Japan, where the suicidal stated found similarly pure expression.

The National Socialist assemblage clearly involved a state totalitarianism, but 'there are totalitarian states, of the Stalinist, or military dictatorship type, that are not fascist.'[70] The 'localised assemblage' of the state was subjected to an 'abstract machine of over-coding', which order all social flows under a unified, centralised, vertical and hierarchical bureaucratic structure.[71] The dangers implicit to such a formation are clear: an absolute rigidity in sociality; a truth defined from above; collectivised 'values, morals, fatherlands'; the paranoid certainty of purified self-hood as against difference; a politics characterised by fear.[72] Nazism builds a molar line which segments society under rigid uniformity. This verified all the dangers of molarity, but centralisation and macropolitical totalisation did not summate the assemblage. A molecular line articulates the way in which Nazism began as a 'mass-movement: a cancerous body rather than a totalitarian organism'. Historical fascism was 'inseparable from a proliferation of molecular forces in interaction, which skip from point to point, *before* beginning to resonate together in the National Socialist state'.[73] Socially dispersed historical flows allowed its emergence at that particular moment in time and identified why the masses desired it. Understanding the rise of Nazism requires addressing the revolutionary social movement that built its popular appeal out of the failure of Weimar democracy. The National Socialist movement began as a cloud of tiny microfascist formations, wherein flows of signification were segmented into micro-black holes of paranoiac enclosure.

Molecularized paranoia was dispersed in the narcissism of social subgroups, ex-soldiers, cities, rural networks, schools, families and beer halls, before building into the socially resonant political machine, under Hitler's charismatic leadership, which established the Third Reich. Such a machine haunts all social movements, and can leads to a micro-authoritarianism masquerading as its opposite in those which pretend to a revolutionary avant-gardism.[74] But, Deleuze and Guattari argue, there is also microfascism at work in the dynamics of the unconscious, inasmuch as we are prone to allowing our desire to circulate exclusively around particular objects, individuals, ideas, self-images and aesthetic experiences, which act like heavy weights on a rubber sheet, sucking desire into gravitic black holes from which it cannot escape.[75] This is therefore a danger integral to molecularity, of 'reproducing in miniature the affections, the affectations, of the rigid', but also of producing 'a thousand little monomanias, self evident truths, and clarities' which make each of us a 'self-appointed judge, dispenser of justice, policeman, neighbourhood SS man'. Such microfascisms are endemic, and 'have a specificity of their own that can crystallise into a macrofascism'.[76]

The Nazi Party rose to power by harnessing diffuse microparanoia and allowing it to rise up and establish a totalitarian apparatus: this social movement then acted as a resonating echo chamber within the totalitarian state. By containing a supple resonance machine within the closed vessel of the totalitarian state the regime incorporates a fluidity which contrasts fundamentally with the classical centralisation of Stalinist totalitarianism.[77] The Nazi totalitarian state acts as resonance chamber, within which the tangle of microfascisms are put to work.[78] The difference between Nazism and other totalitarianisms is partly a matter of degree for Deleuze and Guattari. All totalitarian states set up a resonance chamber between the centralised and the segmentary.[79] There is always a 'molar side and a molecular side'.[80] Similarly, all totalitarianisms seek to set up a resonant molecularity that does not simply 'seal, plug or block' subversive tendencies, but channels popular flows into the service of state function. Nazism radicalises this conjugation of the lines; molecular segmentarity (a revolutionary social movement) sets up its resonant molar totalitarianism (as opposed, for example, to it finding its genesis in a military coup), and that molecularity was placed at the centre of the Nazi mechanism of rule, giving Hitler an '*unequalled* ability to act upon the "masses"'.[81] Without these resonating microfascisms at its disposal, Nazism would have been unable to achieve such penetration of German social minutia.[82] Up to this point *A Thousand Plateaus* broadly reaffirms *Anti-Oedipus*, adding clarity to the conceptualisation of fascist paranoia. Nazi paranoia was built on two lines (state totalitarianism and microfascism) which are conjugated together when a state totalitarianism builds a microfascist resonance machine, or even worse, when a microfascist social movement sets up a totalitarian state apparatus.[83]

Inasmuch as National Socialism was defined by a molecular social movement, Deleuze and Guattari argue that a war machine took over the state.[84] This Nazi war machine was not simply genocidal but suicidal. Indeed, Deleuze and Guattari's implication is that the whole logic of racial extermination derives from that suicidalism. Nazism was a paradigmatic exemplar of desiring-political suicide:

> Fascism is constructed on an intense line of flight, which it transforms into a line of pure destruction and abolition. It is curious that from the very beginning the Nazis announced to Germany what they were bringing: at once

wedding bells and death, including their own death, and the death of the Germans, they thought they would perish but that their undertaking would be resumed, all across Europe, all over the world, throughout the solar system. And the people cheered, not because they did not understand, but because they wanted that death through the death of others . . . One can always say that this is just a matter of foggy talk and ideology. But that is not true. The insufficiency of economic and political definitions of fascism does not imply a need to tack on vague, so-called ideological determinations. We prefer to follow . . . the precise formation of Nazi statements, which are just as much in evidence in politics and economics as in the most absurd of conversations. They always contain the 'stupid and repugnant cry', Long live death![85]

Deleuze and Guattari do not argue that state totalitarianism short-circuited a war machine and became contingently suicidal in the process of pursuing total war (though this certainly occurred); rather they claim that a suicidal line of flight invested the molecular dynamics of Nazism from the very beginning. Nazi totalitarianism was constructed when a revolutionary movement took over the state. To do so, the movement adopted the characteristics of a war machine, building within the German state a smooth space for the realisation of a palingenetic line of flight that was to give National Socialism its characteristic mass appeal. Resonating within the social body, this war machine exceeded the totalitarian nationalist apparatus that later sought to harness it, and set it to abolition: fascism is a revolutionary nationalism.

Suicide traced the trajectory of this regime. Himmler's suicide preceded Hitler's by three weeks, taking place on 23 May 1945. Several months earlier, Luftwaffe pilots had been asked to volunteer for training in suicide missions – specifically in the art of ramming enemy aircraft. The Nazi suicide squads went into action in April 1945, with 183 suicide planes setting out to challenge thirteen thousand US bombers on 7 April. They had little success, with most being shot down. That suicidalism was, for Deleuze and Guattari, more than a purely ideological matter.[86] It is the potential fate of all revolutionary nationalisms. The war machine established on the resonating segmentarity of German society carried within it an unlimited potentiality which was only fully released with the onset of total war. It constructed suicidalism both at the political and 'the economic level, where arms expansion replaces growth in consumption and where investment veers from the means of production towards the means of pure destruction'.[87] For Deleuze and Guattari, the paradox of fascism is that it was defined, from the start, not by its totalitarianism, but by a 'reversion of the line of flight into a line of destruction' that animated its molecular segmentarity.[88] The Nazi regime carried a deterritorialising desiring-machine inside its narrative of national rebirth. This paradoxical schizoid function within a paranoiac order established a cancerous line of flight (militarised rebirth as a corruption of the mutational impetus). By the 1940s the Nazi state had been set to global war, explicitly pursuing a radical politics of total abolition. The claim here is that a state born of a revolutionary urge that directs it into a totalitarian nationalism is integrally destructive. The molar cannot contain the line of flight which births it, so it co-opts the state and sets it to flight – with an inevitable turn to genocidal purification within, and pure war without.

Deleuze and Guattari borrowed the concept of the Nazi suicidal state from Paul Virilio,[89] but extended it quite differently in arguing that the National Socialist movement had always nurtured a potentially apocalyptic line of flight. The state apparatus ended up as the appendage of this suicidal war machine:

> Paul Virilio's analysis strikes us as entirely correct in defining fascism not by the notion of the totalitarian state but by the notion of the suicidal state: so-called total war seems less a state undertaking than an undertaking of a war machine that appropriates the State and channels into it a flow of absolute war whose only possible outcome is the suicide of the state itself . . . [Hitler's] 'Telegram 71 is the normal outcome: If the war is lost, may the nation perish' . . . it was this reversion of the line of flight into a line of destruction that already animated the molecular focuses of fascism, and made them interact in a war machine instead of resonating in a state apparatus. A war machine that no longer had anything but war as its object and would rather annihilate its own servants than stop the destruction. All the dangers of the other lines pale by comparison.[90]

This is not simply a controversial historical claim about National Socialism, implying that all revolutionary movements risk fascism in their progression within the system of sovereign nations. It also has radical implications for the theory of the desiring-political as such. The concept of a line of flight that was suicidal from the very beginning suggests that deterritorialisation is not universally revolutionary, liberatory and creative. In defining Nazism by its suicidal line of flight, Deleuze and Guattari suggest that deterritorialisation is a very risky business.

Lines of flight have an integral danger (suicidalism), just like molarity (totalitarianism) and molecularity (micro-fascism).[91] Furthermore, Deleuze and Guattari suggest that the danger which belongs to deterritorialisation is the worst of them all.[92] Surely our faith in the revolutionary content of deterritorialisation must be placed in question if lines of flight

> themselves emanate a strange despair, like an odour of death and immolation, a state of war from which one return broken . . . self immolation . . . the line of flight crossing the wall, getting out of the black holes, but instead of connecting with other lines and each time augmenting its valence, turning to destruction, abolition pure and simple, the passion of abolition.[93]

Deleuze and Guattari argue that it is 'the destiny of the war machine' per se to be able to 'turn against itself' and become a 'suicide machine'; fascism simply radicalises this tendency. This seems to problematize any claim to a revolutionary potential rooted in desire's deterritorialisation.[94] The 'third fascist line' in *A Thousand Plateaus* thus appears to present an enormous internal challenge to the theory of revolutionary deterritorialisation in *Anti-Oedipus*. Unsurprisingly, theorists who are generally broadly sympathetic to Deleuze and Guattari have developed extremely critical readings of this concept.

John Protevi argues that recognising the fundamental difference between the two volumes of *Capitalism and Schizophrenia* is a condition for the possibility of a good reading: the theory of the desiring-political, he argues, shifts significantly between the two texts.[95] The imputation of a basic dangerousness integral to deterritorialisation appears to break from the straightforwardly dualistic account in *Anti-Oedipus*. Nick Land similarly argues that this disjunction between the texts represents a fatal problem for the remobilisation of their thought. The idea of a line of flight gone wrong betrays the anti-paranoiac spirit of the earlier text.[96] The schizoanalysis of *Anti-Oedipus* was a call to 'always decode . . . and extinguish all nostalgia for belonging'. As such 'schizoanalysis shares in the delicious irresponsibility of everything anarchic, inundating, and harshly impersonal, seeks a fringe of experimentation that knows no bounds, pushing to the edge of capitalism . . . it is a dissolution of identity.'[97] The admittedly crude value of the account lies precisely in the dichotomy between molecular, revolutionary, schizophrenic or creative, and molar, reactionary, paranoid or fascistic – in sum, 'between the dissolution and reinstitution of the social order'.[98] *Anti-Oedipus* simply *is* the challenge of the paranoiac and repressive with the schizophrenic and creative.[99] Abandoning this rigid dichotomy, for Land, implodes the entire theory of the desiring-political. This leads Land to posit that, as a consequence of an all too credulous reading of Virilio, Deleuze and Guattari have been led astray in their interpretation of the National Socialist assemblage, and accordingly, that the suicidal line of flight is a defective concept. Land argues that the implication that Nazism was in some way a matter of letting go is simply implausible.[100] Nazism is the definition of a paranoiac tendency for Land, defined by the proliferation of enemies and paranoid subjectivities, gloom, oppression, the love of obedience, leadership and symbols,

> the icons of molar identity . . . nostalgia for what is maximally bovine, inflexible, and stagnant: a line of racially pure peasants digging the same patch of earth for eternity [and] above all, resent everything impetuous and irresponsible . . . to eliminate the disorder of uncontrolled flows, and persecute all minorities exhibiting a nomadic tendency.[101]

This is a coherent reading of the Nazi regime, but it is a misleading critique of Deleuze and Guattari; the concept of a 'fascist line of flight' in no way detracts from the fact that Nazism was a revolutionary nationalism, and thus an assemblage with heavily paranoiac tendencies.

Eugene Holland develops a more sophisticated iteration of Land's critique, suggesting that Deleuze and Guattari's account of fascist suicidalism makes for a misunderstanding of the regimes historical character.[102] For Holland,

> [an] apocalyptic moment of Hitler's sheds little or no light on the emergence of the fascist movement that depended for part of its support on rapid

acceleration of the development of productive forces and on the massive integration of unemployed and underemployed populations into the workforce.[103]

The Nazi regime pursued the mobilisation of the entire economy to war precisely by extension of its original promise to restore self-confidence in the German nation. 'What had not been possible to maintain (or attain quickly enough) through the development of productive force alone increasingly required the pursuit of power and domination (scapegoating at home and conquest abroad) to achieve.'[104] Whilst it is clear from Telegram 71 'that the fascist regime eventually reached a point at which Hitler could see its imminent demise and would have preferred its total destruction to defeat', this was peculiar to the contingent historical progression of World War II. Holland concludes that we have no reason to assume there was anything 'intrinsically "suicidal" about historical fascism . . . rather, the Nazi State turned to total war and then pure destruction for contingent historical reasons.'[105] His point is that extending the theory of a suicidal line of flight from Hitler's Telegram 71 mistakes the historical specificities of the National Socialist event for a universal truth about fascism and, even more unsustainably, desire as such. We must therefore simply abandon the theory of the suicidal line of flight as a conceptual aberration, and concentrate on the political dangers of molar and molecular striation.

The problem is that Deleuze and Guattari state variously (and emphatically not only in the context of National Socialism) that the danger on lines of flight is important not only in its scale (of destructive consequence) but also in its significance to their work as a whole.[106] Deleuze and Guattari do not come up with the concept of the suicidal line of flight by universalising the particular idiosyncrasies of Nazism. Rather, they view National Socialist suicidalism as an exemplar of the danger integral to deterritorialising desire. In this sense their claim must be distinguished from Helmut Thielicke's theory of fascism as nihilism.[107] Thielicke argued that the suicidal dimensions of the Nazi assemblage should be understood as indicative of cynicism amongst the National Socialist leadership.[108] Hitler simply disguised his nihilistic convictions with ideological baggage 'in order to give them the value of spiritual suggestion'.[109] Deleuze and Guattari, by contrast, see in the Nazi lionisation of death a true desire for self-mortification, and argue that is characteristic of the kind of revolutionary political line that the Nazi state exemplified. It is, they claim, a peculiarity of any absolute political deterritorialisation that it may turn suicidal in some contexts and thus become autoannihilating. The issue at hand is whether it is more credible to interpret these Nazi statements as simple fakery, and so inoculate the urge to revolution of any apocalypticism, or to find in the event a disturbing potential of the revolutionary urge itself. Deleuze and Guattari's theory of fascism challenges us to face our distaste for admitting to the revolutionary dimensions of such movements.

The idea that the fascist ticket is a "blatant and insistent" lie is shared with Adorno and Horkheimer, but is also implicit to Carl Schmitt's classification of fascist ideas as politically useful myths.[110] Deleuze and Guattari's claim, then, is highly contentious. It is, however, less difficult to substantiate than the claim to a secret nihilistic cynicism. Comparative empirical support is available, in the form of historical assemblages which are characterised by typologically similar constellations of lines, which suggests that the suicidal state concept is at least a plausible supposition. The Meiji state provides just such comparative backing. The institutional roots of the Meiji constitution lay in the forcible opening of Japan to external influences by Commodore Perry, which brought about the end of the much more supple and segmented Shogunate system in 1854. Following this catastrophic event, a wholesale remodelling of the Japanese internal order was pursued under the guidance of domestic elites, with the explicit aim of constructing a strong centralised state that would be able to resist foreign incursions in the future. Postconstitutional Japan was organised around the figure of the emperor, who was framed in messianic terms as the representative of the rebirth of the Japanese nation. The Meiji constitution established a totalitarian apparatus which initiated a program of interventions at the social, cultural and institutional levels. These reforms sought to westernise the Japanese social order and set up a European style state-bureaucracy. Traditional practices were deemphasised whilst the traditional folk religion was steadily overcoded by state-nationalist discourse. The genetic identity of the Japanese was emphasised and a military nationalist and colonialist discourse promoted.[111] The Meiji totalitarian state apparatus was established gradually, over a far more extended historical period than the corresponding institutional formation in Nazi Germany. It was founded by a relatively small group of oligarchs rather than the upswell of a microfascist social movement. Similarly, the institutional format and content of Meiji totalitarianism was clearly unique to its particular historical and cultural milieu, and notable for its exceptional focus on the quasi-deified figure of the emperor. Nevertheless its assemblage was clearly defined by the totalitarian organisation of social, cultural and religious practices, institutional and military structures, and ethnic/religious identity. It entailed, as such, a powerful molar charge of reterritorialising desire.

Emiko Ohnuki-Tierney constructs her superb analysis of how the kamikaze emerged by reference to a political aesthetic circulating around the cherry blossom imagery. She traces how 'successive state machineries' deployed the cherry blossom imagery, a symbol with a long history of cultural associations with Japanese identity, until it became the 'dominant political and military symbol'.[112] It became, in state national discourse, an identifier of the particular Japanese essence or soul. This was gradually incorporated into the discourse of colonial expansion: foreign territories were now claimed for Japan on the grounds that the cherry tree had been found there. In colonised spaces, the cherry tree was exported to 'symbolically stamp areas as spaces for Imperial Japan'.[113] This was, however, not simply a molar ideological structure into which the individual pilots were subsumed. The cherry blossom had long been associated with a wide milieu of significations within Japanese culture, constituting a supple marker of selfhood. The cherry blossom as cultural signifier was implicated not in a single set of meanings, but in a complex of relationships. Its anthropological connotations incorporated life and death, but also reproduction, fertility, time and norm subversion.[114] Rather than seeing this as purely a regime of signs constructed by the totalitarian state to support its molar order, Ohnuki-Tierney shows how this aesthetic brought into play a supple segmentarity to build a dynamic and supportive resonance machine for the organisation of desire within the closed vessel of the totalitarian state. That the cherry blossom aesthetic from the very beginning incorporated multiple quanta of deterritorialisation suggests that it was always defined by an abstract machine of mutation rather than overcoding, and so exceeded the functions assigned to it by the totalitarian state. Its dynamic interpretative mutability was to almost fatally limit the ability of the totalitarian state to stabilise the aesthetic under the imperial referent. The state overcoded the cherry blossom aesthetic with a military connotation, marking soldiers' uniforms, to characterise the 'blooming life' of the soldier. Gradually the flower came to be identified with the idea of a 'beautiful' martial death for the emperor.[115] It would become the "exclusive visual symbol" of the kamikaze.[116]

During the progression of World War II, the Yasukuni Shrine was at the centre of a molar ideological strategy, aestheticizing martial death for the emperor through the narrative of heroic military dead being reborn at the shrine as falling cherry blossoms.[117] This military overcoding of the cherry blossom signifier was increasingly distributed throughout the capillaries of the Japanese social order – a ' "stupid and repugnant cry", Long live death!' appearing in school textbooks, songs and novels under the cherry blossom motif; a dispersed microrepetition of state militarism, bound into a supple register of patriotic sentiment associated with the cherry blossom aesthetic.[118] This seems to confirm Deleuze and Guattari's claim that 'the stronger the molar organization is, the more it induces a molecularization of its own elements.'[119] The state developed a molecular cultural resonance machine that bound Japanese society to the totalitarian project through an aesthetic militarism, binding the molar formalisation of desire around the emperor into a molecular resonance machine that was far more supple. This clearly, as Ohnuki-Tierney argues, explains the diversity of individual participation in the kamikaze strategy, but it does not explain why and how the state assemblage as a whole set out on so manifestly suicidal a line. No war machine social movement preceded crystallisation into the Japanese totalitarian state. Japan's fascist assemblage thus ran a different course to that under Nazism, but its conjugation of molar and molecular lines with a resonant war machine would also sow the seeds of an intense line of flight towards state suicide. An aesthetic war machine took form within the molecular resonance machine built by the Japanese state. It was this war machine which gave birth to the kamikaze by tipping the entire state assemblage into suicidalism.

Assigned a military connotation by the state, to legitimate its military practice this aesthetic war machine was set to flight and captured the entire assemblage to its function. All elements of the assemblage, from the individual pilots to the emperor himself, were swept up by its line. The military associations of the aesthetic would now fatally haunt the Meiji regime. As in Germany, the poor progress of the war, as opposed to any essential cultural characteristic of Japanese desire, would allow the full actualisation of a suicidal line of flight. What Ohnuki-Tierney fails to fully recognise is that in turning this aesthetic into the pillar of its own legitimation, the totalitarian state had surrendered its legitimacy to its military apparatus (the cherry blossom marking the uniforms of soldiers and sailors) and the concept of martial death. To refuse the logic of its practical extension would be to jettison its aesthetic legitimation qua molecular resonance machine. The issue here is thus more than the tragic misrecognition, by the individual pilots, of a totalitarian state ideological strategy. The cherry blossom aesthetic had become a war machine overcoded by its destructive supplement, to which the Japanese state apparatus was now surrendered. The small group of military officers responsible for developing the strategy, who presented it to the state bureaucracy, acted as representatives of the military-aesthetic war machine staging a takeover of the entire assemblage. This aesthetic war machine would now set out on an unlimited line of flight into pure war (victory or death), dragging with it the whole of Japanese society. The Meiji assemblage became an appendage of its war machine's suicidal flight. State suicide was not a product of totalitarian state logics; it was a politics of pure war. Deleuze and Guattari point out that the 'reversion of the line of flight into a line of destruction [. . .] already animated the molecular focuses of fascism' in the German case.[120] Similarly, the emergence of the special attack methods cannot be understood without reference to the aesthetic war machine that the totalitarian state had set to resonate within society. A line of flight was built on the supple molecularity of the cherry blossom aesthetic, and set to destructive resonance by the state totalitarian apparatus, which carried the entire assemblage towards pure abolition.

One cannot overstate the psychological effect of the special attack methods on the Americans.[121] The practice was taken to prove the incomprehensibility of the enemy.[122] Morris argued that the special attack strategy 'produced indignation and rage out of all proportion to the tactical importance', and so likely contributed to the decision to drop the atomic bombs. It seemed to prove the likelihood of fanatical Japanese resistance to invasion.[123] In this sense, the special attack methods directly drove the very real possibility of collective abolition that faced Japan at the close of World War II.[124] By the end of the war, it seemed to its adversaries, that Japan 'no longer had anything but war as its object and would rather annihilate its own servants than stop the destruction'.[125] Yet, unlike Nazi Germany at the very brink of abolition, following the atomic bombings of Hiroshima and Nagasaki and the equal if not greater devastation wrought by strategic bombing, Japan's state apparatus reasserted control over its war machine and surrendered. Virilio, commenting on the fall of Japan, argued that if it 'were not for Hirohito, who was a fairly intelligent individual, the militarists would have carried out a national suicide: an entire country committing mass suicide.'[126] Certainly much of the military establishment would have indeed have fought to the last man, and most of the officers involved in the special attack operations committed suicide rather than surrender with their emperor. Zizek observes that amongst Japanese expatriates in Brazil, a group calling themselves Shindo Renmei refused to accept that defeat was anything but enemy propaganda, going so far as to fake magazine covers to provide evidence that Japan had won the war. 'The perpetrators of the fake stuck to it fanatically, were ready to sacrifice their lives from it. They knew that their denial of Japan's surrender was false, but they nonetheless refused to belief in Japanese surrender.' This suggests no ciphered nihilism, rather here we see the suicidal line of flight continuing long after the totalitarian state apparatus had dissolved.[127]

Paul Virilio argued that a Japanese state suicide would have been even more drastic than the National Socialist one because it would have formed a collective pact based on the cultural-aesthetic machine rather than an injunction from the despot.[128] The cherry blossom aesthetic might certainly have bound the population directly to any potential plunge into state suicide, but the dynamics were not as alien to our culture as Virilio and others have insisted. Whilst undoubtedly the supple segmentations of the cherry blossom aesthetic built on a uniquely Japanese cultural milieu, the construction of the Japanese suicide state only took place via the contingent assemblage of the three lines, not according to some Japanese essence.[129] In turning to the uniqueness of Japanese culture to explain the suicidal line of Meiji, Virilio's claim is quite different from Deleuze and Guattari's. There should be no doubt about the cartographic singularity of the German or Japanese suicide states. The Nazi state was constructed by a war machine (the National Socialist movement), which was then set to violent resonance within the state. It should be unsurprising that it was unable to pull back from a suicidal conclusion to its trajectory. The Meiji desiring-assemblage, realising that it must rein in its war machine or follow its line of abolition, was able to return to its paranoiac foundations in the molar line (the emperor) to pull itself back from the brink of the abyss. Hitler, riding at the head of the war machine, thrust on into utter desolation.

This explains Deleuze and Guattari's claim that challenging paranoia with lines of flight is never sufficient. The suicidal danger that is proper to lines of flight is, Deleuze and Guattari state categorically in *A Thousand Plateaus*, much more terrifying than the totalitarian centralised power built on a conjugation of the molar and molecular, which was paradoxically in the end to save Japan from self-abolition, as Virilio noted. This brings us, however, no closer to confirmation of Deleuze and Guattari's imputation that political lines of flight per se have suicidal excess as their integral danger. This is a matter which goes beyond any actual (fascist or nonfascist) political assemblages, and concerns rather the cartography of the desiring-political as such.

Revolution and annihilation

Rather than seeing historical fascism as the product of modernity's compression of the totalitarian mind, Deleuze and Guattari drew a much more unsettling implication. What distinguishes fascist from totalitarian assemblages is the former's possession of a revolutionary line. Does this mean that all revolutions are destined for the same fascist fate, that revolutionaries are integrally prone to turning out badly? No less than Deleuze and Guattari, Alain Badiou and Slavoj Zizek are occupied by the problem of the integrally suicidal revolution. Each, in seeking to think of revolutionary politics as a matter of passionate commitment, reaches this common insight; creative revolution always implies its opposite, extravagant annihilation.

Badiou and Zizek's accounts both build directly on the Lacanian architecture of lack, which was rejected so emphatically in *Capitalism and Schizophrenia* for putting death into desire. This conceptual choice determines their disagreement from Deleuze and Guattari, but it cannot explain the radical divergence in their individual critiques.

Badiou has presented his work as a direct challenge to Deleuze's philosophy.[130] There is no doubt that on many issues there is little space between these thinkers.[131] The similarities of their two problematizations regarding revolutions and destructive annihilation, however, stand in stark contrast to the choice between a metaphysic of lack and metaphysic of excess that draws them apart.[132] Badiou's work is explicitly organised around the problematic shared with Deleuze and Guattari: the relationship between creation and destruction in revolutionary events. This is clearest in *Theory of the Subject*, where revolutionary subjectivity is deemed identical with the need to terminate the place from whence that subject emerges.[133] Badiou's central concern in this text is for how the party can fulfil its role as 'the leader to come of its own termination'.[134] *Theory of the Subject* is an explicitly Lacanian text.[135] In it, Badiou views the combination of integral or ontological lack and an always destructive departure from the place of origin as essential to the revolutionary act, with the emphasis being explicitly on the 'topology of destruction'.[136] Creation occurs at the 'border of lack', but it is destruction which makes possible a revolutionary 'mastery of loss'.[137] Inasmuch as the revolutionary subject appears in an operationalisation of destruction, the similarity to Deleuze is apparent.

Badiou recognises these resonances, but argues that because Deleuze completely refuses lack he is driven to recentre the political subject on excess.[138] This framing of lack versus excess is a crucial distinction that will become increasingly significant throughout Badiou's work and as his debate with Deleuze evolves. In his early work, *Theory of the Subject*, Badiou argues that a radical commitment to revolution as such, courage, is a key operator in actual revolutionary events. This lays the grounds from some questionable politics. Badiou, as Hallward points out,[139] in relying on pure confidence in the face of the anguish necessary for revolution, sets no limits and no restraints. He thus ends up being an apologist for reeducation campaigns as the terrorising price paid for revolutionary novelty.[140] The barbarism of destruction integral to revolution is a continuous theme in Badiou's work.[141] Revolutionaries are always 'anxious to exceed the excess in the act of interruption'.[142] Because this is a necessary side effect of the need to destroy the place of revolutionary subjectivity, we must accept this 'vital risk of interruption'. This is the source of the 'superego of terror' which has haunted every revolutionary project.[143] Badiou's responses to this vital risk in *Theory of the Subject* are pretty unconvincing.[144] Politics is a matter of commitment, passional not logical, to a revolutionary project. He recognises that this means an inevitable danger of (auto)destructive excess. Badiou rejects the 'vulgar moralism' of many anti-Stalinist arguments of his day for missing this fact: 'the essence of terror is political.'[145] Indeed, for Badiou, only revolutionary courage itself can save us from fatalism, passive nihilism or the embrace of radical dissolution and crisis.

Yet given that 'the essence of confidence is having confidence in confidence,' it is hard to see how courage can preclude the 'rise of a purely destructive 'nihilism' amidst the revolutionary 'gesture of abandonment'.[146] *Theory of the Subject* is defined by a single problematic: Revolutionary politics tends to go badly precisely because it is an ontologically passional matter.

The inherently risky or destructive potentialities in revolutionary politics exposed, but not really addressed, in *Theory of the Subject*,[147] drives Badiou, in his subsequent *Being and Event*, to invent a concept of lack reinvigorated by a mathematical ontology of the void. The central point of Badiou's set-theoretical ontology of the 'void-set' or 'multiple-of-nothing' is that it allows him to think in multiplicities without any organising unity or speculative metaphysics of the one.[148] There is a kind of axiomatic decision here, marking a fidelity to the mathematical theory of the void (associated with Cantor) which now comes to condition Badiou's entire project.[149] The mathematics of the void provides a means to articulate the messianic activity of lack with respect to destructive revolutionary excess. Indeed, the function of the void in Badiou's new framework is to limit the need for destruction in revolutionary political events, by allowing novelty to emerge literally ex nihilo from lack itself.[150] This entails turning away from the problem of subjectivity to the question of truth. Truth processes are generic for Badiou. Political, artistic, amorous, scientific truths are always exceptional; they are never part of the objective state of affairs, what Badiou terms the situation. Truth is indiscernible, excessive and explosive for the situation. Truth is thus quite different from knowledge: it is precisely that which exceeds the knowable in the situation – an event. Truth is an event which takes place always at a site which is specific to but not specified by the situation.[151] This site, in the generic process of truth, is the 'edge of the void' which haunts every concrete historical situation.[152] The void in a situation is that which defines it without being part of it. It is that which, subtracted from the situation, gives it its difference. Subjectivity is the affirmation of or fidelity to the event of truth: For Badiou, 'a subject is a militant of truth.'[153] Fidelity to a truth involves naming it the site of its event (naming the proletariat as the site of the void in capitalism, for example). This, once again, requires courage. Faithful commitment to living a truth is forcing 'the situation itself to confess its own void'.[154] Fidelity to the event is a matter of naming or 'sounding' the 'site of the unpresentable' lack in the situation and being faithful to all its implications.[155] Fidelity is slow and steady continuation of the event through to the destabilisation and alteration of the state of the situation; it is the praxis of lack by which (for example revolutionary political) subjects are formed.[156]

Badiou clearly continues to skirt the fanaticism of 'blind faith'.[157] Badiou is attempting to root the revolution in an assertion or pure passion for revolution itself; he cannot but risk disastrous commitment. It is all too easy to see how a subject utterly absorbed in fidelity might arise. Badiou argues that the dynamics of creative events are indeed prone to becoming hysterical, and in the end a pure destructionism of self and other. Resonances, therefore, continue to be apparent with respect to Deleuze and Guattari's vision of the line of flight descending into abolition.[158] The similarities here are confirmed when we see that it is fascism for Badiou, like Deleuze and Guattari, which represents the primary case of such excessive fidelity to the void as such. Badiou argued in *Ethics*,[159] in quite an explicit contradiction of Deleuze and Guattari, that the Nazi event was, in line with Thielicke, a matter of fakery – the simulacrum of an event – and that this was the source of its terror.[160] 'Nazi politics was not a truth process'; it simply mimicked a real revolution.[161] Its reactive mimicry of the revolutionary truth process was not, however, Nazism's most disastrous ethical feature. It was the attempt to fill out the void, to name it as such which defined Nazism's definitive horror. In naming the Jew as the void, Nazism set out to eliminate the void from its situation.[162] Nazism attempted to name the unnameable void itself; this is what makes it paradigmatically evil for Badiou.[163] Evil is 'naming the void'.[164] This risk or problem of evil is integral to any truth event, the result of which is the 'obscurantist subject'.[165] Such subjects seek a total truth by naming and evaluating 'all the elements of the objective situation'.[166] Evil is the suicidal absolutization of the truth event's power. It can be avoided only by categorically refusing to name and so fill the void. Badiou has, by *Ethics* and *Being and Event*, completely abandoned the idea that destruction is itself a 'necessary part of the newness' in an event.[167] Destruction is no longer the kernel of the generic event of truth. When destruction takes place it is only a matter of the contingent state of the situation. It remains pragmatically, but not essentially, functional in some, and especially political, events.

There can be no fail-safe against the possibility of naming the void.[168] We, as subjects, must simply decide to allow lack to remain lack: The central principle here seems to be recognition of our limits or finitude.[169] We must refuse to seek total truth if we are to prevent disaster. The sites on the edge of the void, named so as to allow fidelity to their truth event, must retain an aspect which is unnameable. The unnameable is that element in truth which conditions its infinite process; it is the lack that prevents truth from becoming a completed excess. By remaining unnameable, the truth of a situation remains incomplete. As long as lack remains lack, destruction may be limited only to pragmatic necessity. In politics, the key connotation here is that we must withhold naming the community which revolution seeks to establish, in the same way that one must avoid objectifying one's lover. Truth is never total and must be appreciated as such if it is not to be totalitarian or fanatical. This limitation on truth is an act which only a subject can effect, so Badiou presumes the post facto limitation of truth by a subject constituted by fidelity to that truth. This is a very awkward move, which assumes that a kind of revolutionary cynicism is necessary, which surely counteracts the fidelity-courage-affirmation by which Badiou founds the subject.[170] It also requires some historically questionable faith in the restraint of existing revolutionary subjects. Badiou seems to recognise that his solution in lack remains unsatisfactory; the political still opens always onto barbarism. Violent barbarity is the integral risk in all truths.

In Badiou's more recently translated *Logics of Worlds* (2009b), the analytic of fascism (as radical evil, the obscure) is extended to apply to the Jihad. This is a significant move. Furthermore, *Logics of Worlds* seems to return curiously to the argument of *Theory of the Subject* inasmuch as destruction once again becomes part of the kernel of the truth event. In *Logics of Worlds*, the idea of an essential link between that destruction and the subjective capacity is revived; the revolutionary must put 'to death its own over-existence'.[171] Suicidal destruction is now deemed essential, as well as subtraction, to destroy the appearance of the situation (or World) as necessary; the ordinary social idea must be destroyed for new subjects and new worlds to appear: Destruction is the princedom of the subject.[172] This reembrace of destruction is tied to Badiou's description of subjectivity as a wager, or leap, which can always go wrong and become obscure by naming the void.[173] The obscure subject is represented today by the Islamist, which Badiou understands as an occultation of desire which, over-enamoured by the absolute, seeks to nurture it everywhere and develops a 'hatred of every living thought, every transparent language and every uncertain becoming'.[174] A conservative impulse 'displayed in the world by the rebel body and its emblem'; under the banner of the new event, political Islamism hides a 'descent of this present' into the past.[175] Badiou argues that we observe here a pseudo-revolutionary event – what Deleuze and Guattari might term a reterritorialisation masquerading as a deterritorialisation.

Excessive destructionism is the most definitive characteristic of the obscure:

> The obscure body engineers the destruction of the body: the appropriate word is fascism, in a broader sense than the fascism of the thirties. One will speak of generic fascism to describe the destruction of the organised body through which the construction of the present (of the sequence) had previously passed.[176]

Islamism, as the contemporary modality of the fascistic-obscure, for Badiou, is a violent negation which involves a kind of monstrous fidelity that 'crushes the past in the name of the sacrifice of the present'.[177] In this way, the obscure subject is suicidal in its extravagant embrace of destructive excess; it utterly destroys the organised body. It should be clear that Badiou's thesis has now moved remarkably closer to Deleuze and Guattari's, at least on this specific topic.[178] The danger which haunts Badiou's thesis is that of an excessively destructive subject over-enamoured by the void, which 'lives for an idea' but allows that idea to drive into utter horror and desolation by its occultation or naming of the void. This is suggestively similar to Deleuze and Guattari's account of a line of revolutionary flight which goes suicidally excessive and descends into abolition by becoming over-enamoured by its objective trajectory into a black hole. Badiou confirms that (auto)destructive excess is a danger integral to the desiring-political itself. Politics is to live for an idea for Badiou, which always risks taking it too far, becoming swept away by its absolutization; believing the idea is complete. For Deleuze and Guattari, the line of flight is a deterritorialisation of desire (not semiosis or truth). This conceptual divergence suggests that it is natural to that deterritorialisation for one to become enamoured by the movement itself, embracing in the process a seductive potentiality for extravagant self-abolition.

These two conceptual vocabularies frame politics as a passional matter which assumes the danger of excessive (auto)destruction. What distinguishes Badiou from Deleuze and Guattari is his quite different vision of how that extravagant excess is to be restrained. For Badiou, the refusal to name the void or insistence that lack remains lack prevents us from becoming fascistic, excessively or destructively over-enamoured in all our truth processes. In refusing lack, Badiou accuses Deleuze of being unable to contain destructive excess.[179] Under Badiou's conceptual architecture the lack which must stand unnamed in a truth is all that prevents our fidelity to it from becoming fascistic. Lacan's concept of lack thus remains the determinant influence on Badiou, as he makes clear at the end of *Logic of Worlds*: 'Life is what gets the better of the drives.'[180] Badiou disavows Freud's death drive as a recipe for disaster,[181] accepting Lacan's conceptual improvement, which Deleuze and Guattari challenged. The consequences are predictable. For Badiou, we become infinite in living for an idea.[182] This is a kind of heroism rooted in our desire to live, by which new worlds are rendered possible.[183] Through the 'inevitable death in the injunction of the event' which destroys the place from whence the revolutionary subject appears, the infinite subject in fidelity to an idea becomes possible: 'Finitude is not a natural attribute of being.'[184] Yet we reach infinity by fidelity to an idea which we must accept as defined by a lack. Recognition of an idea's imperfection or lackingness is what keeps us from embarking on a fascistic fidelity. As such, inasmuch as he argues that it is in pursuit of infinity conditioned by our appreciation of ontological lack that we commit to an idea, Badiou is simply providing more efficient counter-mnemotechnic tools through which to forget our mortality; fidelity is a life strategy for denying death/becoming immortal, but through an appreciation of ontological lack we can avoid getting overexcited in that project (i.e. too destructive. Badiou's thought, like Lacan's, is conditioned by the fear of death.

This explains why Badiou thinks that Deleuze's interpretation of death and desire is profoundly nonrevolutionary.[185] He accuses Deleuze of a theistic gesture which amounts to an obsession with mortality or human finitude: The implication is that Deleuze and Guattari develop a metaphysics of excess, which underpins their politics, and amounts to little more than a submission to the animalistic becoming-finite of any body. In this sense, Deleuze and Guattari's vision of desire's deterritorialisation amounts to being-for-death. Badiou's marks here a key feature of Deleuze and Guattari conceptual grammar; it precisely does not facilitate an immortalising project conditioned by recognition of ontological lack. Deleuze and Guattari's political philosophy is an assault on all architectures of lack. The opposition between their conceptual projects is starkly evident.

Slavoj Zizek acknowledges that what is at stake here is the politics of mortality, but develops an almost diametrically opposed critique of Deleuze and Guattari to that articulated by Badiou. This is curious, since Zizek is also a Lacanian, and an admirer of Badiou. His main divergence from the latter is on the subject of death.[186] For Zizek, Badiou's greatest insight concerns precisely the injunction '*mieux vaut un desastre qu'un desetre*: better to take the risk and engage in fidelity to a Truth-Event, even if it ends in catastrophe.'[187] He accuses Badiou of failing to follow through, however: of obstructing the revolutionary passage of the act inasmuch as he rejects (explicitly in his most recent work) the problem of finitude and the death drive.[188] A mathematical faith in the unnameable void as such misses, for Zizek, our revolutionary engagement with the undead real of the death drive which stands behind it. Zizek argues that Badiou ignores Lacan's explicit claim that in an experience of the void the 'subject finds himself confronted with the death drive at its purest' and that confrontation is prior to the sublimation that might institute a revolutionary event.[189] Following Lacan, Zizek argues that the undead real is indeed unnameable, but that events nevertheless really do intervene in this unnameable core.[190] The event, if it occurs, is never simply a matter of truth unnamed, but of our direct experience of the undead real as fiction. Revolutions which go extravagantly and suicidally destructive are not simply an integral danger to be avoided (which results from naming the void), but literally intrinsic to their reality as expressions of the undead drive. The revolutionary political event is the moment when the

> opposition between a 'crazy' destructive gesture and a strategic political decision momentarily break down. This is why it is theoretically and politically wrong to oppose strategic political acts, as risky as they might be, to radical 'suicidal' gestures a la Antigone, gestures of pure self-destructive ethical insistence with, apparently, no political goal. The point is not simply that, once we are thoroughly engaged in a political project, we are ready to risk everything for it, inclusive of our lives, but, more precisely, that only such an impossible gesture of pure expenditure can change the very coordinates of what is strategically possible within a historical formation.[191]

Truly revolutionary events involve surrendering to the destructive undead drive.[192] Radically this means embracing the most terroristic dimensions of revolutionary politics. In what runs the risk of being read as an ode to irresponsibility, Zizek closes *The Ticklish Subject* (2008) with the observation that whilst we must resist the temptation of trying to 'directly provoke a catastrophe' in the hope that an 'act will somehow occur' – a strategy he associates with the Red Army Faction and the Unabomber – 'one should no less firmly resist the opposite temptation of the different modalities of dissociating the act from its inherent catastrophic consequences.'[193]

It seems clear to Zizek that 'one should *insist on the unconditional need to endorse the act fully in all its consequences,*' even the most destructive ones.[194] Zizek thus radicalises Badiou's implication that there is 'something inherently terroristic in every authentic act, in its gesture of thoroughly redefining the rules of the game, inclusive of the very basic self-identity of its perpetrator' because 'a proper political act unleashes the force of negativity that shatters the very foundation of our being.' Terror is not simply integral to the revolutionary act but even sometimes good.[195] This seems to supply cogency to Krips's claim that 'rather than simply misreading Badiou's politics, Zizek perverts it to the point that it loses touch with the domain of the political.'[196] Zizek articulates what is at stake in the relationship between death and lack: In challenging Badiou's faith in the moderating effects of the unnameable void, Zizek suggests that a politics of revolutionary desire is always a politics of terror. Once we see terror as rooted even deeper in the essence of the political than in the (for Badiou, evil) practice of naming the void, that is to say, as rooted in the undead real of the revolutionary act itself, we are left with the inevitable conclusion that the desiring-political is always a matter of extravagantly self-destructive excess to the exact same degree that it is a matter of revolutionary natality or creation.

When talking of the dangers of deterritorialisation in *A Thousand Plateaus* Deleuze and Guattari also explicitly rejected any idea of the destructive revolutionary act which needs to be followed closely by rational processes of political reconstruction. They embrace a concept of permanent revolutionary becoming, but they do not embrace a vision of revolutionary events as irrevocably terroristic. This is because, for Deleuze and Guattari, man or woman's creative potentialities are not predicated on the existence of ontological lack – either undead drive or awful horror of our mortality. Deleuze and Guattari argue that the lesson of political deterritorialisation's integral terror is precisely the opposite one taken by Zizek: We must take care. We don't want to 'blow apart the strata', but rather to reconstitute it, carefully, delicately, creatively; to make it shift and become-other. This is not, they argue, a matter simply of step-by-step transformations in society; the aim is a revolutionary 'great rip' like 1968, but reaching such a rip is absolutely a matter which takes caution if it is not to become suicidal. As such, like Badiou, they are concerned to limit the destructive consequences of revolutionary events, whilst recognising their integral capacity for excess. Becoming-revolutionary is not a characteristic of desire, or a type of desire (fidelity to an idea); rather all assemblages have revolutionary lines. The point is to make them take flight. This involves 'dismantling the organism' which is a process in which 'one courts death', and as such requires an art of caution:[197] 'If you blow apart the strata without taking precautions, then instead of drawing the plane you will be killed, plunged into a black hole, or even dragged towards catastrophe.'[198] The hesitancy that Zizek sees in Badiou is given explicit framing in Deleuze and Guattari, but because they dispense with Lacan's reactionary architecture, their reasoning moves outside Zizek's field of vision.

Too sudden destruction and the machine will 'turn immediately into a body of nothingness, pure self-destruction whose only outcome is death'.[199] Deterritorialisation takes care. In other words, one can recognise the terror which lies at the heart of the political without becoming its resigned cheerleader. Above all, Deleuze and Guattari argue, we need 'a minimum of strata' if we are to 'prevent the plane of consistency from becoming a pure line of abolition and death, to prevent the involution from turning into a regression to the undifferentiated'.[200] The crucial point is that a vision of caution as immanent to the revolutionary process of deterritorialisation itself is necessary because Deleuze and Guattari cannot rely on a consciousness of our ontological lack to provide restraint. We are, they argue, integrally full to bursting; this is what it means to be alive. In stark contrast to Badiou, an understanding of death which does not lack is at the heart of what

Deleuze and Guattari mean a cautious revolutionary politics. Zizek thus argues that Deleuze and Guattari's refusal of lack thus amounts to a disavowal of the reality of castration; they refuse the father figure that is the brute fact of our actual finitude and death.[201] The result for Zizek is that Deleuze and Guattari leave us without orientations, trapped in an endless circular rush of novelty and recreation.

Deleuze and Guattari may be, as Zizek argues, decidedly unencumbered by the problem of human finitude, but they are certainly not unconcerned with it.[202] The strange copresence of two opposite critiques: from Badiou, that Deleuze and Guattari reject lack and become theorists of being-for-death; and from Zizek, that they reject lack and deny finitude altogether, are only possible due to their shared antipathy to a nontragic account of the relationship between death and creativity. The metaphysic of lack, Deleuze and Guattari suggest, is a trick played by power to keep us from becoming revolutionary. In accepting the tragic dictate, critical thinkers have played the supporting role in repressing any strategic vision of creative political action. With the same gesture, they restrict our capacity to grasp the politics and disturbing attraction of fascism.

Mishima's revolution

The novelist Yukio Mishima claimed that the postwar constitution's repudiation of its war machine left Japanese culture grossly distorted by an extradition of the death impulse.[203] He founded the Tatenoki or Shield Corps principally to return war, and with it death, to its rightful place in the Japanese cultural milieu. Modelled on the right-wing secret societies of Japan in the 1930s, down to its kitsch brown uniforms with brass buttons, and lead by devoted student leader Morito, the Shield Corps' earnest imitation of the war machine seemed as unserious as their mission to provide a shield for the divine emperor.[204] That it was an entirely serious matter, at least as far as Mishima was concerned, became very apparent with his suicide in 1970.[205] On 25 November, he arrived at an army base in the centre of Tokyo with four of his most devoted followers. He was brought in to see the presiding officer, a testament to his national profile, carrying an antique samurai sword. He and his four followers proceeded to tie the general to his chair, and then barricaded themselves in his office. A group of officers attempted to storm the room and were attacked by a furious Mishima welding his fourteenth-century blade. After Mishima threatened to kill the general and commit seppuku the officers retreated and rang the police. Mishima demanded, through the door, that the soldiers of the camp be assembled on the parade ground outside the office balcony, and that they maintain silence so he might speak to them. The police arrived, and the soldiers assembled. Mishima stepped out onto the balcony to deliver his final speech. He lambasted recent pacifist youth protests, which embodied the spirit of 1969 in Japan, and in particular, lamented the failure of the politicians to bring the army in to quell them. He spoke of a missed opportunity for the military forces to step in, take power and rewrite the constitution. He called for these gathered elements of a suppressed war machine to rise up with him, overthrow democracy, and restore the emperor to his rightful place.[206] The speech was interrupted by heckling, catcalls, helicopters circling and a general lack of comprehension from the crowd assembled below. In receiving such a decisive negative, Mishima softly declared 'I have lost my dream' and turned on his heels. Walking inside, after commenting that 'they had not heard him very well,' he knelt.[207] Driving a blade into his abdomen, he pulled it across his belly, neatly emptying himself onto the floor. Morito then attempted, ineffectually, to cut his head off, before following him in death.

Mishima's suicide, the first seppuku to have taken place since the end of World War II, was greeted by national and international astonishment. The political meaning of his act is held as profoundly in question by most biographers. Indeed guilt over repressed homosexuality is often deemed a prime mover.[208] Susan Napier responds that Mishima's suicide can only be understood within the sociohistorical conditions of postwar Japan, to which his literary creations were also closely linked.[209] For Mishima, she argued, the emperor was a symbol of continuity across break point that World War II represented. His entire work is a romantic recasting, though fantasy, in search for 'venues of escape from the wasteland of modern Japan'.[210] Mishima's characters' preferences for excessive action embody a quest for restored identity that would find fulfilment 'in the imagery of the Imperial house'.[211] Mishima, with his suicide, sought to fill the void left by the war.[212] Piven counters that Mishima's historic-political commentaries were simply a cipher for an underlying psychodynamics of lack.[213] There is certainly little doubt that, as Piven suggests, sexuality and death are closely related throughout Mishima's fiction. His characters are rarely sympathetic, and tended to annihilation and trauma, and in this context suicide was a sustained concern.[214] The connotation Piven draws is simply that Mishima's politics mirror a psychosis which idealised powerful father figures, alongside the erotic killing of younger men,[215] playing out the fantasy of murdering a weak self-image under the guidance of the superego. Mishima is the classical masochist, for whom the 'eroticization of death is defence against its terror'.[216]

Whether one sees the desire for the emperor orientating his suicide as a mask for underlying psychopathology, or a response to sociohistorical reality, matters little. A totalitarian urge forces Mishima take flight from the fractured self into unity.[217] Either way, Mishima is categorically molar; aiming to defeat his powerful consciousness of lack, with the emperor naming the ideal of molarity or wholeness.[218] Suicide is Mishima's attempt to fill the void. His consciousness of lack can only be sublimated as a masochistic urge to transcendence, seeking to kill death with death.[219] An implicitly Badiouian reading of Mishima as fascist thus defines the extant literature. Thielicke provides a key reference here. He, like Badiou, defined fascism as asserting or naming 'a vacuum, *the nihil*, [because] the assertor himself is oppressed and afflicted by his own nothingness'. In this sense, Mishima's suicide becomes the result of his being 'oppressed by the breakdown' that is consciousness of death.[220] Hypermasculinity and the emperor are ciphers for a despairing reactive nihilism.[221] All fascists, and Mishima may be deemed exemplary here, seek to conquer death by naming the void.[222]

The problem with this reading is that Mishima's extensive writings on politics and death reveal him as no creature of totalitarian lack.[223] Indeed, it is clear that it was precisely his desire for a transformative action that made him a fascist. Badiou's Lacanian assertion that fascism is naming the void is clearly inadequate in the task to politically theorising Mishima. Mishima's obsession with the war machine appeared directly out of the delight in ambiguity that runs throughout of his literature and personality.[224] Where authors seek the empty root in his work and life, they miss the active play of masks in which he was constantly engaged.[225] In search of a true, if absent, centre, we see only what we look for: the reactive attempt to resolve fractured being. By contrast, Mishima's fluid transitions of identity, from the popular film star, to the bodybuilding narcissist, to the fascist agitator; his obsession with costumes, from Hawaiian shorts to military uniforms; his simultaneous adoption of the pose of media celebrity and samurai, suggests a much more active embrace of schizophrenic molecularity than the assumption of a sovereign lack allows.[226] Mishima's obsession with war explicitly emerged within his dynamic play with mask and role.[227]

Mishima claimed he started reading the *Hagakure* during the war, and argued it was the blueprint for his entire oeuvre.[228] Written by a samurai turned priest named Tsunetomo Yamamoto, and recorded by his retainer, the *Hagakure* only became publically available during the Meiji era. Its most famous line – 'the Way of the Samurai is death,' immediately became the slogan of the kamikaze.[229] Amidst postwar guilt, many copies would be burned. It was the ethos of the samurai recorded in this text that attracted Mishima, not the totalitarian function to which it was put by the Meiji regime. Indeed he lamented at length the use of the *Hagakure* for political indoctrination during the war, arguing that it radically exceeded the modernist ideology of the state.[230] Indeed, Mishima saw Meiji as precisely a capitulation, and he rejected any attempt to capture the *Hagakure* to this project. Indeed, as his highly despondent attitude to the emperor confirmed, he was never really a state thinker. The emperor who in 1946 had denounced his divinity as 'imaginary and harmful notion' is roundly denounced even as Mishima offered him a shield.[231] Mishima read in the *Hagakure* a radical critique of both Meiji and the emperor, a frame for his loathing of the pacific status quo, but also of the Meiji past with its surrender to modernity. Mishima's fantasy is not conformism, but a revolutionary nonconformity to all prior and existing registers.[232] Mishima's reading of the *Hagakure* is no ode to the head of state; it is a critique, indictment and demand, written from the perspective of his bounded war machine. The most deterritorialised military elements of the Meiji assemblage, those which finally exceeded the state, are seen as the only route to a vital future for Japan. Mishima reads the *Hagakure* as revealing the presence of an affective exuberance and freedom that escapes all rigidly striated social and moral forms:[233] The military line of flight is vitally prior to totalitarian bureaucratic or cultural concretisation.

Mishima read in the *Hagakure* a revolutionary model of life organised around the desiring-politics of the decision to die.[234] In seeing death as the 'womb of his literary oeuvre', Mishima outlines a distinctively fascistic theory of creation, claiming that 'if art is not constantly threatened, stimulated by things outside its domain, it exhausts itself.'[235] To create, he argued, is always to decide on death in conditions you cannot have chosen. Mishima's central enemy in this task was technocratic bureaucracy, which reduces each individual to a mechanism in a pacifying social machine.[236] The problem is that 'one may neither live beautifully nor die horribly' in a bureaucratic 'age of technicians'. Creative events are simply no longer possible, since they require decisions made moments of mortal crisis. The secret of the Samurai, as Mishima reads the *Hagakure*, is that in any crisis of decision between life and death, one must always decide on death. The affective energetics of the decision explains why this is the case, for only 'self-destruction has to do with a man's free will . . . When one breaks through the constricting forces by choosing to die, one is performing an act of freedom.'[237] Only by deciding on death in a moment thrust upon you from the outside is subjectivity brought to its creative self-excess.[238] The secret to a philosophy of life that is 'strong, vivid, and brimming with energy'[239] is to see 'life and death as two sides of one shield'.[240]

As such, it seems inevitable that Mishima would lionise in Meiji that which he saw as approximating Tsunetomo Yamamoto's decisionism: the kamikaze pilots.[241] What was distinct about these pilots, he argued, is precisely that they did not choose to take part. They were placed by the state in a moment of crisis. Only in their being thrust into that moment of decision were they able to express, in a passion that exceeded them, that which is the essence of the vital: a destructive self-excess. Nowhere more clearly than this does Mishima declare himself for fascism.[242] He reads the *Hagakure*, with echoes of Marinetti, as guided by 'a glorification of energy and passion. Energy is good, lethargy is evil . . . Here there can be no such thing as going too far'.[243] Mishima's was thus 'a philosophy of extremism' which recognised only 'energy as the motivating principle of action'.[244] To be prepared to die, to have complete resolution in whatever belief one has, is the only marker of subjectivity. Mishima notes that the *Hagakure* 'makes no distinction between major and minor beliefs'; in other words, the idea in question is irrelevant. Being is actualised in action: War is thus closest to the fundamental nature of being inasmuch as its integral mania for death establishes a being literally overflowing with vitality.[245] The consequences of death (victory or defeat, success or failure) are as irrelevant as the meaning of death;[246] what matters is the passional energy of its pure action.[247] Existential philosophies of lack are explicitly the object of critique here. To be brimming with vital strength is the very opposite of the manner in which the *Hagakure* was mobilised intellectually during the war to offer solace to those who were set to die.[248] Subjectivity, for Mishima, is at its most intense only when the subject embraces its own energetic proliferation. In this sense, the only true act is one in which you are destroyed.

The kamikaze suicide squadrons did not, for Mishima, glean their vital politics from individual commitment to the ideology of the Meiji regime. Semiosis and significance are completely irrelevant. Mishima assumes they were, in large part, simply forced to take part. He simply rejects the distinction between chosen death and obligatory death in this context. No man is perfectly free to choose death, he claimed, but neither can he be 'completely coerced into it'.[249] A real decision 'can only be made in the cool grim reality of an individual facing death; it is a question of the human spirit in the ultimate state of tension'.[250] Mishima claims 'we are unable to come face to face with death until we are cornered between fate and our choice, and in the final form of death their clings eternally the covert struggle between human choice and superhuman destiny.'[251] This is why 'ultimately we cannot choose death,' for in choosing it we become something else.[252] The 'I' falls away. In death, the sovereign will that might choose dissolves in the face of its own vital proliferation. This is a vision of subjectivity as an action realised only at the point of its explosion.[253] This is why Mishima rejects the 'illusion that we are capable of dying for a belief or a theory'. What matters is the subjective energetic decision by which our significations no longer have any purchase.[254]

Mortal action is the essence of a revolutionary moment for Mishima, indeed the 'revolution *is* action'.[255] His fascism, as such, is no ideologeme of molar identity. Indeed, it has nothing to do with totalitarian semiosis. For the same reason, Mishima's sees suicide as neither political technology nor a metaphysics for the transcendentalization of a political project. The fascism of his suicidal politics lies in its search for a revolutionary transgression of the self by establishing a moment of self-excess. Whereas his suicide is treated in the literature as the autonomic act of an individual, as a flawed or impossible attempt at self-legislation, by territorialising the autos, the self and the imperial sovereign, Mishima understood his own act as a revolutionary flight into fracture. This same suicidal movement defined, in his view, the politics of the kamikaze. Politics did not reside in the fact that the pilots were tragically forced by the state, nor that they were happily committed to their duty; rather, their participation in a fascist line is the result of placing them in a necessarily fatal moment and declaring that there is always something productive there.[256] Fascism finds its vital measure in the purity of its catastrophism, its departure from intentionality and semiosis by way of the institution of a fatal line that carries the world along with it.

We need not assign Mishima with any tangible expectation that the army would rise up as a consequence of his suicide.[257] Mishima's revolutionary actionism rejected any and all logics relating to consequences.[258] His fidelity was to the absolute movement of a war machine, to the excessive energy, passion and intensity of pure war. For Mishima the revolutionary event takes on a radically postinstrumental form. In fully fascist assemblages such as this, success and failure, natality and destruction, occupy the same exterior moment. This inexpungible moment of political life establishes the risk of fascism as politically integral: The revolution as suicide, catastrophe as creation.

Notes

1. Essay reproduced in H. Scott Stokes, *The Life and Death of Yukio Mishima* (New York: Cooper Square Press, 2000), pp. 225–226.
2. Ibid., p. 226.
3. Admiral Nagano put forward this quandary clearly: 'It is agreed that if we do not fight now, our nation will perish. But it may well perish even if we do fight'. See R. Inoguchi, *The Divine Wind: Japan's Kamikaze Force in World War II* (Annapolis: Naval Institute Press, 1958), p. 220.
4. Ibid.
5. A reference, from the period, to the destruction on Kublai Khan's 1274 invasion fleet by a huge storm or *Divine Wind*.

6. Pilot Saburo Sakai quoted in R. L. Rielly, *Kamikaze Attacks of World War II: A Complete History of Japanese Suicide Strikes on American Ships, by Aircraft and Other Means* (Jefferson, NC: McFarland, 2010).
7. US Navy Vice Admiral C. R. Brown suggested that it is thus 'not given to Westerners to understand it' (Inoguchi 1958, p. iv).
8. Rielly 2010, p. 4. See also A. Axell and H. Kase, *Kamikaze: Japan's Suicide Gods* (London: Longman, 2002); R. Lamont-Brown, *Kamikaze: Japan's Suicide Samurai* (London: Arms and Armour Press, 1997).
9. Axell and Kase 2002, p. 9.
10. Rielly 2010, p. 8; E. Ohnuki-Tierney, "Kamikaze," in *Cherry Blossoms, and Nationalisms: The Militarization of Aesthetics in Japanese History* (Chicago: University of Chicago Press, 2002).
11. Rielly 2010, p. 9.
12. R. Benedict, *The Chrysanthemum and the Sword: Patterns of Japanese Culture* (New York: Houghton Mifflin Harcourt, 1967).
13. Rielly 2010, p. 11.
14. E. Ohnuki-Tierney 2002.
15. Ibid.
16. E. Ohnuki-Tierney, *Kamikaze Diaries: Reflections of Japanese Student Soldiers* (Chicago: University of Chicago Press, 2006), p. xvii.
17. Ohnuki-Tierney 2002. This is why Ohnuki-Tierney argues that, if we are to explain their desire to participate, we must recognise the central role played by a failure of symbolic communication – which made it possible for the regime to present the practice as sublime. Leveraging individuals' misrecognition, 'the tokkōtai pilots and other student soldiers [were absolved from needing to] come to terms with the discrepancy between what they perceived and what the state intended' (p. 31).
18. Inoguchi 1958, p. v.
19. Ohnuki-Tierney 2006.
20. Whilst on the one hand the state machine was clearly formidable and insisted on absolute obedience, the collection of diaries translated and assembled by Emiko Ohnuki-Tierney (2006) shows that the individual pilots sought to illuminate and make sense of their situation in a number of ways – from Tadao, Hachiro, or Norimitsu who were deeply invested in philosophical existentialism and romanticism, to Hayashi Ichizo's Christian humanism (p. 179), or Nakao's Liberal individualism. These were the intellectual crème de la crème of Japanese youth – in many cases able to read Nietzsche and Kant in the original German – and naturally sought to make sense of their suicides drawing on their studies.
21. As the first *tokkōtai* bomber put it: 'I am not going on this mission for the emperor or for the empire. I am going because of my beloved wife' (Axell and Kase 2002, p. 12).
22. By contrast with earlier interpretations of nothingness in Japanese philosophy, often that reflected neo-Platonic themes in framing it as the unified pre-Being from which all things emanate and to which all things return.
23. H. Tanabe, *Philosophy as Metanoetics* (Berkeley: University of California Press, 1990), p. lix.
24. Inoguchi 1958.
25. Ibid., p. 206.
26. Rielly 2000, p. 300; Inoguchi 1958, p. 186.
27. G. Deleuze and F. Guattari, *Anti-Oedipus* (London: Continuum, 2004a), p. 366; see also F. Guattari, *Chaosophy* (Los Angeles: Semiotext(e), 2009), p. 70. Though it is worth noting that Deleuze was not exclusively critical of Freud, in *Coldness and Cruelty* he refers to Freud's *Beyond the Pleasure Principle* as a 'masterpiece of philosophical reflection' (G. Deleuze, *Masochism: Coldness and Cruelty*, New York: Zone Books, 1999, pp. 114–115). The text's ambiguities, such as the oscillation between dualism and monism, are seen here as highly elucidatory rather than objectionable. The critique in *Anti-Oedipus* should not, therefore, be taken to mean that Deleuze and

Guattari are calling for a final discard of Freud, as Dufresne does (T. Dufresne, *Tales from the Freudian Crypt*, Stanford: Stanford University Press, 2000).

28. A claim shared with Marcuse (H. Marcuse, *Eros and Civilization. A Philosophical Inquiry into Freud*, London: Abacus, 1972). See Deleuze and Guattari 2004a, p. 73. Ironically, this is the accusation Badiou will, in turn, level at Deleuze and Guattari's philosophy.
29. For Deleuze and Guattari, belief in Oedipus boxes up the life of the child, distorting it under the assumed truth of its 'dirty little secret' (2004a, p. 25); Guattari 2009, p. 198.
30. Their terming the death instinct 'ridiculous' must be recognised as a little misleading; Deleuze and Guattari rework Freud's thesis on the unconscious, but the problem of death and desire is far from simply rejected as ludicrous (see Dufresne 2000). To summarise Freud's account briefly: Freud introduced the death instinct to account for 'mysterious masochistic trends' he identifies in the ego, a basic compulsion towards morbid inertia or the repetition of suffering (S. Freud, *Beyond the Pleasure Principle, Group Psychology and Other Works*, London: Hogarth Press, 1955, pp. 14, 36, 37, 40) which he opposed to an opposite instinctual drive towards the conservation of life. In this framework, the ego acts as a mediating surface between these two basic drives and reality, as modulated by a pleasure principle. Both these instincts are in principle conservative, aiming

> to re-establish a state of things that was disturbed by the emergence of life. the emergence of life would thus be the cause of the continuation of life and also at the same time of the striving towards death; and life itself would be a conflict and compromise between these two trends. (Freud 1955, p. 41)

To this end it constructs a superego to help the ego master the two fundamental unconscious desires, and thereby keep energetic cathexis at a minimum. The central function of the superego is to hold at bay our irrational urges so that we can function in the world. The superego is defined by the 'first and most important identification' undergone by the individual (with the mother and father), which invariably follows the pattern of desire and perception of obstacle exemplified in Sophocles's famous tragedy (S. Freud, *The Ego and the Id and Other Works*, London: Hogarth Press, 1961, p. 31). Resolving the Oedipus complex requires the construction of this internal prohibitory figure which can act as a channel or mediator for the unconscious. The strength to master the unconscious drives is 'borrowed' from the father, and as such the superego is an internalisation of the father's authority. Identification with the mother or father fixes the disposition and genders the individual. The super-ego is thus the 'heir of the Oedipus complex and . . . also the expression of the most powerful impulses': the death instinct. The concept of the death instinct ensured that the ego is defined as the flight into neurosis, where hysterical or nervous dispositions are simply relatively domesticated expressions of the basic drives. The ego is identified by its constitutive diversions of the basic instinctual passions under to the structural constraints of the Oedipal dynamic. Our personality traits (neuroses) are clearly as much a source of suffering (inasmuch as they divert the desires) as pleasure, but the only alternative to their cultivation is the descent into psychosis through surrender to the drives (the loss of self). Structural guilt results from the internalisation of authority, as a sublimated expression of the instincts, manifesting as a certain perverse satisfaction in suffering which Freud termed primary masochism (p. 49). Diverted, or sublimated, manifestations of the drives paradigmatically occur in perverse fusions of the sex and death instincts at the level of desire: secondary masochism and sadism (pp. 164–165). The flight from the instincts which calls up the superego is the source of individual morality or ethical sense, but also of all social conceptions of authority. Freud argues that moral and social order result from the extension of the same logic which establishes primary masochism: a prohibitive rechannelling of the death instinct in particular (p. 168). Civilisation, like the ego, must

keep in check the primary passions, especially the destructive death instinct, through reaction-formations (S. Freud, *Civilisation and Its Discontents*, London: Hogarth Press, 1969, p. 49). Sublimating Eros though a cultural injunction to sociality, civilisation inhibits aggression by sending it back into the individual ego. The construction of a cultural superego or collective guilt reflex, sublimating the destructive death instinct, is indispensable if we are to achieve social stability at the cost of inevitable permanent unhappiness. Without the process of sublimation, civilised society would be unable to keep in check aggression consequent to the death instinct. This was markedly demonstrated in World War I (Freud 1969). The death instinct thus dooms us to an absolutely necessary program of self-repression at both the individual and the collective levels. For Freud, therefore, we must resign ourselves to perpetual discontent (Freud 1961, p. 36).
31. 'Oedipus . . . is the image or the representation slipped into the machine, the stereotype that stops the connections, exhausts the flows, puts death in desire, and substitutes a kind of plaster for the cracks; it is the Interruptrice (the psychoanalysts as the saboteurs of desire)' (Guattari 2009, p. 98).
32. Ibid., p. 146.
33. Deleuze and Guattari 2004a, p. 365.
34. Ibid., p. 342.
35. For whom the social effort to free Eros for the pursuit of pleasure can absorb the force of destructive impulse (Marcuse 1972, p. 187). Or for that matter, Norman O. Brown, who develops an alternative dialectical resolution to the problem of death in desire; understood as representing the integral sickness of man. See N. O. Brown, *Life against Death: The Psychoanalytical Meaning of History* (Middletown, CT: Wesleyan University Press, 2012).
36. See G. Lambert, *Who's Afraid of Deleuze and Guattari?* (London: Continuum, 2006), p. 77. This requires a radical reworking of the problematic of death and desire.
37. Dufresne 2000, p. 115.
38. For Lacan 'the constant pursuit of an illusory unity' which lures us away from recognising our integrally fractured nature 'is surely related to that agony of dereliction which is man particular and tragic destiny', and this, he argues, is 'how Freud was lead to his deviant concept of a death instinct'. Abandoning the meta-biological parameters of Freud's account, Lacan reinterprets the concept of the death instinct as the consciousness of our mortality (structural lack) which drives the fiction of self in ego psychology (J. Lacan, "Some Reflections on the Ego," *International Journal of Psychoanalysis* 34, no. 1 (1953): 11–17, 15; J. Lacan, *Ecrits: A Selection*, New York: Norton, 1977; J. Lacan and J.-A. Miller, *The Seminar of Jacques Lacan*, Cambridge: Cambridge University Press, 1988).
39. M. Heidegger, *Being and Time* (Oxford, Blackwell, 1962).
40. The death instinct becomes the term Freud used to mark the 'symbolic order in travail, the process of coming, insisting on being realised' which establishes the fractured subject and insures '*Je est un autre*' (Lacan quoted in Dufresne 2000, p. 119).
41. N. Land, "Making It with Death: Remarks on Thanatos and Desiring-Production," *British Journal of Phenomenology* 24, no. 1 (1993): 66–76, 74; D. W. Smith, "The Inverse Side of the Structure: Žižek on Deleuze on Lacan," *Criticism* 46, no. 4 (2004): 635–650, 643.
42. For Deleuze and Guattari, far from being structured like a language with lack at its heart, there is no universal syntax of desire, just as there is no rock bottom of foundational instincts which underpin all formations of desire. Death is in no way 'in' it.
43. In this sense, Freud is 'taking part in the work of bourgeois repression at its most far reaching level' (Deleuze and Guattari 2004a, p. 53).
44. This is why Deleuze and Guattari's use of the term Oedipus as a signifier for any concept by which the self is deemed to be preorganised rather than contingently assembled. Whilst the Western cultural location of Oedipus is important, different representative

mechanisms can fulfil oedipal or counter-oedipal functions. The concept of the ego in the work of the early twentieth-century Islamic scholar Said Nursi as a hypothetical and accordingly insubstantial line drawn by God, upon which divine qualities assemble, and which accordingly has no essential meaning or independent existence, might be read as a counter-oedipal model. S. Nursi, *The Words 1: From the Risale-i Nur Collection*, (London: Truestar, 1993).
45. Smith 2004, p. 642.
46. Guattari's work as a therapist at the De Borde clinic in France mobilised this insight to great effect (2009).
47. Mothers, fathers, breasts, phalluses, anuses, etc.
48. Desire is not for reterritorialisation or deterritorialisation; these are immanent processes.
49. William Connolly is thus right to note the 'vague essentialism' of this claim; desire is deterritorialised; this is a founding ontological commitment (W. E. Connolly, *Capitalism and Christianity, American Style*, Durham, NC: Duke University Press, 2008, p. 81).
50. Deleuze and Guattari 2004a, p. 197. In this way, psychoanalysis prevents the appearance of an 'overly creative machinic unconscious [which] would exceed the "good behaviour"' upon which contemporary production relies. Oedipus represents the industry of normalisation which organises the capitalist socius with only very limited direct coercion (p. 202). The oedipalized individual is the delegated agent of consumer capitalism. With contemporary consumer capitalism's assemblage with New Age or Evangelical representations of the prestructured self (soul) it is easy to see how, in this sense, Oedipus functions today in various non-Freudian semiotic regimes. New age discourse repeats post-Fordist norms of self-reliant, individually responsible, fixed-ego, reality-actualising, consumption-orientated identity. In psychoanalysis, the schizophrenic is viewed as departing from ego unity in surrender to the drives. He or she is ill precisely because she is no longer defined by the oedipal structure. This is to interpret desire's natural deterritorialisation as sickness: The capitalist axiomatic 'transforms the breakthrough into a breakdown'. The sick 'schizo' is the result of the productive unconscious being 'led off course, brutally interrupted' by oedipal representation: '[The schizo] is not suffering from a divided self or a shattered Oedipus, but on the contrary, from having been brought back to everything he had left' (p. 135). In this context, capitalism is a social organisation unlike those which have historically preceded it (which sought to rigidly organise or constrain revolutionary flows of desire according to hierarchical classes, castes or ideational structures): Capitalism is defined by 'the task of decoding and deterritorializing the flows' (p. 35). In this sense, capitalism possesses an integrally revolutionary character, a claim held in common with Marx. Capitalism's mode of operation is an axiomatic commitment to deterritorialisation. No transcendent codes survive capitalist monetarization. This is more than a commitment to free liberalised markets or capital mobility; value contingency is applied to all social codes. These themes are common in postmodernist cultural theory, the central insight of which being that consumer capitalism feeds from the fluid identitarian shifts of the population as mediated through popular culture (see for example the works of Zygmunt Bauman, including *Liquid Modernity*, Cambridge: Polity, 2000). This deterritorialisation constantly threatens to destabilise power's (cultural, economic, etc.) distribution in society. Capitalism thus puts in place a whole register of collective infrastructures, generally through media and advertising, which channel the flows of desire in the population into useful, consumption orientated, tasks and which therefore 'constantly counteract, constantly inhibit [the] inherent tendency [towards deterritorialisation] while at the same time allowing it free reign'. In this way, capitalism 'never ceases to interfere with the most intimate levels of subjective life' (Deleuze and Guattari 2004a, pp. 202, 37). A key element in this process is the reoperationalisation of archaisms, such as national identity or religion, which implement collective reterritorialisations simultaneously to the deterritorialisations that are its condition of functioning. William Connolly, for example, argues that an 'evangelical-capitalist resonance machine'

organises production in America today, increasingly defined by an ethos of revenge. That resonance machine functions precisely to suppress deterritorialised tendencies in a society through the 'centred calmness' of family, church, and heterosexual normativity, whilst emphatically supporting a deterritorialising cowboy economics which leads to such insecurity that it ends up fostering ressentiment and militarist obsessions, and promotes ecological disaster (Connolly 2008, pp. 9, 29). The most important, however, is the generalised reification of the individual qua consumer (Deleuze and Guattari 2004a, p. 279). Deleuze and Guattari's schizoanalysis forms an immanent critique of capitalism: so 'Capital cannot disown schizoanalysis without defanging itself' (Land, 1993, p. 67).

51. Guattari 2009, p. 47.
52. R. Mackay and A. R. Avanessian, *#ACCELERATE: The Accelerationist Reader* (Falmouth: Urbanomic, 2014), p. 488. For a critique of the "accelerationist" position from cultural theory, see B. Noys, *Malign Velocities: Accelerationism and Capitalism* (London: Zero Press, 2014).
53. As such, for Deleuze and Guattari, 'social revolution is inseparable from a revolution of desire' (2004a, p. 382). See also Guattari 2009, p. 72.
54. E. Holland, *Deleuze and Guattari's* Anti-Oedipus: *Introduction to Schizoanalysis* (London: Routledge, 1999), p. 304.
55. This is not to advocate an orgy of revolutionary destruction which then might be followed by some kind of 'second stage, of organisation, functioning, serious things', as in traditional models of revolution. Rather, revolutionary politics is dislocated from the normal places, moved into schools, universities, workplaces and prisons, where tendencies in this direction are already in place (Guattari 2009, p. 277).
56. The first volume of *Capitalism and Schizophrenia, Anti-Oedipus*, is often interpreted as being for molecularity. There seems little doubt that, in the text, what are referred to as molecular lines of reterritorialisation or striation are deemed suppler and less prone to rigid organisation. Molecularity is understood as open to becomings, or thresholds, of various kinds. The second volume, *A Thousand Plateaus*, is more explicitly focused on the becomings themselves, and distinguishes molecularity from lines of flight or deterritorialisation, which nonetheless emerge from the supple character of molecular striations.
57. Virtuality is a concept which is highly important in Deleuze's solo work (especially Deleuze, G. (2004c). *The Logic of Sense*. London and New York, Continuum and Deleuze, G. (2006). *Bergsonism*. New York, Zone Books). It is distinguished from the actual. In this context virtuality refers to the fact that the diagrams charted in *Anti-Oedipus* do not purport to be descriptions of specific (i.e. actual) historical forms. In the very same way that they reject the oedipal paradigm as representing something essential about the structure of the unconscious, Deleuze and Guattari reject any understanding of the social field as defined by essential structures for the flux.
58. Primitive regimes operate a flexible molecular segmentarity, defined by ancestral law, the constrained institution of chieftaincy, which allows a limited nomadism. This prevents the decoding of cultural identity whilst deterring the formation of a hierarchical social order.
59. G. Deleuze and F. Guattari, *A Thousand Plateaus* (London: Continuum, 2004b), p. 253.
60. Ibid. The war machine is a virtual diagram, and is not to be confused with the desiring-machines or actual assemblages it builds.
61. See I. Khaldūn, *The Muqaddimah: An Introduction to History* (Princeton, NJ: Princeton University Press, 1969).
62. Deleuze and Guattari 2004b, p. 253.
63. J. Reid in B. Jahn, *Classical Theory in International Relations* (Cambridge: Cambridge University Press, 2006), p. 294.
64. 'Fascism is largely addressed architectonically, as a pole of desires . . . fascism is on the side of paranoia and reterritorialisation, the counter-pole to schizophrenia and deterritorialisation' (J. Protevi, "A Problem of Pure Matter: Fascist Nihilism in *A Thousand Plateaus*," in *Nihilism! Monsters or Energy*, ed. K. A. Pearson and D. Morgan (London: Macmillan, 2000), p. 168).

65. J. Protevi, "A Problem of Pure Matter: Fascist Nihilism in *A Thousand Plateaus*," in *Nihilism! Monsters or Energy*, ed. K. A. Pearson and D. Morgan (London: Macmillan, 2000), p. 167.
66. For Michel Foucault, *Anti-Oedipus* was the account and critique of 'the fascism in us all, in our heads and in our everyday behaviour, the fascism that causes us to love power, to desire the very thing that dominates and exploits us' (Foucault in Deleuze and Guattari 2004a, p. xv).
67. See Land 1993, p. 73.
68. Protevi 2000, p .167.
69. As Benjamin Noys points out, futurism avowed its suicidalism, as a desire for perpetual replacement, to be thrown in the dustbin by the next avant-garde. See Noys 2014, pp. 22, 70, 74.
70. Deleuze and Guattari 2004b, p. 236.
71. Ibid., p. 254.
72. Ibid., p. 250.
73. Ibid., p. 236.
74. N. Thoburn, "What Is a Militant?," in *Deleuze and Politics*, ed. I. Buchanan and N. Thoburn (Edinburgh: Edinburgh University Press, 2008), p. 99.
75. Deleuze and Guattari 2004a, p. 237.
76. Deleuze and Guattari 2004b, pp. 251–252.
77. Ibid., pp. 236, 246.
78. Ibid., p. 247.
79. Ibid.
80. Ibid., p. 248.
81. Ibid., p. 236 (emphasis added).
82. Ibid., p. 246.
83. Ibid., p. 253.
84. Ibid., p. 254.
85. Ibid.
86. Of course, this is not to deny that national socialist state propaganda deployed an ideology of glorious death for the fatherland, as exemplified in Munich's Tomb of the Martyrs.
87. Deleuze and Guattari 2004b, p. 254.
88. Ibid., pp. 253, 255.
89. P. Virilio, "The Suicidal State," in *The Virilio Reader*, ed. J. DerDerian (Oxford: Blackwell, 1998).
90. Deleuze and Guattari 2004b, pp. 255, 253.
91. The three dangers which combined to define Nazism as an assemblage of desire.
92. Deleuze and Guattari 2004b, pp. 252, 255.
93. Ibid., p. 253.
94. Ibid., p. 392.
95. Protevi 2000.
96. Land 1993.
97. Ibid., p. 67.
98. Land 1993.
99. Ibid., p. 70.
100. Ibid., p. 75.
101. Ibid.
102. E. Holland, "Schizoanalysis, Nomadology, Fascism," in Buchanan and Thoburn 2008.
103. Ibid., p. 79.
104. Ibid., p. 83.
105. Ibid.
106. Deleuze and Guattari 2004b. See especially p. 252 but also pp. 122, 178, 180, 192, 221, 227, 298, and 330.

107. H. Thielicke, *Nihilis, Its Origins and Nature with a Christian Answer* (London: Routledge, 1961).
108. Ibid., p. 32: 'National Socialism quite emphatically did not think of itself as a revolution of nihilism. On the contrary it affirmed certain absolutes. For instance it made the people (Volk), the absolutely normative court of appeal for all ethics (what is good for my people is good) and declared the biological basis of history to be the one constant, abiding, and absolute quantity. It was, therefore in complete accord with the basic principle of all isms in that it made an absolute of certain aspects of creation. If, then, we declare with regard to such a movement that it is nihilistic, we are saying not only that what it calls an absolute is a pseudo-absolute, a pragmatic composition, but also that the responsible representatives of the movement are quite aware of what it is – without however, betraying the secret. In this case we speak of a camouflaged or "ciphered nihilism".'
109. Ibid., pp. 33–34.
110. See D. Lebow and R.N. Lebow, *Weber's Tragic Legacy* (forthcoming). See also M. Horheimer and T. Adorno, *Dialectic of Enlightenment* (Stanford: Stanford University Press, 2002), p. 172.
111. Ohnuki-Tierney 2002.
112. Ibid., p. 102.
113. Ibid., p. 122.
114. Ibid., p. 57.
115. Ohnuki-Tierney 2002.
116. Ibid., p. 165.
117. Ohnuki-Tierney 2002.
118. Ibid., p. 128.
119. Deleuze and Guattari 2004b, p. 237.
120. Ibid., p. 255.
121. R. O'Neill, *Suicide Squads: Axis and Allied Special Attack Weapons of World War II: Their Development and Their Missions* (London: Salamander Books, 1981); E.P. Hoyt, *The Kamikazes* (London: Robert Hale, 1983).
122. T.W. Zeiler, *Unconditional Defeat: Japan, America and the End of World War II* (Wilmington, DE: Scholarly Resources, 2004), p. 109.
123. I. Morris, *The Nobility of Failure* (London: Secker and Warburg, 1975), p. 168.
124. See also D. Rees, *The Defeat of Japan* (Westport, CT: Praeger, 1997), p. 161; Zeiler 2004, p. 168.
125. Deleuze and Guattari 2004b, p. 255.
126. P. Virilio, *Pure War* (New York: Semiotext(e), 1997), pp. 212–213.
127. S. Zizek, *Living in the End Times* (London: Verso, 2010), p. 130.
128. Virilio 1997, p. 213.
129. A common theme in the literature, see O'Neill 1981; Lamont-Brown, 1997; Benedict 1967.
130. A. Badiou, *Deleuze: The Clamor of Being* (Minneapolis: University of Minnesota Press, 1999).
131. R. Brassier, "Stellar Void or Cosmic Animal? Badiou and Deleuze on the Dice-Throw," *Pli: The Warwick Journal of Philosophy* 10 (2000): 216. The details of Badiou's critique are primarily aimed at Deleuze's *Logic of Sense*, a text that will be dealt with in some detail in subsequent chapters. Here only the relations between political creativity, fascism, death and lack will be emphasised.
132. On this point I am indebted to Peter Hallward (*Badiou: A Subject to Truth*, Minneapolis: University of Minnesota Press, 2003).
133. A. Badiou, *Theory of the Subject* (London: Continuum, 2009a), pp. 131, 247.
134. Ibid., p. 247.
135. Badiou 2009a.
136. Ibid., p. 131.

137. Ibid., p. 138.
138. Ibid., p. 287.
139. See Hallward 2003, p. 40.
140. Badiou 2009a, pp. 143, 144, 231. Peter Hallward also notes the implicit acceptance of the necessity of popular terror to maintain the revolution in this context (2003, p. 40).
141. Badiou 2009a, p. 146.
142. Ibid., p. 170.
143. Ibid., p. 172.
144. Astonishingly Badiou argues that excessive ravaging desubjectivizations are associated with 'the widespread conviction that action is impossible', he also, bizarrely, assumes 'courage appeals to justice' (ibid., p. 258).
145. Ibid., p. 294.
146. Ibid.
147. Something which Badiou recognised; see translator's introduction (ibid., p. xi).
148. A. Badiou, *Being and Event* (London: Continuum, 2005a), pp. 23, 67, 69.
149. Ibid., p. xviii.
150. Hallward 2003.
151. Ibid., p. 177.
152. Badiou 2005a, p. 175.
153. Ibid., p. xiii.
154. Ibid., p. 183.
155. Ibid., p. 111.
156. Ibid., pp. 238, 396, 406.
157. Hallward 2003, p. 129.
158. A. Badiou, *Ethics: An Essay on the Understanding of Evil* (London: Verso, 2001), p. 161.
159. Badiou 2001.
160. S. Zizek, *The Ticklish Subject: The Absent Centre of Political Ontology* (London: Verso, 2008).
161. Badiou 2001.
162. Ibid., p. 75.
163. Ibid., p. 80.
164. Ibid., p. 161.
165. Ibid., p. 67.
166. Ibid., pp. 83–84.
167. A. Badiou, *Infinite Thought: Truth and the Return to Philosophy* (London: Continuum, 2005b), pp. 132–133.
168. Hallward 2003.
169. Ironically a point which Badiou will mobilise as a critique of Deleuze in his later work.
170. Hallward 2003.
171. A. Badiou, *Logics of Worlds* (London: Continuum, 2009b), p. 379.
172. Ibid., p. 380.
173. Ibid., pp. 54–56.
174. Ibid., p. 61.
175. Ibid., p. 59.
176. Ibid., p. 72.
177. Ibid., pp. 61, 72.
178. Badiou's suggestion that fascist subjects belong to pseudorevolutionary events is compatible with Deleuze and Guattari's book inasmuch as they argue fascism assembled various lines of reterritorialisation with deterritorialisation.
179. Badiou 2009a, p. 287. The flavour of Freud's argument that we must desire our own repression as a consequence of the death instinct seems to rear its head here.
180. Badiou 2009b, p. 509.
181. Zizek 2008, p. 186.

182. Badiou 2009b, pp. 511–512.
183. Ibid., p. 514.
184. As he claims is proven by his set-theoretical capacity to think the infinite multiple as a void-set (ibid., p. 71).
185. Both Badiou (2009b) and Zizek (*Organs without Bodies: On Deleuze and Consequences* [London: Routledge, 2004]) argue that Deleuze and Guattari's book is essentially indissociable from capitalist rationality.
186. J. Delpech-Ramey, "An Interview with Slavoj Zizek 'On Divine Self-Limitation and Revolutionary Love,'" *Journal of Philosophy and Scripture* 1, no. 2 (2004).
187. Zizek 2010, p. xv.
188. Zizek 2008.
189. Ibid., p. 197.
190. Ibid.
191. Zizek 2004, p. 204.
192. Zizek 2008, p. 193.
193. Ibid., p. 463.
194. Ibid., p. 464.
195. Ibid., p. 465.
196. H. Krips, "Sexuating the Political: From Badiou to Lacan," in *Event and Decision: Ontology and Politics in Badiou, Deleuze, and Whitehead*, ed. R. Faber, H. Krips, and D. Pettus (Newcastle Upon Tyne: Cambridge Scholars, 2010), p. 270.
197. Deleuze and Guattari 2004b, p. 177.
198. Ibid., p. 178.
199. Ibid., p. 180.
200. Ibid., p. 298.
201. Lambert 2006, p. 99.
202. Ibid., p. 100.
203. Mishima frames this issue in explicitly psychoanalytical terms, as a suppression of the death element in Japanese culture. As he saw it, 'the death impulse must eventually explode.' For the same reason he rejected socialism and welfare as ending always in the death of freedom. So long as the 'impulse to resist and the impulse to surrender . . . or the impulse to be free and the impulse to die' are out of balance, Japan will be unable to be true to its cultural heritage: 'our enormous frustration at not being able to die is mounting fast'; death has become our 'only unsatisfied desire' (Y. Mishima, *Yukio Mishima on Hagakure: The Samurai Ethic and Modern Japan*, London: Souvenir Press, 1977, p. 25).
204. Given the emperor had denounced his divinity twenty years prior.
205. As Wolfe notes, 'Mishima planned his death so thoroughly that the morning of 25 November 1970 he told various members of the Tokyo media corps exactly where and when he would die'. See P. Wolfe, *Yukio Mishima* (New York: Continuum, 1989), p. 43.
206. 'Let us restore Nippon to its true state or let us die. Will you value only life and let the spirit die . . . We will show you a value which is greater than life. Not liberty, not democracy. It is Nippon. The Japan we love' (quoted in Scott Stokes 2000, p. 42).
207. Ibid., pp. 46–47.
208. Wolfe 1989, pp. 18, 42. Henry Scott Stokes, a friend and biographer, and the only westerner to attend his funeral (Scott Stokes 2000, p. 245), rejected the idea that Mishima was simply mad, but, in a manner that has been reflected in numerous commentaries, did contend that Mishima's 'homosexuality . . . was a key to his suicide.' He speculates that an affair with Masakatsu Morito, admittedly grounded on entirely circumstantial evidence and second-hand sources, stood at the root of the action. Certainly Morito idealised Mishima. Scott Stokes blames him for goading Mishima into action (p. 247), framing the act as a kind of love-suicide pact. Scott Stokes goes on to suggest that seppuku was for Mishima 'a supreme sexual act – the ultimate masturbation' in this context.

209. S. J. Napier, *Escape from the Wasteland: Romanticism and Realism in the Fiction of Mishima Yukio and Oe Kenzaburo* (Cambridge, MA: Harvard University Press, 1991). Napier sees it as odd that homosexuality is seen as such a key issue in explaining Mishima suicide, given the broader resonance of his later act with abiding themes in his writing.
210. Ibid., p. 9.
211. As Napier notes, it as odd that homosexuality is so often seen as such a key issue in explaining Mishima suicide, given the resonance of his later act with abiding themes in his writing (ibid., p. 221).
212. Ibid., p. 12.
213. Ibid., p. 19.
214. In support we can note, with Scott Stokes (2000, p. 25), that 'Mishima endlessly rehearsed his death', with acts of seppuku taking place in the 1960 short story "Patriotism," and in the film of same name (acted in by Mishima), in 1968 *Runaway Horses*, and 1969 again Mishima acted the part in a film where he commits *hara-kiri*.
215. J. S. Piven, *The Madness and Perversion of Yukio Mishima* (Westport, CT: Praeger, 2004). For Piven, Mishima's suicide and writing repeat the trauma he experienced in early life. His literature gives us the chance to 'lay [. . .] bear Mishima's soul' alongside the explanation of his act. For Piven,

> Mishima withstood sequestration from his parents, a virtually psychotic grandmother who held him prisoner in a dark silent room amidst her illness and hysteria for 12 years and an essentially absent father who abused him when present. Mishima suffered a suffocating infantilisation, the excruciating absence of his mother, and humiliating derogation from a father obsessed with Nazism. (p. 8)

These established conditions which were bound to manifest in madness and perversion. From these early experiences, Piven derives an inevitable hated of women and a love of death, bound up with some classical psychodynamics, whereby Mishima sought to punish 'bad internal object killing some bad qualities, being reborn purified, and reunited with loved ones who now forgive one for those evil qualities he had in life'. In his literature and then in his suicide Mishima sought, for Piven, to convert childhood trauma to adult triumph. 'For Mishima sexuality disguises and restages fear and suffering, erotic vengeance and triumph, simultaneous memorialisation and eradication of traumatic sexual history, transforming humiliation and terror into orgasm, vengeance and victory' (p. 12). Mishima's works of violent fantasy 'reflect tortured internal conflicts' deriving from an 'almost inconceivably painful early life' (p. 13). For Piven, literature both enacts 'his madness and suspends it in inaction, it is a means of expression and survival'. Certainly Mishima's literature contains themes of misogyny and exhibitionist masculinity, or 'phallic narcissism' (p. 24). His fantasies represent 'femininity as incessantly controlling, hostile abandoning, castrating, nauseating, excremental, engulfing' (p. 32). In this sense, 'Mishima is a maker of misogyny myths.' For the same reasons, Mishima's visions of the erotic are saturated with death – Mishima has catastrophic death complex, expressed through metastasis of women by infantile annihilation and anal sadism (p. 34). Surveying this literary architecture, Piven argues that it is 'likely that his ritual suicide was a sexual fulfilment in which he played the victim and voyeur'.
216. Ibid., p. 73.
217. This is why, for Piven, reading Napier, we see in his suicide a 'mask worn to disguises he erotic fantasies and complexes, his obsession with magically transcending death and decay through murdering the mortal body', and all the patriotism and emperor worship is nothing but a 'conduit to disguise and enact fantasies of deeper psychological significance' (ibid., p. 125). This transcendent ideal fulfilled an intense psychological need by providing Mishima personally with 'a symbolic immortality project, an emotional rescue from the terrors of death' (p. 127).

218. Ibid., p. 113.
219. Indeed, drawing on Lacan, Napier reads Mishima work explicitly as a politics of lack seeking to be filled by the emperor.
220. Thielicke 1961, p. 54.
221. R. Starrs, *Deadly Dialectics: Sex, Violence and Nihilism in the World of Yukio Mishima* (Sandgate: Japan Library, 1994), pp. 188–189: The 'active' quality of fascism 'was always a sham . . . an 'elaborately constructed mask to cover passive nihilistic despair'. Mishima's actions were the 'ritual of a passive nihilist disguised by the mask of an active nihilist'.
222. This act of naming, for Badiou, explains the scale of fascism's horror.
223. The Meiji regime, he claimed, was a capitulation to Western corruption. Similarly, he felt comfortable criticising the emperor for not fulfilling his authentic function.
224. Scott Stokes 2000, p. 224.
225. Piven 2004; Napier 1991.
226. Scott Stokes 2000.
227. Piven 2004, p. 2.
228. Y. Mishima, *The Way of the Samurai: Yukio Mishima on Hagekure in Modern Life*, trans. Kathryn Sparling (New York: Basic Books, 1977), p. 5.
229. Ibid., p. viii.
230. Ibid., pp. 40, 99.
231. Wolfe 1989, p. 17.
232. See Napier 1991, p. 223.
233. Mishima 1977, p. 7.
234. Mishima 1977.
235. Ibid., p. 9.
236. Ibid., p. 21.
237. This is recognised that this is 'an idealized view of death', but 'the formula death-equals-freedom is the ideal formula of the samurai' (ibid., p. 46).
238. Ibid., p. 39.
239. This, he argued was the Japanese image of death: 'The Japanese concept of death is straight and clear, and in that sense it is different from the loathsome, fearful death as seen by westerners', which he contrasts with medieval European death with scythe and Aztec death 'overgrown with luxuriant summer growth'. Japan's vision of death is 'not that kind of rough, wild death, but an image of death beyond which their exists a spring of pure water, from which tiny streams are continuously pouring their pure waters into this world, has long enriched Japanese art' (ibid., p. 100).
240. Ibid., p. 40.
241. 'Death for Jocho has the strange, clear, fresh brightness of blue sky between the clouds. In its modernised form, it coincides oddly enough with the image of the kamikaze squadron, which has been called the most tragic form of attack used during the war. The suicide squadrons were called the most inhuman methods of attack, and after the war the young men who had die in them were dishonoured. However, the spirit of those young men who, for the sake of their country hurled themselves to certain death is closest in the long history of Japan to the ideal of action and death offered in *Hagakure*, though if one were to examine their motives individually, one would certainly find that they had their fears and their hardships. I suppose some people will say that the Kamikaze suicide pilots, despite their high sounding name, were forced to die. And certainly these youths not yet out of school were forced by the national authorities to proceed to their death against their will. Even if they went of their own will, they were rounded up into attack forces almost by coercion and sent to certain death' (ibid., p. 101).
242. With the exception of Mishima's 1968 play entitled *My Friend Hitler*. Y. Mishima and H. Sato, *My Friend Hitler and Other Plays of Yukio Mishima* (New York: Columbia University Press, 2002). See, for a good discussion of the play, D.C. Goodman, "Mishima Yukio's *My Friend Hitler*," in *Inexorable Modernity: Japan's Grappling*

with *Modernity in the Arts*, ed. H. Nara (Lanham, MD: Lexington Books, 2007), p. 151.
243. Mishima 1977, p. 7.
244. See ibid., p. 61. 'There is no such thing as an excess of energy. When a lion runs full tilt, under his feet the fields disappear; he may even pass by the prey he was chasing at the far end of the field. Why? Because he is a lion' (p. 44).
245. Ibid., p. 69.
246. 'One can fail to accomplish mission – *Hagakure* is simply expression the relativistic position that rather than to live on as a coward having failed ones mission, having failed in one's mission it is better to die' (ibid., pp. 104–105).
247. Ibid., p. 83.
248. Ibid., p. 93.
249. Ibid., p. 102.
250. Ibid., p. 103.
251. Ibid., p. 102.
252. Ibid., p. 104.
253. Mishima is explicit about this: 'If life is not something we have chosen for ourselves, then maybe we are not ultimately free to die'; we can only affirm our fate in action 'what is important is purity of action . . . and any death thus arrived at' (ibid.).
254. Ibid., p. 105.
255. Ibid., p. 160.
256. See R. Esposito, *Bios: Biopolitics and Philosophy*, Vol. 4 (Minneapolis: University of Minnesota Press, 2008), p. 145. This claim can be usefully linked with Esposito's reading of Nazism as three interlocked immunitary logics: the first defined by the superimposition of medical and political-juridical power, to prevent future contagions (Molar); the second defined by the physical evacuation of 'diseased' elements in the body of the German community (Molecular); and the third concerning the morbid genesis of life. This final element, reveals the kernel of fascism in 'a kind of excess whole full sense we have yet to understand' (p. 143) – the extremity of the Nazi attempt to control the procreative process through sterilisation, castration and abortion amidst a simultaneous national 'pro-natalist campaign', reveals precisely the Nazi belief in the necessity of fully superimposing death and birth: Subjecting creation (birth) to destruction (death).
257. This is why Starrs concludes that the very 'futility of the whole affair made of it a nihilistic act par excellence' (1994, p. 159). My suggestion is that this reading misses the point entirely.
258. Ibid., p. 161.

2 Self-burning

Immolāre

Most academic works dealing with self-burning in political protest are found in psychiatric journals where a 'political' dimension is seen simply to distinguish it therapeutically from other suicides.[1] Its modern practice is often dated quite precisely from Thich Quang Duc's self-incineration in Vietnam in 1963. The printing of the image of Quang Duc's self-incineration in broadsheets certainly impacted powerfully upon US domestic support for the Diem regime, fostering imitators worldwide. Ten more Vietnamese monks followed Quang Duc's lead in the subsequent two years, alongside several Americans, including Norman Morrison – whose act Robert McNamara credited as having transformed his and his family's opinions on the war.[2] The practice continued in Vietnam in 1966–67, with a further seventeen self-burnings, alongside six more Americans and a Russian. The year 1969 witnessed the passage of the practice into Europe, the United States, Soviet Russia, and South Korea.[3] India has seen the largest number of self-burnings in the last three decades, often in protest at political-economic conditions.[4] Other notable groups of cases have been amongst Kurds outside and within Turkey, Romanians, Chinese, and Pakistanis.[5] A continuing campaign of self-incinerations by Tibetan Buddhist monks appears to protest Chinese rule and the erosion of Tibetan cultural and political-economic autonomy: Since 2010, it has been suggested that as many as several hundred male and female monks of various ages have set themselves alight to this end.[6]

Inasmuch as a wide variety of ideologies, individual aims or collective projects are associated with protest self-burnings, the act itself seems associated with diverse political intentions. Equally remarkable is the variance in its apparent effects or political consequences. Jan Palach's explicitly political public self-burning in Prague in 1969, which will be examined in more detail below, had little real consequences beyond the domestic outpouring of grief and public contemplation, in sharp contrast with the international political consequences of Thich Quang Duc's. The ongoing Tibetan campaign of self-burning has received only muted coverage, in part due to the control of information flowing out of the region, and so similarly contrasts with the widely documented and apparently revolutionary connotations popularly assigned to Mohammed Bouazizi's self-burning on 17 December 2010. Given the spectacular consequences associated with Bouazizi's act in various literatures, it is appropriate that this event be subjected to particular study. It appears to be the exemplary recent case of a political self-destruction, and as such constitutes a good case with which to illuminate the subject disembodied in such acts.

A young fruit seller from the town of Sidi Bouzid, Mohammed Bouazizi, following an altercation with the local authorities in which his scales or produce were confiscated on the ostensive grounds that he had no permit, and possibly after being physically slapped by a female police officer, went to the local magistrate threatening to set himself alight.[7] Being there disregarded, he doused himself with petrol and set himself alight in front of the audience attracted by the commotion.[8] The police officer accused of abusing Bouazizi was later cleared of wrongdoing, but interviews with family members assert that a highly masculinised sense of personal insult provided part of the now likely forever opaque reasons for the act.[9] The intentions standing behind his self-incineration were undocumented, and so could play little role in determining its political consequences. It seems difficult to reach any definitive conclusions about causality. What we do know is that Bouazizi's self-burning became a rallying point for protests throughout the town, centring on poverty and widespread unemployment. As these protests increased in scale, the Ben Ali regime attempted to suppress them, blockading media reports; but aided by the publication and popularisation of Bouazizi's act on Facebook and in other social media, this resulted only in their exacerbation. Protests spread into neighbouring towns.[10] Western media outlets describing the unfolding events also narrated Bouazizi's act as of central and founding importance. As the protests continued to increase in scale, Ben Ali had himself photographed with the now dying Bouazizi. This clumsy attempt at retrieving command of the narration of events succeeded only in exacerbating collective opprobrium.[11] Bouazizi's death on 4 January sparked nationwide protests. Lethal responses by the authorities were recorded on camera phones and disseminated. In the face of broadening revolt, a series of increasingly cowed speeches by Ben Ali in January culminated in a promise not to seek a sixth term on 13 January. To the chorus of popular rejection the next day, gently pushed by the military establishment, Ben Ali departed the country, crowning what was christened the Jasmine Revolution by media outlets.

This sudden collapse of an entrenched autocratic regime and security establishment was unanticipated. A spirit of revolutionary excitement spilled over borders, with protests emerging in neighbouring countries. The collapse of the regime in Tunisia is thus seen as having given birth to what has been termed the Arab Spring, explicitly suggesting resonances with Prague 1968. Revolutionary upheavals swept the region, taking in Libya, Egypt, Yemen, Bahrain and Syria. Tunisia becomes case zero in an international series, and Bouazizi's act the point of initiation. Commemoration of Bouazizi's act has thus bound him indelibly to the subsequent international events, but it is critical to recognise that Bouazizi himself declared no ideological aims whatsoever. Bouazizi's voice is absent from the signifying regimes that defined the subsequent revolts. It is for this reason that Karin Fierke argues that 'it is less the intentions of Bouazizi, than the effect of his act, and how it was given meaning, that are of interest'.[12] What is critical, Fierke argues, is that a sacrificial connotation was assigned to Bouazizi's act by others, which is what allowed him to unintentionally give birth to an emergent revolutionary condition in the region. The political content of Bouazizi's act was formed through processes of semiotic contestation and capture after the fact.

A self-sacrificial (as opposed to suicidal) connotation was assigned to Bouazizi's act by others, which allowed him to give birth to an emergent revolutionary condition in the region. It is widely assumed that only the subsequent assignment of a sacrificial connotation can supply political meaning to self-destructive acts. One result of this is that self-burning in protest, often along with hunger striking and suicide bombing, is often referred to as self-immolation.[13] The term self-immolation is derived from the Latin stem *immolāre*: to sprinkle with sacrificial meal. To immolate is to offer up a sacrifice, with immolation traditionally referring to the slaughter of a sanctified victim.[14]

As a forceful demonstration of strength of feeling about a particular political issue, self-immolation is interpreted as a direct expression of an experience of suffering.[15] The finality of the act directs attention to the embeddedness of the actor in structures outside his or her control.[16] Indeed, Crosby et al. argue that self-burners should be understood as expressions of structurally produced group desires.[17] Historical clusters of self-burnings are epidemics within collective behaviour emerging when times are particularly unsettled.[18] This is suggestive of the work of Emile Durkheim,[19] for whom acts of self-burning may be neatly packaged under the category altruistic suicide, who are 'mechanically compelled by society, or the group, to end their lives, with little or no individual will involved', as when an old person commits suicide to avoid becoming a burden on his or her family.[20] Anthony Giddens,[21] reading Durkheim, suggested we might distinguish a unique form of sacrificial subjectivity or agency in this context. Where Durkheim's model assumes a mechanical lack of agency on the part of the self-burner, a conscious intention to further a cause on behalf of others often seems significant in such events. Terming these acts sacrifices or immolations allows an expansion of Durkheim's category to articulate the peculiar quality of consciously choosing to die on behalf of others for a political cause.[22] Framing the act as a sacrificial offering indicates that the political subject is defined by his or her conscious intention to die on behalf of any cause.

This cannot, however, provide a satisfying account of Bouazizi as a political subject. It is likely that Bouazizi's act *was* meant as an indictment of the social inequality and limited opportunities provided in Tunisian society under Ben Ali, but there is little or no compelling evidence to suggest this was an act which occurred on behalf of others. Bouazizi seemed to be engaged in a distinctly personal, if very much publically articulated, protest. Indeed, as Fierke notes, all that can be said of Bouazizi's act was that it was interpreted after the fact as having been on behalf of society at large, and that this interpretation by others is what produced its enormous political charge. Bouazizi's intentions must remain opaque. Indeed intentionality is almost always ambiguous in such events, since it is almost always impossible to confirm the motives of self-annihilating subjects after their act.[23] This question mark over intentionality is unproblematic if we see sacrificial acts as acquiring their content through subsequent attachment to the symbolic architecture of social life. In this sense, meaning is identical with a semiotic functionality that is necessarily formed through the wider social interpretation and contestation after the act. Sacrifices glean their social significance by being interpreted as referring to symbols which are sacred inasmuch as they epitomise in some way the values and affective cohesion of a group.[24] Intentionality is thus less important than socially assigned sacrificial meaning.

Such an account finds its grounds in the work of social anthropologists Hubert and Mauss,[25] who claimed that the designation of sacrificial offerings is the central means by which social norms are created and maintained in traditional societies. The unity of the sacrificial system is located in a procedure which 'consists in establishing a means of communication between the sacred and the profane worlds through the mediation of a victim, that is, of a thing that in the course of the ceremony is destroyed'.[26] The referent sacrifice confers a sacred character on a victim, who becomes the means of transmission between divine and profane. The victim separates and unites the profane and divine spheres so that a productive exchange can take place – thus the victim's famous ambiguity.[27] For Hubert and Mauss the institution of sacrifice is intrinsically bound up with production of the myths and narratives that underpin social life: the genesis of the ideas which are deemed to exist outside, yet condition sociality, and with which individuals seek to enter into relationships with so as to find strength and assurance.[28] Sacrifice is a mechanism of exchange by which the transcendent imaginary or narrative architecture of society is engendered and then sustained.[29] We find in religious sacrifice the template of political sacrifice, since it is in its relation to the mythic foundations of social life that the constructive force of the practice is located. Immolations are not defined via intentionality, as illusory personal outputs of theological or ideological fantasy or fanatical overidentification with their social context; they acquire their reality with relation to the social facts which are instituted as a result.

The potency of sacrificial rituals is that they allow imaginary social things to achieve a transcendent reality. Self-sacrifice is an engine for the production of the founding myths present in all sovereign collectivities.[30] Sacrificial substitutions reinforce 'pre-existing social relations and spiritual beliefs' but are also '*constitutive* for the community in terms of its particular social dynamic and ideals'.[31] Self-sacrifice is a molar politics, a site for the imagining of a community of desire, particularly under conditions of oppression or occupation.[32] Thus self-immolation amongst Crimean Tatars in the 1970s could become the interpretative site for the ideal construction of a homeland.[33] The continuing campaign of self-immolations in Tibet are sacrificial rites inasmuch as they sustain sacralised collective identity in the face of the perceived threat to cultural autonomy posed by Chinese control of the region,[34] drawing international attention to their plight but also actively participating in the imagining of an independent Tibet. It should be clear that the intentions of the actor are at least partly irrelevant to the assignment of political content, for it is the imaginary social forms constructed through later semiotic capture that give political meaning to sacrifice, not the intentions of the subjects themselves. Self-sacrificing subjects acquire political content by being interpretatively folded into an imaginary/mythic totality, and thereby immortalised through memorialisation as martyrs.

For Karin Fierke, what identifies a family of self-sacrificial political acts is their role in the 'creation of alternative forms of identity and belonging' through an act of radical communication.[35] For Fierke, 'self sacrifice . . . is an "act of speech" in which the suffering body communicates the injustice experienced by the community to a larger audience'.[36] In this context, whilst 'sacrifice in a political context implies a community for which the sacrifice is made and an audience to which it speaks . . . The self-sacrifice . . . is about the restoration of the nation in circumstance in which sovereignty has been curtailed'.[37] The speech act becomes political inasmuch as it is received by others as embodying a desire for communal sovereignty, emerging in response to the humiliation of its lack.[38] The 'agent of political self-sacrifice, often referred to as a martyr' is political, for Fierke, only inasmuch as they can be interpreted as the 'embodiment of the suffering nation'.[39] This is the signature of a political self-sacrifice across different cultural contexts. The politics of self-burning relies on their interpretation as an embodiment of a counter or restored sovereignty, through an affective reconstruction of ontological security: 'The self-sacrifice of the individual body becomes an expression of the loss of collective sovereignty, which materialises the injustice experienced by the community and thereby creates the condition for its restoration'.[40] Politics, here, is an emotional 'response to a loss of equilibrium or a loss of value'; a sense of 'the need to restore dignity', which is retrospectively read as the connotation of the act of self-incineration by audiences engaged in interpretative contestation around its meaning.[41] In this way, Fierke argues, 'in the Arab Spring, various acts of self-sacrifice contributed to the construction of community and the nation'.[42] Bouazizi's act became political inasmuch as it was interpreted as affirming collective identity, embodying the sovereignty of a repressed 'liminal communitas' that opposed the entrenched autocratic regimes. Mohammed Bouazizi is a self-sacrificial political subject because his act was retrospectively understood as having taken place on behalf of a wider community dissatisfied with the Ben Ali regime; his perlocutionary act was received as performing a new social imaginary or narrative body politics, promising the restoration of sovereignty through a communalising affect.

Self-sacrifices are political inasmuch as they allow 'communities of recognition [to be] constituted and reconstituted through the movement and circulation of emotion, evoked by the bodily self-sacrifice, and given resonance and power through memory'.[43] Through the construction of memory around the figure of the martyr, a community of desire can take form and reclaim sovereignty over itself.[44] Fierke's account is therefore a classically dialectical analysis of political resistance, articulated as the contradistinction of two incommensurable (hegemonic and counter-hegemonic) structures of meaning and authority.[45] Self-sacrificial subjects are political inasmuch as their speech act is interpreted as a declaration of the sovereignty of an affective community that seeks to instantiate an antistructure. That is to say, the politics of self-sacrifice are wholly a question of their semiotic potential vis-à-vis restoration of the sovereignty of a liminal transcendent community.[46] Fierke argues that the assignment of self-sacrificial content assumes an appeal to preexisting patterns of meaningfulness (an existing language game).[47] In other words, self-sacrifice, to become political, must tap into a pool of historical memory. This certainly explains how it can be a conservative mechanism for '*restoring* sovereign community',[48] as in Ireland where a historical tradition of struggle through sacrifice was explicitly appealed to by Bobby Sands in his eloquent explanations of his hunger strike in the early 1980s.[49] A transformative or revolutionary charge is however also implied by self-sacrifice inasmuch as it allows the counter-structure of political meaning and rules to emerge in 'opposition to the formalized dominant structures'. This assumes that the liminal affective community will 'by definition [have] a less formal identity, which fluctuates'.[50] Fierke's account thus assumes the retrospective allocation of politicality to the act of self-destruction, by reference to its potential as an interpretative site for the pursuit of sovereign political projects. Acts of self-sacrifice become political inasmuch as communities use them to create a space by which to engage in constructive political conversation about the rules by which they live, and so seek to restore sovereignty in conditions where it is perceived as lost.

If the act is politicised by the patterns of signification and affective resonance that preexist and then solidify in the space which succeeds it, the political subject that self-annihilates must remain inaccessible and ontologically empty; she gains her politics only through retrospective assignment of a martyr signification and the construction of a sovereign semiosis that draws a molar line. Clearly subjects are sometimes interpreted as martyrs after the fact and, in this sense, acquire sacrificial meaning after the fact, often through their folding into preexisting narratives. Self-destructive acts may be assigned retrospective political content via imaginaries that promise alternative rules of social order, but such imaginaries can only be assigned to the act in the aftermath of an immanent challenge to the extant sovereign order of meaning. Retrospective semiosis simply cannot provide us with an account of the rupture that is identical with the subject that self-annihilates, unless we surrender it entirely to the degree to which they are captured by patterns of affect and signification in consequent interpretative contestation, and in the process eject from political space any number of self-destructive subjects on the consequentialist grounds that they fail to result in the institution of language games that relate to the restoration of sovereignty.[51] In such a case, there can be no question of a nonsovereign politics.

Political acts of self-annihilation seem to elude our grasp in terms of causal instrumentality, means and ends, intentions and consequences. Oscillating in the contemporary media space, the narrative and affective consequences of any image or speech act are always uncertain.[52] Contingency certainly played a critical role in the interpretation of Bouazizi's act, with key issues, including the apparently gendered element of his protest, absent from most popular narrations. In this context, Neville Bolt has cogently recognised that for this reason, contemporary self-immolations cannot be reduced to their narrative products. Indeed, as noted above, the central problem for propagandists of the deed[53] has always been the impossibility of maintaining control over the narratives that emerge from their violent events.⁵⁴ Bolt notes that propaganda of the deed now occurs in a complex and uncontrollable space of global media interactivity, where the proliferation of meanings and dissemination of images supplies the effects of violent acts with accelerated unpredictability.⁵⁵ The significance of symbolic violence seems to reside in its power to give birth to the uncontrollable proliferation of narratives, myths or affective formations in a virtual space. Causation is unchained from intention and even from content by the new media: As such, the self-immolator can take on the role of facilitator of revolutionary spontaneity and proliferation through the production of iconic violence, but in abandoning any attempt to control the message, they inevitably have unexpected or even contrary communicative effects.⁵⁶ In this way, self-destructive propaganda of the deed is a matter of setting off discursive avalanches that cannot be predicted or mapped in advance, which problematizes the sufficiency of reading such act's politicality in its relationship to an affective community construction. It is simply impossible to ascertain in advance whether an act will necessarily garner one signification or another. Fierke recognises this in emphasising the existence of contestation around the meaning of the act, but argues very clearly that the political enters in only with the attribution of a martyr signification.⁵⁷

Sacrificial rites draw their force from an offer of ontological security under a sovereign formation.⁵⁸ This is why Fierke implies that there is nothing intrinsically violent about self-burnings. Notwithstanding, it is clear that the immediate affective content of many acts of political self-annihilation is the institution of violence and social crisis. In Vietnam following the self-immolation of Thich Quang Duc in 1968, protests by Buddhist monks created a febrile social condition, leading to mass arrests, sectarian (majority Buddhist) protests and riots, a coup (tacitly sponsored by the US), the killing of Diem, and a consequent acceleration of the conflict in Vietnam.⁵⁹ Quang Duc's self-incineration did not appear to increase capacity for a cohesive counterclaim to sovereignty. The aftermath of Quang Duc's self-annihilation was characterised by disordering and disorganised violence, contextualised by a generalised breakdown of popular faith in the legitimacy of the regime at home and abroad. Quang Duc's self-incineration was read as a negation of the sovereign order, but there is little evidence of an emergent positive counter-structure, liminal community formation or interpretative construction of a new sovereign language game, perhaps due to the rapid progression of events.

What this suggests is that the politics of self-burning cannot be sufficiently contained by its potential for retrospective capture under myth through interpretative contestation. These events may create an 'opportunity space'⁶⁰ for sovereign myth-making, and for the affective identification of martyrs, but such processes of narrative capture assume the existence of a prior moment of rupture with the extant semiotic regime. Communities engaging in emotive contestation around the meaning of self-destructive events may well construct a space to engage in political conversation regarding the rules by which they live, but these processes occur after the fact, and so cannot explain any violent break with sovereign order integral to the political subject that self-annihilates. In this way, the sacrificial paradigm averts its eyes from the obscene rupture of social life that attends the act of self-destruction. This follows the broad tradition of thinking on suicide, seeing its taboo character as indicative of the impossibility of a politics expressed in flight from the world. Unless mapped onto a broader project of mythic narrativization that continues after the fact, self-destruction can only be a departure from political space.

When Rene Girard discussed the sacrificial paradigm he argued that its function is to construct social order in precisely this sense.[61] His innovation and critique of Hubert and Mauss was in observing the circularity in their argument, and its consequential deficit of explanatory value.[62] Hubert and Mauss failed to recognise, Girard argued, that the sacrificial rite functions through substitution to preclude the eruption of social disorder in other forms, most notably as mob violence. The sacrificial rite is thus a socially mediated mechanism for the managed expression of social violence, and this is what allows it to become a means for the symbolic ordering of social life. It institutes imaginaries of stability to contain the ever-present risk of violent disorder that is an inevitable condition for a society of mortals. Ironically, the events marked out as political sacrifices in postpositivist social science tend to have more correspondence with what Girard referred to as sacrificial crises – events which, as reminders to primary violence (essentially, death), spark processes of social rupture and disorder, and which in traditional societies elicited sacrificial offerings in the hope of their management through mythic substitution.

Self-burnings, like hunger strikes to death or suicide bombings, appear to be inverted sacrifices in this sense: institutions or formations of primary violence that rupture and break with extant social order, without promising any resolution in an alternative social order or sovereign semiosis. These acts embody or symbolise violent disorder, not its resolution. Any counter-hegemonic myth-making, I have shown above, necessarily comes after the fact, as part of a process of capture and social ordering through, for example, the identification of martyrs by surviving audiences. The object of the sacrificial ritual, from a Girardian perspective, is a presocial excess that threatens to rupture social order by bringing it face to face with its underlying groundlessness (qua death). It is that fatal excess or foundational crisis which is constitutive of the subject that self-annihilates, not any stabilising (hegemonic or counter-hegemonic) semiosis that might be constructed in its aftermath. Indeed, such retrospective semiosis, given the disordered and often violent proliferations that commonly follow acts of self-annihilation, is precisely suggestive of a search for social meaning in the face of its interruption by suicidal death.

Girard argues that with the onset of modernity, the sacrificial institution is no longer needed for ensuring social stability. It is replaced by law, which is a far more effective tool for managing the threat of violent disorder. Principally law remains, however, a mechanism for the social mediation or substitution of violence. The sovereignty of law simply is the assertion that violence (qua right to kill) is restricted to the hand of the state.[63] Inasmuch as legitimate violence is monopolised under law, its generalised social expression is contained.[64] Law is therefore, at its root, a mythic substitution of violence, and fulfils the same basic function as the sacrificial institution. Girard's argument here resonates closely with Walter Benjamin's in *Critique of Violence*, which provides a conceptual toolbox by which the political subject of self-annihilation can be categorically conceptualised as prior to, and so integrally problematizing, any and all sovereign semiosis.[65]

Benjamin also claimed that it is only through myth-making that the sovereignty of law and therefore social order can be sustained. Law must monopolise violence to function, and this reveals law's paradoxical reliance on and foundation in violence. Sovereign law is the continuation of violence as opposed to its denial, a violence given transcendent or ideal status as myth. As Jacques Derrida observed, Benjamin suggests that 'the authority of law rests only on the credit that is granted it'.[66] The critical point here is simply that law is always an 'act of Faith . . . One believes in it; that is its only foundation'. There is, therefore, something integrally mystical about law, and this is precisely because it is founded on and sustained by violence. For this reason, Benjamin suggested, in some disagreement with Girard,[67] that violence integrally maintains the capacity to shatter, if only momentarily, the force of law.

Benjamin distinguished the mythic violence of law from what he termed divine violence.[68] The mythic violence of law, which orders, constructs communities and institutes heroic narratives of sovereignty, is opposed to a divine violence which destroys law or more importantly faith in the sovereignty of law. Divine violence is law-breaking, antimythic violence that creates space for instantiation of a radically new order. It is, as such, fully revolutionary. Benjamin clarifies this distinction via the difference between the strike and the general strike. The strike is a form of political violence that hinges on a withdrawal, generally of labour.[69] The strike is conditional and grounded in the logic of exchange; it is sustained until a change to the mythic/legal order is negotiated. It challenges, for example, claims of criminality on the grounds that it views that assignation as illegitimate, and so insists upon a change to the law. The general strike, on the other hand, is an absolute withdrawal, and so, Benjamin argues, anarchistic. It breaks absolutely with the extant social order, and asks for no modification of the existing legal code, simply denying the figures of law any legitimacy whatsoever. Unconditional withdrawal frustrates all concepts of defined legal political ends – mobilising violence as a pure means. The refusal of any logic or ends or instrumentality is the marker of divine violence.

The hunger striker unto death or self-burner similarly goes beyond the alteration of the law/mythic order through exchange or bargaining process; after all, they will never witness any such alteration.[70] Like the general strike these are rites of violence in which no exchange is offered. Death stands unredeemable, and as such institutes a rupture with law as such. Understood in this way, self-annihilation is an act without positive or sacred ends: It is violence as a pure means. As Benjamin makes clear, only sacred violence leaves positive markers in myth and legal order. Divine violence leaves no traces; it breaks the cycle of myth, embodying an excess that brings social order to its presemiotic origin. Mythic forms may follow, and a new legal order may be created after the fact, but that order is born in flight from the radical subject of divine violence. Self-burnings and hunger strikes to death consecrate an offering that embodies crisis without resolution. Mohammed Bouazizi, unlike Bobby Sands, did not even attempt to predetermine his mythic effects, strategically preframing his act within a poetic project of transcendent imagining. He articulated no identifiable ends. It is its radical negativity that gave his act fertility and force. Bouazizi is a political subject of divine violence; his self-burning was a pure means, without heroic ends or positive intentions, which as such opened a space for the subsequent proliferation of myth. This suggests a suicidal political subject, who needs no transcendent referent or connection to a sovereign semiosis to occupy political space.

Ben Ali correctly identified in Bouazizi's suicide a radical challenge to his authority. We can understand the act in this context as a precise inversion of the logic of sacrifice: Its political ontology is a function of its exposure of a socially immanent violence (death). As opposed to seeing a political subject given form in the semiotic construction of new myths of sovereign order, a transcendent counter-structure or liminal communitas, Bouazizi's self-immolation embodied and unchained a socially immanent disorder. Bouazizi's act shattered popular faith in the Tunisian regime, and in turn led to the establishment, in the surrounding states, of a condition of collective faithlessness. This event exposed 'every act of government [a]s nothing but a way of not losing control'.[71] Popular faith in authoritarian law dissolved in the face of an unconditional gift of auto-annihilation. To understand this as a sacrificial offering is to see only the mythic capture of divine violence after the fact, and to confuse the political subject of auto-annihilating violence with our attempt to make sense of its politically constitutive excess.

Death and desire

Each body has its own model of death, which determines the productivity of its lived experience.[72] This is simply to recognise that individuals think about their deaths in diverse ways.[73] Our mortality, the fact that we die, and individual finitude are not the same thing, but rather interact to singularize us. We are circumscribed in countless ways, by time, talent, experience, understanding, intelligence, passion, and perseverance and in all else.[74] The ubiquity of our finitudes is the definitive feature of being; it defines the particular assemblage of affective capacity which is a life. Our model of death is as singular as the assemblage of affects that defines each body:

> The meanings that men give to death hinge on the meanings they give to their lives. The conceptions of death are as variegated and complex as those of life. Death has no essence. It has no core of its own. Its substance is all borrowed, is wholly circumstance. Its shape is utterly determined by what manner of life it ends.[75]

To say each body has its own model of death is simply to recognise that a body is defined by what it can do.[76] A body's affects are the condition for its relations with other bodies; racehorse-rider-bet, oxen-farmer-cart, flea-dog.[77] The model of death is, very simply, what it means for a body to be dead; no more biting, no more running, no more loving, no more writing, no more eating. Bodily intensity = zero. The machine stops. A model of death is thus singular; each body has its own. The model is not an object or different understanding of the body; rather it allows us to think what a body can do as the recording surface upon which any particular assemblage of affects (desiring-machines) that makes up a body takes place. It is not a place for assemblage, rather it occupies space as an immanent matrix of intensities, upon which the stratifications or materialisation that organise or disorganise a body can occur.[78] The model 'can be occupied, populated only by intensities', because it is the unformed, nonstratified field for those intensities to pass by and into each other, to pulse or intensify.[79] The model of death is the body in its most reified state of potentiality, prior to affect, and so defines the body's assembled finitudes.[80] The model of death is the positive limit of what a body is capable of as the source-point of all intensities.[81] Badiou argues in *Logics of Worlds*[82] that 'death is not a category of being' but of appearing; a logical and not an ontological matter, and so cannot be spoken of in itself.[83] Beings are not integrally mortal, but rather simply have death as one of their possibilities; as the contingent 'minimisation of its identity, and thus of its degree of existence'.[84] Deleuze and Guattari agree that the model of death is the minimisation of the body's affects.[85] What they dispute is any claim that this implies a primary identity or preorganisation. Organisation or disorganisation, they argue, can only occur on the model. The model is a fully ontological matter in this sense: It is the positive matrix for all that a body can be. The model of death is the register of possibility.

Desiring-machines distribute themselves on the model of death, and determine the capacity for a body (individual or collective) to add to its affects: arm for grabbing, mouth for speaking.[86] The model of death thus conditions the possibility of affective recombination and proliferation.[87] It is the matrix for the construction of new relations on a body. This implies, as Badiou notes,[88] the self-organisation of an intrinsically surging body by way of its free assemblage, but it is decidedly *not* a derivation from negative totality. The model resists any and all preorganisation, and only as such, is it the motor for bodily autopoesis.[89] The model of death = all affects at zero. The model provides the contingent surface on which affects are attracted to each other in new formations. That explosion of self is the 'experience of death'.[90] Every deterritorialisation involves such an experience, involving the transformation of our model of death.[91] By allowing the model to disorganise the body, it is released for its productive reassemblage.[92] Desiring-production is this break-flow process, crossing affective states.[93] This is not a vision of endless departure: A body moves from affective limits to the redefinition of those limits.[94] Life is the oscillation from model to experience and back again.

Creation always takes place from the architecture of death.[95] In *Anti-Oedipus*, Freud's account of death has been radically reconfigured as the perpetually remodelled condition for the possibility of life as a creative experience of dying.[96] This implies we need not live in ontological dread of death as the liminal condition of our freedom, but rather actively transform what it means to die. Fear is simply one way in which mortality may be experienced.[97] Play with our experience of death is the practice of life, and requires self-knowledge to the degree that modelling death is the substance of practical embodiment (it defines what a body can do). Put simply, dying takes effort. The becoming of desire is inseparable from a concept of death as self-created.[98] This is not a matter of simply choosing death. Indeed, for Deleuze as Guattari, it is not so much that we *can* choose death as that the experience of death is the *only* process.[99] When Deleuze and Guattari state that the model can't ever truly be reached because it is a limit, they make it clear that this is not about the actual reduction of affects; the point is not that we should simply destroy ourselves, but the experience of dying is nonetheless what is at stake.[100] The experience of death may or may not be about the enlargement of affective capacities – the enlargement, in other words, of our model. There is no such thing as death per se.[101]

Where is the human subject in this account? If the model of death is a motor for the proliferation and mutative transformation of our desiring machines, there surely seems little space for human subjectivity.[102] Surely, as Land claimed, humanity can only surrender its place to a machine function.[103] Freud is certainly indicted for insisting that 'you will be a subject' and inventing the conceptual tools to 'nail us down as one'.[104] Subjectivity appears almost exclusively as a target for machinic disarticulation.[105] Creative subjectivity is the art of becoming the residuum of our death; this is precisely a question of suicide. It is only in the play of our subjective masks that life becomes productive. Death is differencing, machinically assembling novel chains on the model we have constructed for ourselves.[106] The subject is an ambulant activity on the recording surface.[107]

The human subject here is defined only by the inevitability of its becoming-other.[108] All firm representations of the self are illegitimate enclosures of desiring-production into territorial forms. Whilst this subject is perhaps a leftover, it does not lack.[109] The residual subject is full of affects-realising as a recombinatory multiplicity.[110] Through its operationalisation of death, desiring-production enacts a subject scattered 'around the entire compass of its cycle, a subject that passes by way of all becomings correspondent to the included disjunctions'.[111] Subjectivity dwells in possibility,[112] as 'an intense feeling of transition'.[113] It is constantly productive and, as such, becoming-revolutionary: Lines of subjectivization are 'lines of fissure, lines of life-death which, when they fold over and re-divide, form at the interior an outside'.[114] This is a condition in which death changes nothing; that is to say, it is already there.[115] The experience of death thus implies a kind of extra-being, already there as the nascent and all-pervasive matrix of desiring-production.[116] Revolutionary lines of flight are expressions of continuity precisely inasmuch as they are the expression of discontinuity with the body (experiences of death). Subjectivity is always suicidal, it seems.

The problem of suicide which *A Thousand Plateaus* makes explicit is thus already explicitly at issue in *Anti-Oedipus*. A creative subject is necessarily one step away from a suicidal one, because it is by definition dissolving. Subjectivization is autodissolution. When Deleuze and Guattari argue in *A Thousand Plateaus* that 'in dismantling the organism there are times one courts death,' they directly extend their account of subjectivity as a machinic oscillation between model and experience of death.[117] This is why Deleuze and Guattari raise in that later text the need for an 'art of dosages'. It is all too easy to overdose on death.

> You don't do it with a sledgehammer; you use a very fine file. You invent self destructions that have nothing to do with the death drive. Dismantling the organism has never meant killing yourself, but rather opening the body to connections that presuppose an entire assemblage, circuits, conjunctions, levels and thresholds, passages and distributions of intensity, and territories and deterritorializations measured with the craft of a surveyor.[118]

Furthermore:

> You have to keep enough of the organism for it to re-form each dawn; and you have to keep small supplies of significance and subjectification, if only to turn themselves against their own systems when the circumstances demand it . . . and you need to keep small rations of subjectivity in sufficient quantity to enable you to respond to dominant reality.[119]

Building oneself a model of death and deterritorialising requires caution, for reasons integral to the process itself.

Some machines are more productive than others; plainly not all models of death are productive. One can, obviously, live in permanent despairing dread of death or live life as a morbid absurdity; the question is how productive will you be. *Anti-Oedipus* makes it clear that you can't deterritorialise without making a model of death, *A Thousand Plateaus* is concerned to demonstrate that it is entirely possible to botch it, creating fruitless or barren experiences of death. A botched model seeks to reduce the body's affects rather than expanding them.[120] Rather than attracting desiring-machines to circulate anew on its matrix of intensity, an 'Empty' model repels them along with the organism, destroying the organism with so 'violent an action' that 'you blow apart the strata' entirely. The consequence is that 'instead of drawing the plane you will be killed, plunging into a black hole, or even dragged towards catastrophe.' The empty body is a too 'organised death', a life that is closed to novelty and refounded in suicidal identity.[121] The model of death obviously sets out criterion for a breakdown of the body as well as the organism. We can become anorexic,[122] masochistic[123] or alcoholic, and in the process set about the reduction of bodily affects to nil. The other way of botching it is going fully cancerous and fascistic; a death-machine sending its tanks outwards under a Promethean promise.[124]

There are many ways to botch the model. We can only take care always to add to our affects rather than embrace the purity of subtraction; a condition of too heavy deterritorialisation. To reach a point where 'there is no longer an I,' accessing the model of death so as to release the proliferating desiring machines, cannot be achieved through an ethic of purification. Accelerating too fast may lead to a 'body of nothingness, pure self-destruction whose only outcome is death'.[125]

Experienced as uncertainty and self-critique, the paranoid organism is constantly battling to keep its underlying disorganisation under wraps. Some models drive reactive stratification, as the fear of disorder materialised. Organisation is a reaction to the primary risk of violent deterritorialisation; this applies at both the individual and social levels. The danger represented by the seductive purity of a full subtraction of affects is irrevocable. The appeal of submitting to disintegration is integral to being, but not because it is an unconscious drive.[126] All creative experiences skirt real abolition: the demented reduction of a body's affects to zero or the unrestrained pursuit of a desire's line of flight into a black hole. Each subject is a residuum of their death.

Events and death

Badiou's statement that Deleuze's 'philosophy of life is essentially . . . a philosophy of death' is clearly borne out in *Capitalism and Schizophrenia*.[127] Badiou seeks to distinguish himself firmly from Deleuze inasmuch as for him 'death is not, and can never be, an event'.[128] Deleuze's Stoicism is certainly unnerving for anyone hoping to mobilise him in pursuit of a politics.[129] This is at the root of claims that Deleuze is a thinker of pure contemplation who can observe change, but is unable to provide grounds for agency.[130] The accusation of political passivity or ascetic contemplation finds its grounds in a real, if conventional, paradox. Deleuze argues that all action takes place in a bind of radical absoluteness. One is never fully author of one's own existence, but defined by a matrix of forces and trajectories which predetermine our actions. The Stoic response is that the only possible act is one animated by *amor fati* – the affirmative willing of one's unwilled existence. *Amor fati* is not a matter of resignation to the flows which exceed us, something Deleuze equates with Nietzschean ressentiment.[131] Rather, for Deleuze, there is an integrally revolutionary political agency located in the Stoic position.

This agency is curious. For Deleuze the actor doubles the event by embodying in our will that which has already been caused such that we become 'the quasi-cause of what is produced within us'.[132] This counter-actualisation 'limits, moves and transfigures' the event itself.[133] Something is added by counter-actualising an event.[134] This something is clearly important for Deleuze inasmuch as he argues that counter-actualisation is the way in which all transmutations happen.[135] Counter-actualisation is the virtual dimension of the actual situation which affirms its becomings, deterritorialisations or lines of flight. How could such an affirmation add anything to the event?[136] How, in other words, is this not identical to resignation in practice, if achieving a metaphysical, or indeed mystical agency? This surely is the definition an apolitical gesture, indulging whatever actual forces the institutions of power have assembled.[137] The implication seems to be that causing radical change is impossible.[138] If all events are evental only inasmuch as they are counter-actualised, no revolutionary modification of, or break from, a state of affairs can be achieved.[139] We act only by supplying affirmation to our being swept up by events' extant becomings. For Badiou this is only resignation to the impossibility of action through a 'dogma of our finitude, of our carnal exposition to enjoyment, suffering and death': a surrender to what happens.[140]

Deleuze's response to this charge is contained in his reading of Maurice Blanchot, a reading that hinges on the theorisation of suicide. Maurice Blanchot asked the seemingly obvious question, 'Can I die'?[141] He argued that to die, to really, affirmatively die, one must do so twice. One 'must be mortal twice over: [be] sovereignly, extremely mortal'.[142] The problem of death's impossibility is that of the impossibility of having consciousness of the disappearance of one's consciousness.[143] Suicide is the hope that, in the autorealisation of one's death, death will reappear to the self 'in the form of power'.[144] Blanchot argues that such an 'action here is only the mask of a fascinated dispossession': It is impossibility. 'The weakness of suicide lies in the fact that whoever commits it is still too strong'. A suicide seeks to be a 'great affirmer of the present', he seeks 'an apotheosis of the instant', a voluntary affirmation of something which 'one can look neither back upon nor forward to'.[145]

It is the structure of this problem which interests Deleuze because, he argues, it is reflected in all events. For Blanchot the impossibility of suicide derives from the doubled character of death:

> There is one death which circulates in the language of possibility, of liberty, which has for its furthest horizon the freedom to die and the capacity to take mortal risks; and there is its double, which is ungraspable. It is what I cannot grasp, what is not linked to me by any relation of any sort. It is that which never comes and towards which I do not direct myself . . . to kill oneself is to mistake one death for the other.[146]

Because death is doubled in this way:

> Suicide remains essentially a bet, something hazardous: not because I leave myself a chance to survive, as sometimes happens, but because suicide is a leap. It is a passage from the certainty of an act that has been planned, consciously decided upon, and vigorously executed, to something which disorientates every project, remains foreign to all decisions – the indecisive and uncertain, the crumbling of the inert and the obscurity of the non-true.[147]

Blanchot thus argues that suicide must therefore be understood as animated by the wish to 'eliminate death as future'. Deleuze claims that this is only 'defining the illusion', when it is the double ontology and leap that are really significant.[148] The illusion simply 'is not where the problem resides'.[149] For Blanchot 'you cannot make death an object of the will'; we can only contain in experience the borderlands of its phenomenality.[150] For Deleuze it is obviously true that attending to death per se is impossibility, but it is precisely this which makes our own model and experience of death the inevitable object of the will.[151]

The reasons for this claim can also be traced to Blanchot, for whom the attempt to bring the two deaths together is closely linked to the creative process. Suicide is an illusion or madness, but 'it is madness we could not be spared without being excluded from the human condition'.[152] For Blanchot, the artist 'is linked to his work in the same strange way in which the man who takes death for a goal is linked to death'.[153] This shocking comparison between art and suicide highlights the operationalisation of impossibility is essential to them both.[154] The artist and the suicide 'succeed in doing something only by deceiving themselves about what they do'. They enact a constitutive leap into the unknown, into the impossible, and without that leap, artistic creation would be impossible. 'The act of dying itself constitutes this leap' as a 'radical reversal', whereby at the end, where the promise of mastery (of death) stood before the consciousness of the actor, he or she is cast 'out of [his or her] power to begin and even to finish'.[155] The impossible is the object or terminus of a suicide. This same impossibility, however, acts as the origin of the work of art. The work of art emerges from, or rather dwells in the negligence which the suicide denies. The negligence of the double is the gamble or risk out of which a work necessarily originates. The creative work emerges from an essential risk where being is put at stake on the power to die.[156]

Deleuze, in *The Logic of Sense*, reworks Blanchot's claim in stating that to creatively will any event is fundamentally to 'accept war, wounds and death':[157]

> The ambiguity [of events] is essentially that of the wound and of death, of the mortal wound. Death has an extreme and definite relation to me and my body and is grounded in me, but it also has no relation to me at all – it is incorporeal and infinitive, impersonal grounded on in itself. On the one side there is the part of the event which is realised and accomplished; on the other hand there is that part of the event which cannot realise that accomplishment. There are thus two accomplishments, which are like actualization and counter-actualization. It is in this way that death and its wound are not simply events among other events. Every event is like death, double and impersonal in its double.[158]

To will an event is a self-effacement mirrored at the doubled heart of the event itself; it is the leap into impossibility which is the experience of death.[159] Events are doubled: 'With every moment, there is the present moment of its actualization, the moment in which the event is embodied in a state of affairs, an individual, or a person', but there is also another sense of the event which exceeds the individual completely.[160] Here we see the creative dance of the individual with his or her utter contingency.[161] Here we become-other; deterritorialising is a leap into autodissolution. To will the event is to commit to our departure.

This apparently gives weight to Badiou's accusation of Deleuze's event as being simply the play of unlimited becoming, bound by historicity and futurity to be a work from beyond the body, enacted by the universal in the celebration of mortality.[162] Building a productive model of death is certainly a labour of disintegration; but the leap cannot and should not be disentangled from the singular for Deleuze. It is not a pure ahistorical break, but a leap into univocity on that singularity. The experience of death is univocal, voiced as one in its decision on deterritorialisation.[163] This is not to say that death is one and same for every being. Beings are multiple and different, but inasmuch as they are 'an occurring', they are necessarily crossed by univocal extra-being, a becoming-other. Badiou's articulation of Deleuze's event as simply a fractal of the One is misleading.[164] Deleuze's claim is that the event is coextensive with all becomings as a process of deterritorialisation, but 'unity is said of the multiple so that the One says *nothing but the multiple*'.[165] Badiou's phrasing of univocity (admittedly moderated somewhat in *Logics of Worlds*) as the transcendent ordering of the multiple, severs deterritorialisation from the singularities that are deterritorialised.

Counter-actualisation is the speculative leap into 'the splendour of the event itself': creation by self-negligence.[166] To will is precisely to become the double of that which assembles us; that is to say, to become the residuum of the univocal movement scattered across its reverberating possibilities. We *must* risk suicide because the creative leap or experience of death has exactly the same structure as the ultimately antiproductive gesture. A creative event cannot simply be actualised, it must be counter-actualised, lived as an autodestruction; this is what it means to will. To will an event is to will my undoing (becoming-other).[167] Events are never private or personal, but rather singularities which bind the private to the collective, the particular to the general, and so are 'neither individual nor universal'.[168] Like acting (in the theatrical sense) a part or role so as to give it its thematic meaning, to will the event is to bring the moment embodied in a state of affairs, or person who is subject to it, into contact with its future and past – not its history, but the virtual movement that 'overwhelms me, scattering its singularities all about' and opens to deterritorialisation.[169] Counter-actualisation is a fourth-person experience; the experience of a 'they', whereby an event's impersonality is embodied in one's person.[170] It is, in other words, fidelity to one's deterritorialisation.[171] This is why there is danger integral to every willing of the event. Deleuze in *The Logic of Sense*, like Badiou in *Being and Event*, thus sees the need for restraint.[172] As in *Capitalism and Schizophrenia*, what is at stake in *The Logic of Sense* are the risks of actual politics: the dangers integral to the creative as such. The counter-actualising will constitutively risks falling victim to its own morbid logic.[173]

Willing the event must open to suicide because it precisely reproduces its logic.[174] Deleuze terms this problem the eternal truth of the wound. To act politically is to counter-actualise/wound the self, which is to risk suicide. Political life is a 'process of breaking down': It is a cracking, a deterritorialisation, an embrace of forces outside, indeed the resolute affirmation of such forces though a leap into my impossibility. To counter-actualise is to 'risk [...] something and [go] as far as possible in taking this risk' as a kind of 'irrepressible right' written into the fabric of events as such.[175] Actual self-destruction is written into the very logic of political creation. Inasmuch as this makes clear that actual suicide is a central problem of Deleuze, criticisms that his work only passively observes creation seem at least partially redressed; Deleuze advocates constant autodestructive engagement in the actual. Indeed one might suggest that the problem is even more profound than his critics have recognised. For Deleuze, counter-actualising transformation seems to invariably precipitate real self-destructions. Accordingly, the problem of politics for Deleuze is that of how we might become 'a little alcoholic, a little crazy, a little suicidal, a little of a guerrilla – just enough to extend the crack, but not enough to deepen it irremediably'.[176] Events are deterritorialisations, experiences of death which are held short of catastrophism.[177] It is not accidental to political action that suicide emerges. The logic of political events has the architecture of death at its heart.

Badiou categorically distinguishes political events from artistic events, love events and scientific events, whilst seeing their truth processes as generic. Deleuze and Guattari distinguished between philosophy, art and science, but leave politics out of the typology; this is because these fields are already integrally political.[178] Art, they argue, is revolutionary because it too carries an integral risk of suicide. This is an explicit deviation from Blanchot, for whom art is politically inadequate. Blanchot argued that 'the work itself is essentially a risk' because the impersonality of death operates as the necessary origin of the work.[179] A work of art always tends towards that incessantly deferred horizon 'which once reached, makes the work impossible'.[180] The artist is beleaguered by the demands of this necessary horizon. In a series of discussions of literary figures, Blanchot demonstrates what this means. The artist or writer, because the work depends on his or her exposure to impersonality, must be understood as at risk, endangered by the very 'pressure which demands that he writes'.[181] The writer's work is the opening of a space which is alien to him, to which he is always an alien. The demand of the work amounts to a 'nullification of oneself', a self-incineration.[182] Artistic creation is experimental: 'It is a search – and investigation which is not undetermined but is, rather, determined by its indeterminacy, and involves the whole of life, even if it seems to know nothing of life'.[183] One is invariably changed by art: 'We are according to what we write'. There are no creations without internal transformations that threaten self-abolition.[184] The work of art is a 'movement of dispossession'. Creation embraces a fatal risk as 'the truth of the experience'.[185] The artist must not only embrace his inevitable failure – the impossibility of fully reaching the actual, but affirm that extreme experience.[186] It is risk for its own sake, permanent exile, the impossibility of every being *at home* in being.

In *A Thousand Plateaus*, literature, music and painting are assigned just such an integral riskiness. For Deleuze and Guattari, reading Blanchot, artists are necessarily on the edge of cracking-up. This argument appears most clearly in their lauding of 'the Anglo-American novel'. They locate, in Lawrence, Miller, and above all Melville, a trajectory that amounts to a radicalisation of the line of glorious error which Blanchot identified in Mallarme, Kafka, Rilke and Holderline. Man's openness to fatal enrapture has certainly been the recurring theme in literature, art and music. Herman Melville's *Moby Dick* stands, Deleuze and Guattari argue, as the defining expression of an attempt to capture the dangerousness of becoming. Ahab's pursuit of the Whale takes him into the absolute, seeking to reach completion by touching the unique and anomalous as such. The reader stands witness, in the unfolding of his obsession, to an excess that belongs to all absolute commitment. Ahab's death is no longer his. His decision for the Whale in all its fatal connotations ensures that Ahab is met at the borderline by a pure externality. Pursuing the whale takes Ahab into celebrant abolition. Throughout the Anglo-American novel 'the same cry rings out: go across, get out, break through, make a beeline, don't get stuck on any point. Find the line of separation, follow it or create it, to the point of treachery'.[187] Deleuze and Guattari praise the Anglo-American novel for knowing 'how difficult it is to get out' and 'how tempting it is to let yourself be caught', and thereby for devoting itself to crossing the wall at the price of becomings.[188] The novel is not seen following Blanchot as an end in itself.[189] For Deleuze and Guattari, as a project of autodissolution, the novel is never a 'work which *is*, and nothing more'.[190] The insufficiency that Blanchot saw in artistic activity 'at decisive hours' distinguished for him the work of art from the pressures of political action. For Deleuze and Guattari, no such insufficiency exists: 'The point is to get out of it, not in art, in other words, in spirit, but in life, in real life'.[191] 'Art is . . . only a tool for blazing life lines'.[192]

The Anglo-American novel, in seeking to dismantle the stable subject of representation, is peculiarly engaged with the fundamentally political problematic of an integral risk. The madness that is a definite danger for all artists is the risk of politics.[193] This point goes beyond the observation that artists need to suffer for their art. The creative work functions by dismantling strata, felling trees or breaking through walls, and replacing all these (striated, arborescent, molar) structures with lines of creative flight. Such projects are necessarily traced by the risks of abolition (alongside more straightforward blockages, and short circuits of artistic creativity).[194] Fitzgerald's novella *The Crack-Up* is viewed as exemplary precisely because it is so explicitly concerned with this issue. It addresses the strange crack which crosses and explodes all the territories of life. This is a purely deterritorialised line; a line of rupture.[195] The novella's insight, revealed in its 'despairing tone' is that 'the line of rupture or true flight ha[s] its own danger, one worse than all the others? Time to die.' Fitzgerald is integrally concerned with the impersonal risk of the work as such.[196] The question 'Are you going to crack up?', integral for the artist who must risk negligence of the impossible to create, is identical to that of 'What is your model of death?' and in turn 'What are your Lines? . . . Are you deterritorializing? Which lines are you severing, and which are you extending or resuming?'[197] At this point, Deleuze and Guattari's state their disagreement with Blanchot clearly: Art is the demonstrator of the key schizoanalytical precept that politics precedes being.[198] The risk integral to art is precisely the political question of lines and their assemblage.[199] Politics is first philosophy.

In a latter section of *A Thousand Plateaus* entitled 'Becoming Music' it is observed that

> music has a thirst for destruction . . . [for although] music is never tragic, music is joy . . . there are times it necessarily give us a taste for death; not so much happiness as dying happily, being extinguished . . . [and this is] . . . a dimension proper to its sound assemblage to its sound machine, the moment that must be confronted, the moment the transversal turns into a line of abolition.[200]

76 *Self-burning*

In other words we see exactly the problematic of an integral risk in music as the experience of deterritorialisation. Deleuze and Guattari are explicit here: On musical lines into abolition we see the 'danger inherent to any line that escapes, in any line of flight or creative deterritorialization: the danger of veering towards destruction'.[201] It is crucial to recognise that this is not a reading of music as pure deterritorialisation; clearly all music, even improvisation, requires a certain striation. Expertise is the necessary criterion for improvisation not simply being noise. Music pulls towards the extinction of self. As Deleuze and Guattari recognised above, we need to keep enough of our body to reform each dawn, to avoid a pure cacophony.

Deleuze and Guattari follow these comments about music directly with the question 'Is the situation similar to painting, and if so, how?'[202] They make clear that this is not a question of the essence of art per se ('Art is a false concept'), and affirm the fundamental differences between the constitutive problems in literature, music and painting. Rather, the question is that of the politics of any creative process; in other words, 'in each case we must simultaneously consider factors of territoriality, deterritorialization, and reterritorialization'.[203] Creativity is political.[204] What is being raised here is less an issue of technique, as recognition that the leap is constitutive of art, and artists are therefore always politicians of a sort. The painter, the musician and the writer are challenged by the leap on the model of death which is the creative process, and in that leap the question of the desiring-political is posed ('What is your model?'). A revolutionary becoming *is* to the extent that it can confront 'its own danger, even taking a fall in order to rise again'.[205] The madness of artists (their fondness for cracking up) is the function of art's integral politicality. Art, literature and music are already political, and for the same reason, all carry the risk of suicide.

Palach's revolution

On 16 January 1969, Jan Palach, a philosophy student at Charles University, set himself alight in Prague's Wenceslas Square. Suffering third-degree burns over eighty-five percent of his body, he died three days later in hospital. His suicide note explained his action as an attempt to restore the flagging spirits of the Prague Spring, the term given to the assemblage of economic and political reforms and cultural and intellectual ferment which had been interrupted by the invasion of Czechoslovakia by the other signatories of the Warsaw Pact that August:[206]

> Because our nations are on the brink of despair we have decided to express our protest and wake up the people of this land. Our group is composed of volunteers who are willing to burn themselves for our cause. It was my honour to draw lot number one and thus I acquired the privilege of writing the first letter and starting as the first torch. Our demands are 1) immediate elimination of censorship, 2) prohibition of the distribution of Zpravy. If our demands are not fulfilled within five days by January the 21st 1969, and if the people do not support us through a strike of indefinite duration, more torches

will burn. Remember August. In international politics a place was made for Czechoslovakia. Let us use it. – Torch Number One.[207]

The act resulted in a collective outpouring of emotion and mass reflection,[208] but it did not lead to the sovereign reinvigoration Palach had clearly hoped for.[209] Indeed, in this regard, Palach's suicide may be seen as a critical point in the cartography of the Prague Spring as an assemblage of desire.[210] Palach's suicide was a conclusion of the movement, but also its fulfilment in excess. It was a suicide in more ways than simply an individual death, bringing an end to a collective movement of creative political desire. Palach, in this regard, seems to embody the paradoxes of the politics of suicide: Here a line of flight went suicidal without being in any way fascistic.

Stalinism brought to Czechoslovakia the predictable political trials of the 1950s, a party monopoly, the concentration of power, an insistence on blind obedience, opaque decision-making, arbitrariness, a semi-autonomous police system and the injunction to ideological unity.[211] It drew, in other words, a rigid molar totalitarian line across the socius, setting up a resonating molecular apparatus that spread the reach of the party's authority through society.[212] The bureaucratism of this diagram lead to a number of the economic problems which would support the drivers of the Prague Spring, but the student, literary and artistic movements of the 1960s cannot be reduced to the play of structural forces.[213] Despite the tendency in the West to ascribe the decline of Stalinism to the (economic) contradictions of communism, the Prague Spring found its contingent origins in an event that by rupturing the molar caused desire to take flight. Khrushchev's disclosure of the Stalinist personality-cult idea at the 1956 Twentieth Congress confirmed suspicions which communist intellectuals like Jaroslaw Putik had previously dismissed only for their quite evident absurdity.[214] The abortive initiation of de-Stalinisation produced time bombs which exploded differently in different countries.[215] The year 1956 produced an analytical flight (of self-understanding), but more specifically a flight at the level of desire (characterised by communist guilt in relation to the political trials of that decade). The event of the Prague Spring was thus no absolute break in Badiou's sense: It was an accelerating deterritorialisation.

De-Stalinisation was swiftly blocked by Antonin Novotny, then party leader, but ambivalence and contradiction had now been introduced to the system. In the newly smoothed space, communist writers, artists and intellectuals began to work more freely.[216] The shock of 1956 was transmuted to black humour and literary absurdism in theatre and poetry.[217] Communist literary and artistic circles nurtured their lines of flight.[218] The steady refusal of communist eulogization, development of critical views of society and opposition to party standards through literary humour and satire indicated a steady molecularization was underway, accompanied by a diffuse dissatisfaction with molarity which manifested, in particular, in the birth of the student movement.[219] Art and literature demolished the Stalinist idea of culture as an instrument for reeducation.[220] The 1960s saw a new wave of Czechoslovak cinema, but also the explosion of small theatre groups, musicians and fine arts. This movement of molecularizing desire was aided by

Novotny's relaxation of censorship in 1962–63 under pressure from the cultural upsurge and liberal party members. No preset ideational structure organised this movement. Though significant censorship remained active, with artists enjoying much more freedom than cultural journalists, what was evident was a steady challenge to the molar line through the emergence of a molecular 'feeling' expressed through 'humour, farce, escapism, beat and all that jazz'.[221] Journals like *Literarni Noviny*, *Kulturny Zivot* and *Kulturni Tvorba*, which during the 1960s had a circulation of three hundred thousand in a population of fourteen million, were crucial mechanisms in that movement.[222] Writers like Laco Novomesky,[223] Josef Skvorecky,[224] Dominik Tatarka,[225] or the future president Vaclav Havel, expressed clearly not only an awareness of the political function of the artist, but also the risks involved.[226] Rather than posing the function of the artist and intellectual as avant-garde for a revolutionary movement to come, we see the artist here as already revolutionary. By the mid-1960s it was evident that an existential threat to molar organisation was in the process of emerging. A sustained assault on the molar line seemed to come from everywhere at once.[227]

In the face of that critique Novotny had allowed limited decensorship in the early 1960s, which of course accelerated the molecularization. By the mid-1960s he set out to reverse these steps with arrests, condemnation of 'intellectual malice' and 'ideological chaos', and general harassment of the journalists of the key publications.[228] Publishing rights were withdrawn from *Literarni Noviny*, and a party-controlled gazette set up under same name.[229] The clumsiness of this attempt at redrawing the line simply ensured that resistance by artists and intellectuals was now joined by an accelerating program of youth protests and demonstrations.[230] The economic climate certainly played a role in facilitating this social unrest.[231] Novotny's eventual deposition in 1968 was in a palace coup. His replacement, Dubcek, initiated the reforms which are loosely termed the Prague Spring. The reforms themselves had been largely developed in the years previously by party intellectuals like Mlynar and Vaculik at the political level, for the introduction of checks and balances, legal safeguards, decentralisation of power, democratic appointments, the allowance of pressure groups and civic society. Dubcek was concerned that the centralism of the Novotny regime had alienated the people from socialism; his actions may be seen as deriving from a principally conservative desire to shore up the party regime as it was swept away. Only after the reform's introduction in 1968 did most citizens beyond the students really take notice. Whilst the reformers had little intention to challenge the party model and sought, at most, slow change, the basic logic of the reforms clearly ran in the opposite direction. Decentralisation lead to unprecedented enthusiasm beyond these limits in society at large.[232] The party machine itself was caught up. Unsought, the reforms set free the deterritorialisation of desire in society at large.

The reforms principally aimed to limit state interference in economic organs. The idea of worker participation in elected management through the construction of enterprise councils had particularly radicalising effects.[233] Even before the reforms had been enacted, workers begin electing councils, and through this democratisation in action, reformism turned into a mass movement. In this way, the deterritorialisation which began in cultural circles spread first to the students and then to the workers, a line of flight traversing the social field. It should perhaps have been less surprising when, in August 1968, the Warsaw Pact invaded. The detailed Soviet bureaucratic negotiations which lead to the invasion are peripheral here.[234] What drove the invasion was paranoia in its formal sense: fear of contingency. Desire's deterritorialisation threatened the heavy molar line of Soviet-style organisation. There was certainly an ideational aspect in the challenge to the leading role of party, but it was the perception that Dubcek had lost control of the process as such which really worried the Soviets, as recently released documents have confirmed.[235] The movement integrally went beyond the reformism of its bureaucratic enactors.[236] The Soviets saw a process that was integrally unmanageable; a great rip was taking place in the fabric of striation.

The accepted wisdom is that Palach's suicide was an act of extreme disenchantment: The invasion had demonstrated the futility of the Prague Spring, and Palach embodied a collective recognition of that futility.[237] Yet the invasion, far from abruptly cutting short the collective deterritorialisation of the Czechoslovaks, resulted in an explosion of improvised collective action: mass resistance, not despondency. The so-called Prague Winter entailed a mobilisation of large sections of society who had previously been only spectators.[238] A campaign of nonviolent resistance had seriously disrupted supply lines compounding 'the occupying armies' logistical woes'.[239] The invasion was widely perceived to have failed inasmuch as the Warsaw Pact was unable to affect swift regime change.[240] Particularly once Dubcek and his reformist colleagues were returned, having been spirited away by the invading forces, the collective mood was ebullient: 'The people felt that they had won, since the collaborators had failed to overthrow Dubcek's team'.[241] It is this August of which Palach would enjoin remembrance. The implication is that what devastated the movement was not the invasion, but the recognition some time after that their leaders were acquiescing to a rollback of the reforms. As in France 1968, the socialists at home broke the back of the revolution of desire.

On return Dubcek called personally and with apparently heartfelt emotion for the general population to refrain from doing anything that would give excuse to the invaders to remain, or later, to reinvade. Dubcek's calls for caution were pragmatic, and implied that the party would fight for as much of the reformist program as could be salvaged. There was a broad popular acceptance of this bargain, evidenced by a remarkable collective restraint which lasted until October, when a treaty legalising the invasion was passed by the Czechoslovak Party and popular direct action resumed.[242] Yet even this eruption of renewed unrest, a student strike in October, workers' strikes and writers' statements always 'stopped short of making a real challenge' so as not to 'invite disaster'.[243] When resistance emerged, it was hamstrung by the caution which Dubcek had begged for. Pragmatism was effective in a way that direct coercion could not be. The people remolarized themselves. So it was that the line of flight was striated and bound back into a stable formation. That caution allowed the rise of a realist faction led by Husak to dominate the party, with Dubcek and all the key reformers being pushed into retirement, often after disavowing the reformist project. Clearly the party reformists were less avid reformers than the population had believed.[244] Figures such as Dubcek were horrified by the suggestion that they were secret anticommunists: They never intended to challenge the single-party system in Czechoslovakia. Indeed, Dubcek, would, at the January plenum before his deposition, emphasise the need to prevent anarchism and to enforce democratic centralism.[245]

It was crucially at this moment that Jan Palach set himself alight. Palach's act would spur the realists within the party to even more certitude that the situation was out of control.[246] It revealed, precisely, the unlimited deterritorialisation which the reformers had inadvertently got caught up in. The reformers were all too happy to return to the rigid striations of bureaucratic dictatorship. The movement's betrayal by its leaders did produce widespread disappointment. The popular outpouring that followed his act, whilst unifying people for a short time, bore no practical fruit. None of Palach's demands was carried out; his act seemed only to confirm that the break between people and party had truly occurred, and that the Prague Spring as a desiring-machine crossing between them was now over. It is not surprising that Palach has so often been interpreted, in this light, as the embodiment of tragedy, sorrow and frustration.[247] What such an interpretation cannot capture is Palach's explicit aim to give flight to the line by reminding the population of the events of August – to remember the active, spontaneous resistance of the people to the Warsaw Pact's invasion. The act sought to express no sorrowful acquiescence to the end of deterritorialisation, but rather to reinvigorate the desire for its continuation – the act was explicitly meant as a continuation of the Prague Spring. Palach sought to reverse the seduction of the populace to participation in the erosion of movement, with a reacceleration of the Prague Spring as line of flight. He sought a passage through abolition, a movement in the face of its betrayal by the party leaders.

The Czechoslovakian philosopher Ivan Svitak, who was stripped of his citizenship after the event, argued that the Prague Spring was the clash of two contradictory ideas: bureaucratic dictatorship and socialist democracy.[248] He saw Palach's act as the tragic expression of an overstretched desire, a gesture which exceeded its own limited powers. Both Palach and the 'spontaneous creativity' of 1968 marked, in this account, the truth of a democratic socialism that was structurally unrealizable due to wider conditions.[249] For Svitak there was thus a victory even in failure, in Palach's fidelity to another path for the socialist states of Eastern Europe.[250] The event was the event of a new truth's possibility. In this sense, Palach was neither reactive nor obscure (in Badiou's sense of the terms).[251] His act was no denial of the event, nor was it consumed with ideological absolutes. Indeed Svitak's account of Palach has clear resonances with Badiou's faithful subject; the trace of the event which 'welcomes, point by point, the new truth',[252] and in doing so becoming an 'erased body'.[253] As the Soviet archives make clear, there is significant reason to doubt the commitment of the reformers to democratic reform. The reforms themselves were in their early stages when the Prague Spring was cut short, and party discussions were by no means clear about where they were going. Furthermore, in Palach's suicide note there is no reference to a new truth of democratic socialism, only to the spirit of August which he sought to affirm and enjoin remembrance of. His suicide note contained, in this sense, only an expression of fidelity to the deterritorialisation of the Czechoslovak socius. What Badiou sees as the experience of a revolutionary life, the universal comprehension of a theorem, an idea, a truth, seems unable to capture this sense. Palach's suicide was precisely not 'truthful'; it was revolutionary in that it was committed to a desire for truths' decoding. Palach insisted on specific points: end censorship; stop distributing propaganda. The Prague Spring, here, is not defined by reference to the conflict between two opposing ideals, but by the contradistinction of two opposing movements: reterritorialisation and deterritorialisation. Palach explicitly invoked the memory of deterritorialisation: 'Remember August.' The politics of his act are determined by fidelity to that univocal movement and its counter-actualisation.[254]

In this sense, Palach's suicide was an affirmation of the rights of movement which are the nonhuman condition of becoming. A revolutionary finitude, the only evidence of an eternity it offered was the eternity of becomings-finite ('others will follow me').[255] In dying, Palach committed himself to a movement beyond him.[256] Badiou's statement that 'death . . . can never be an event,' and his claim in *Logics of Worlds* that his entire purpose is to 'think existence without finitude', add up to withdraw Palach from political life. It is impossible to think of Palach's fidelity without his finitude. His fidelity was to creative politics precisely though its 'terrestrial writing' that is death.[257] His act was a faithful affirmation of mortality as the writing of life's univocal motion. Here, politics does not reside in commitment to an idea, but in fidelity to deterritorialisation. To this extent Palach's act seems precisely to imply Deleuze's claim that resistance comes first.[258] It is clear that this insight is present, if buried, in Badiou's philosophy. For Badiou, a truth is affirmed, and this is the subject, yet that subject is only faithful if the truth is not subjected to occultation, that is to say, its incompletion as a truth is retained. The infinity which is the object of fidelity is conditioned by the truth's contingent realisation. For Badiou, this indicates its ontological ground in lack, but for all his efforts, truth is here conditioned not by generic logical procedure but by its capacity to deterritorialise: Politics, here, precedes truth.

Nonetheless, we must accept that Palach's act added to the defeatist attitude: a collective tragic sense of an irreversible fate.[259] Palach's act became, retrospectively, the suicide of the movement: The Prague Spring ironically descended into abolition through an act seeking to continue its flight.[260] Was it inevitable that Palach's act would be a failure in this sense – to shock and elicit contemplation, but trigger no flight, indeed to become the symbol of movement's impossibility? Were Palach's antiproductive consequences integral to his politics of suicide, suggestive by a botched and therefore suicidal model of death? The authorities certainly did not think that the act was necessarily doomed to failure. The Warsaw Pact countries rapidly put out propaganda suggesting Western coercion of Palach, that he was a capitalist provocateur or the victim of a trick – having been told that the fluid would not, in fact, harm him when set alight.[261] Palach's grave at Olsany Cemetery became a focus of student vigils, with candles burning constantly. In response, the Czechoslovak authorities removed the bronze death mask from the grave. They then began to put pressure on Palach's mother to relocate his remains from the capital to Vsetaty in central Bohemia. Her refusal to give way prompted the state, on 22 October 1973, after the atmosphere had quietened, to dig up the grave at four in the morning, cremate his body and give the ashes to his mother.[262] The molar authorities clearly saw in the event a potential for revolutionary productivity. We see here a creative politics only as unrealised potential, as Svitak suggested.

Palach's act may have resonated with European Marxists like Svitak in search of a truth with which to respond to the gulags, but this was clearly not the root of its politics. Palach's suicide had convinced a number of party members that the situation really was out of control and the molar apparatus had to reassert itself to prevent disaster. Dubcek's call for caution was reactionary not because it was an attempt to deny the event – indeed he would argue tearfully for exactly the opposite interpretation: It was reactionary because it broke the movement of desire. His injunction to take care was heeded by the students, artists and writers of the Prague Spring, and expressed in their solemnity. Yet the minimal intensity of Palach's actual consequences cannot thereby be reduced to his suicide.[263] It seems clear that the consequences of the act were overdetermined by the promise of a greater catastrophe were there to be a continuance of the movement that Palach demanded. In this sense, a globalised climate of fear supplied the theatre of submission with its seduction. Questions are clearly raised here for Deleuze and Guattari's defence of the concept of caution as more than the calling card of the counter-revolutionary, but as Svitak observed, the event also directs our attention to the presence of a terrifying international suicide machine, without recognition of which the politics of Palach's act remains inaccessible.

On suicide machines

Derrida evoked the thought of

> an event that would bear witness, in exemplary or hyperbolic fashion, to the very essence of an event, or even to an event beyond essence. For could an event that still conforms to an essence, to an essence, or truth, indeed to a concept of the event, ever be a major event? A major event should be unforeseeable and irruptive that it disturbs even the horizon of the concept or essence on the basis of which we recognise an event as such.[264]

Such an event would necessarily remain evasive, resist our experience and suspend our comprehension.[265] A major event is one in which its constitutive wound necessarily remains open.[266] Palach's death, in as much as it embodied a register of possibility displaced, seems to mark just such an injury in history.

The Cold War dyad certainly had more interests in common than apart in keeping the Prague Spring under wraps; the continuation of the line in 1968 would have disturbed the cohesion of both diagrams. The Soviets had been careful to feel out the Western diplomatic establishment before invading. The West's moral outrage was accordingly limited, loud but without content. Indeed, Peking would accuse the USSR of collusion with the US.[267] In this sense, Palach's suicide must be located in relation to a wider machine-process if we are to theorise its politics. Indeed, from this point of view, the suicide of the Prague Spring helped the mechanism of détente, inasmuch as it was absolutely clear after 1968 that all serious discussions needed to go through Moscow.[268] Perhaps then, we must assent to Jean Paul Sartre's acerbic comment that the West was reassured by the invasion, and that public displays of regret are designed only to hide our guilt at having taken part in a 'holy alliance with the USSR [to] maintain order'.[269] Negotiations with the US resumed shortly afterwards, and the "organic unity" of the bloc was recognised as fact by the US until the Carter administration.[270] Svitak observed that 'detente was not an alternative to the Cold War but a continuation of it . . . the normalization of the abnormal, that is, the continuation of the divided world at the expense of smaller nations'.[271] As he went on to point out; this 'perpetuation of the divided world and divided Europe is the result of the atomic weaponry of the superpowers, who cannot guarantee the peace but who do guarantee mutual suicide in case of a world war'. The technology of death ensured that between the West and the USSR, 'differences [were] secondary'.[272]

Svitak here identifies the smooth space constructed by the Cold War machine.[273] As the suicidal state war machines of twentieth-century fascism disappeared, the order that took their place was no less suicidal. Indeed, the global war machine that took shape that emerged after World War II 'assigned as its objective a peace still more terrifying than fascist death'. With the doctrine of nuclear deterrence a full reversal of Clausewitz's famous statement takes place. Politics becomes materialised war, a pure logistics of disaster.[274] The nuclear couplet of the US and Soviet Russia no longer appropriated a war machine so as to set it to the pursuit of national interest; rather they created 'a war machine that takes charge of the aim, appropriates the States and assumes increasingly wider political functions'.[275] Under the deterrent paradigm, war becomes an integral part of peace.[276] Nuclear deterrence did not, in this sense, function as a system of blackmail in relation to the war it promises, but rather functioned through the real peace it promoted and installed. An international regime of social production conditioned by a particular mechanics of death: The war mechanism reigns over a flat global space:

> [This] post-fascist, figure, is that of a war machine that take peace as its object directly, as the peace of terror and survival . . . Total war is itself surpassed, towards a form of peace more terrifying still. The war machine has taken charge of the aim, worldwide order, and the states are now no more than objects or means adapted to that machine.[277]

In surrendering death to an automatic function, the national body politic is subsumed by a suicidal cybernetics: the pure peace of an ever-deferred catastrophe. Total war between states acted as a constant predicate or virtuality of this system. Yet total war itself became less and less likely between the nuclear couplet, replaced rather by a myriad of small scale interventions: precisely like that of the Warsaw Pact in Prague in 1968. It was through such actions that the smoothing of global order was affected. In this sense, 'the fascists were only the child precursors . . . [and] the absolute peace of survival succeeded where total war had failed'.[278]

Faced by the evident madness of the postfascist machine, Gustav Metzger invented an 'autodestructive art', promising an aesthetic event to mirror the wider mechanics of suicide.[279] This was a political aesthetic of revulsion in the face of the overkill of nuclear war. Where death is 'fed into, processed and administered by computers', a society appeared in which destructivity turned always inwards, realising and repeating in multiple diverted expressions.[280] He envisioned autodestructive art as a mass therapy and educational programme, with revolution as its limit. For Metzger, whilst the history of art is pervaded by pulverisations of prior forms, such an aesthetic becomes vital with nuclear deterrence. Built around the use of acids to create self-abolishing pictures, Metzger accessed the temporal kinesis in matter and life: random corrosion as creation, a protest and a subversion of the absolutization of nuclear war.[281] Might we not read Palach's act as autodestructive art, in this vein, his wound marking the impossibility of change authored by the global administration of suicide as international politics? His act becomes a temporal disintegration, a protest and subversion of a global logistics of catastrophe. Was Palach simply providing evidence for the claim that the revolutionary charge of an absolutely deterritorialising acceleration is always more readily 'appropriable as an aesthetic than effective political force'?[282] It is certainly tempting to locate in its aesthetics the key to Palach's frustrated consequences. Blanchot's comments on the inadequacy of the artist, and Deleuze and Guattari's on the need for us to get out 'not just in art but in real life', come together to suggest that the limited effects of Palach's act are precisely the marker of its aestheticism: the artwork of a political impossibility, a perfect expression of the radical immobility of the deterrent regime. Against the firm differentiation of the logics of art and political life, it is clear that Palach's suicide left no doubt regarding the nature of the diagram within which it was embedded. Here his suicide might be read otherwise, as a participant in an autoimmune cycle.[283] Nuclear deterrence offered the promise of collective suicide to immunise life from the possibility of nuclear destruction: Palach commits suicide to construct an escape. This is, in line with Metzger's premise, a suicide levelled against suicide: a politics in reiteration of the autoimmune event. This suggests a viral proliferation of political self-destruction.

The Cold War evidently facilitated the global distribution of suicidal politics, most obviously by seed-funding many of the Islamist organisations that deploy human bombs today.[284] In this direct sense, as Derrida noted, the most dedicatedly suicidal organisations in the world today are the precise embodiment of the 'suicide of those who welcomed them, armed, and trained them' in years past.[285] The end of the Cold War and the consequent diffusion of nuclear terror gave birth to a sense of pervasive threat, a conception of powerful 'anonymous forces that are absolutely unforeseeable and incalculable' in their potential for access to the tools of absolute destruction.²⁸⁶ The victory of the US camp created an even more terrifying condition, where 'there is no longer any limit' on the sources and loci of apocalyptic threat.²⁸⁷ The singular designated enemy essential to the Cold War mechanism was now replaced by an unspecified enemy.²⁸⁸ This new type of enemy is the creature of contingency embodied; a nightmare born of the extension of the logistical imaginary.²⁸⁹ As the global post-Cold War machine 'set its sights on [this] new type of enemy, no longer another state, or even another regime', Deleuze and Guattari suggest 'there arose from this a new conception of security as materialised war, as organised insecurity or molecularized, distributed, programmed catastrophe.'²⁹⁰ The irony here, as Derrida pointed out, is that all attempts to crack down on this unspecified yet admittedly catastrophic threat could only feed and nurture that which it hoped to overcome: 'producing, reproducing, and regenerating the very thing it seems to disarm'.²⁹¹ The end of the Cold War saw an absolutization of the kind of suicidal autoimmune crisis which Palach embodied. It is no accident that political self-destruction proliferates everywhere today.

Notes

1. K. Crosby, J.-O. Rhee, and J. Holland, "Suicide by Fire: A Contemporary Method of Political Protest," *International Journal of Social Psychiatry* 23, no. 1 (1977): 60–69; D. Bhugra, "Politically Motivated Suicides," *British Journal of Psychiatry* 159, no. 4 (1991): 594–595; M. Husni, N. Koye, Z.Z. Cernovsky, and J. Haggarty, "Kurdish Refugees' View of Politically Motivated Self-Immolation," *Transcultural Psychiatry* 39, no. 3 (2002): 367–375; B. Park, "Sociopolitical Contexts of Self-Immolations in Vietnam and South Korea," *Archives of Suicide Research* 8, no. 1 (2004): 81–97.
2. S. King, "They Who Burned Themselves for Peace: Quaker and Buddhist Self-Immolators during the Vietnam War," *Buddhist-Christian Studies* 20 (2000): 127–150.
3. As Park (2004) examines, in South Korea, up to a hundred leftists and trade union activists have self-incinerated since the 1970s.
4. Bhugra 1991; M. Biggs, "Dying for a Cause – Alone?," *Contexts* 7, no. 1 (2008): 22–27.
5. Biggs 2008.
6. Striking, in this context, is the effort China has expended to prevent recorded images of self-burnings from being disseminated
7. P.J. Schraeder and H. Redissi, "Ben Ali's Fall," *Journal of Democracy* 22, no. 3 (2011): 5–19.
8. A. Jacobson, *Duality in Bouazizi: Appraising the Contradiction.* Independent Study Project (ISP) Collection, 2011, http://digitalcollections.sit.edu/isp_collection/1009
9. P. Amar, "Middle East Masculinity Studies: Discourses of 'Men in Crisis,' Industries of Gender in Revolution," *Journal of Middle East Women's Studies* 7, no. 3 (2011): 36–70; Jacobson 2011.
10. Schraeder and Redissi 2011; O. Roy and C. Merlini, *Arab Society in Revolt* (Washington, DC: Brookings Institution Press, 2012).
11. P. Howard and M. Hussain, "The Role of Digital Media," *Journal of Democracy* 22, no. 3 (2011): 35–48; Schraeder and Redissi 2011.
12. K.M. Fierke, *Political Self-Sacrifice: Agency, Body and Emotion in International Relations*, Vol. 125 (Cambridge: Cambridge University Press, 2012), p. 220.

13. G. Sweeney, "Self-Immolation in Ireland: Hungerstrikes and Political Confrontation," *Anthropology Today* 9, no. 5 (1993): 10–14.
14. As such, it connoted mass or communion before any reference to self-destruction by fire. J.A. Simpson and E.S.C. Weiner, *The Oxford English Dictionary*, 2nd ed., Vol. 7 (Oxford: Clarendon Press, 1989).
15. S.R. Craig, "Social Suffering and Embodied Political Crisis." *Hot Spot Forum, Cultural Anthropology Online*. Retrieved from http://culanth.org/fieldsights/97-social-suffering-and-embodied-political-crisis
16. E.E. Sarraj and L. Butler, "Suicide Bombers: Dignity, Despair, and the Need for Hope. An Interview with Eyad El Sarraj," *Journal of Palestinian Studies* 31, no. 4 (2002): 71–76.
17. Crosby et al. 1977, p. 65.
18. M. Bloom, *Dying to Kill: The Allure of Suicide Terror* (New York: Columbia University Press, 2005).
19. E. Durkheim, *Suicide: A Study in Sociology*, ed. G. Simpson, trans. J.A. Spaulding and G. Simpson (London: Routledge & Kegan Paul, 1970) (reprint).
20. Park 2004, p. 84.
21. A. Giddens, *The Sociology of Suicide: A Selection of Readings* (London: Cass, 1971).
22. Park 2004.
23. This is true even where suicide notes, martyrdom videos or the like are prepared in advance. Of course, where the individual does not die, then it becomes possible to ask them.
24. D. Kowalewski, "The Protest Uses of Symbolic Politics in the USSR," *Journal of Politics* 42, no. 2 (1980): 439–460.
25. H. Hubert and M. Mauss, *Sacrifice: Its Nature and Function* (London: Cohen & West, 1964).
26. Ibid.
27. G. Agamben, *Homo Sacer: Sovereign Power and Bare Life* (Stanford: Stanford University Press, 1995).
28. See Hubert and Mauss 1964, p. 88.

> The act of abnegation implicit in every sacrifice, by recalling frequently to the consciousness of the individual the presence of collective forces, in fact sustains their ideal existence. These expiations and general purifications, communions and sacralisations of groups, these creations of the spirits of the cities give – or renew periodically for the community, represented by its gods – that character, good, strong, grave, and terrible, which is one of the essential traits of any social entity. Moreover, individuals find their own advantage in this same act. They confer upon each other, upon themselves, and upon those things they hold dear, the whole strength of society. (p. 102)

29. In this sense, sacrifice often implies a contractual exchange with a figure of transcendence. The latter is no longer 'a god or cosmic engine' but rather a 'secular' formation of myth and narrative. K. Andriolo, "The Twice-Killed: Imagining Protest Suicide," *American Anthropologist* 108, no. 1 (2006): 100–113, 109.
30. As Alex Houen puts it, sacrifice, whether religious or secular, 'institutes an idealism of transcendent justification for a community' which are central to all political formations; ancient and modern. Alex Houen, "Sacrificial Militancy and the Wars against Terror," in *Terror and the Postcolonial: A Concise Companion*, ed. E. Boehmer and S. Morton (Malden: Wiley-Blackwell, 2010), p. 116.
31. Ibid.
32. B. Anderson, *Imagined Communities: Reflections on the Origin and Spread of Nationalism* (London: Verso, 1991).
33. It is precisely through interpretation of these acts that national selfhood was constructed or sustained in the face of Soviet repression. We see therefore, in Uehling's rendition of

the Tatar poetic and narrative rearticulations of self-immolation, the classical terms of political theology. The phrase 'homeland or death' became closely linked to the act as the slogan for opposition to the Soviet forces, and the idea of victory through sacrifice takes centre stage in the narrative of national struggle: 'the emblem of their suffering, invoked as both example and ideal'. Self-immolation here is clearly a form of sacrificial myth-making, imagining political being and sustaining it in the face of threats to collective being. See G. Uehling, "Squatting, Self-Immolation and the Repatriation of the Crimean Tatars," *Nationalities Papers* 28, no. 2 (2000): 317–341, 328.
34. Craig 2012.
35. Fierke 2012, p. 22.
36. Ibid., p. 37.
37. Ibid., p. 38.
38. Ibid., p. 2.
39. Ibid., p. 53.
40. Ibid., p. 79.
41. Ibid., p. 92.
42. Ibid.
43. This attention to the circulation of emotion is intended to demonstrate the influence of postmodernism on Fierke's account (ibid.).
44. Ibid., p. 92.
45. Contrasting with counter-conduct accounts following Foucault, which assume the continuous reimbrications of formations of resistance with formations of power.
46. See ibid., p. 102. This is what Deleuze and Guattari refer to as 'molar desiring-politics', which assumes the construction of identitarian wholes that may be opposed to others through a binary inside-outside logic, and which operate under logics of sovereignty. See G. Deleuze and F. Guattari, *Anti-Oedipus* (London: Continuum, 2004a); G. Deleuze and F. Guattari, *A Thousand Plateaus* (London: Continuum, 2004b).
47. 'Ritualisation is a strategic way of acting in specific social circumstances' (Fierke 2012, p. 43).
48. Ibid., p. 44 (emphasis added).
49. See A. Feldman, *Formations of Violence: The Narrative of the Body and Political Terror in Northern Ireland* (Chicago: University of Chicago Press, 1991).
50. After all, as she put it, a community that has lost sovereignty has 'lost many traditional means of stabilisation' (Fierke 2012, p. 99).
51. Ibid., p. 80.
52. F. Devji, *Landscapes of the Jihad: Militancy, Morality, Modernity* (London: Hurst, 2005).
53. The term coined by the Russian anarchists for the practices discussing here.
54. N. Bolt, *The Violent Image: Insurgent Propaganda and the New Revolutionaries* (London: Hurst, 2012). Thus the reliance on teleology in most theories of revolutionary spontaneity.
55. N. Bolt, D. Betz, and J. Azari, *Propaganda of the Deed* (London: Insurgency Research Group, Kings College, 2008); Bolt 2012; Devji 2005.
56. For example, jihadists' dismay in response to Al Zakarwi's campaign of suicide bombings in Iraq.
57. See Fierke 2012, p. 26.
58. Hubert and Mauss 1964.
59. Which again Fierke recognises: In Vietnam as in Northern Ireland 'further war was the consequence' of acts of self-annihilation (2012, p. 190).
60. Bolt 2012.
61. R. Girard, *Violence and the Sacred* (London: Continuum, 2005).
62. Imaginary forms explain sacrifice and sacrifice creates imaginary forms.
63. See M. Foucault, *Society Must Be Defended* (London: Penguin Books, 2004); M. Foucault and M. Senellart, *The Birth of Biopolitics: Lectures at the Collège de France, 1978–79* (Basingstoke: Palgrave Macmillan, 2008).

64. M. Weber, *Politics as a Vocation*, trans. H. H. Garth and C. W. Mills (Philadelphia: Fortress Press, 1965 [1968]).
65. W. Benjamin, *Critique of Violence. Reflections: Essays, Aphorisms, Autobiographical Writings* (New York: Schocken, 1986).
66. J. Derrida, *Acts of Religion* (New York: Routledge, 2002), p. 240.
67. For Girard, the juridical system is 'infinitely more effective' in containing violence than the sacrificial system (see Girard 2005, p. 23).
68. Benjamin 1986.
69. See also J. Baudrillard and I. H. Grant, *Symbolic Exchange and Death* (London: Sage, 1993).
70. Benjamin 1986, p. 292.
71. The Invisible Committee, *The Coming Insurrection* (Los Angeles: Semiotext(e), 2009), pp. 96, 112.
72. Deleuze and Guattari reconceptualise death as the model and experience of a desiring-production. The model of death is also referred to as the body without organs, a concept borrowed from Artaud. Freud's vacillation between instinctual monism and dualism, identified as crucial by Deleuze in *Coldness and Cruelty* (1989) offered early clues as to this approach; in that text, Deleuze is more sympathetic to Freud's vision than he is in *Anti-Oedipus*. By *Anti-Oedipus*, Freud is seen as having put death in desire to provide an anchor for the fractured self, thereby removing its singularity to a particular life or assemblage of desire (Deleuze and Guattari 2004a, p. 67). The task of schizoanalysis is to destroy Freud's theatre of the unconscious, but only to develop alternative concepts by which to grasp the dynamics of the unconscious understood as a factory of death and desire (pp. 1, 25).
73. As Bergmann observed following extensive discussions with dying patients in a nursing home. See F. Bergmann, "The Diversity of Death," *Annals of the New York Academy of Sciences* 164, no. 3 (1969): 862–870.
74. 'I am finite in both directions, bordered both in the past and in the future. In addition, countless other boundaries circumscribe and hold me. We are limited in talent, in our capacity to experience, in our energy and power, in our ability to sustain emotions, in our endurance of the repetitious, in space and movement, in sympathy and understanding, in intelligence, in passion and in perseverance, and in all else. There is nothing that we possess to an infinite degree, unless it be our capacity to commit errors' (ibid., p. 863).
75. Ibid., p. 864.
76. I. Buchanan, "The Problem of the Body in Deleuze and Guattari, or, What Can a Body Do?," *Body & Society* 3, no. 3 (1997): 75.
77. Buchanan 1997.
78. Deleuze and Guattari 2004a, p. 359.
79. Deleuze and Guattari 2004b, p. 169.
80. Buchanan 1997, p. 79.
81. For Deleuze and Guattari, then, the diversity of our individual understandings of death are not conditioned by death being understood as the limit or horizon towards which we project, rather the anticipation of a reduction of our particular capacities to zero defines our freedom for recombinatory possibility.
82. A. Badiou, *Logics of Worlds* (London: Continuum, 2009b), p. 269.
83. Ibid., p. 270.
84. Ibid.
85. Deleuze and Guattari 2004b, p. 182.
86. Ibid.
87. 'Partial objects [desiring machines] are the direct powers of the body without organs, and the body without organs, the raw material of the partial objects' (Deleuze and Guattari 2004a, p. 359).
88. Badiou 2009b, p. 470.

89. Deleuze and Guattari 2004b, p. 182.
90. 'The functioning appears when the motor, under the preceding conditions – i.e. without ceasing to be immobile and without forming an organism – attracts the organs to the body without organs, and appropriates them for itself in the apparent objective movement. Repulsion is the condition of the machines functioning, but attraction is the functioning itself . . . it all works only by breaking down. One is then able to say what this running or this functioning consists of: in the cycle of the desiring machine it is a matter of constantly translating, constantly converting the death model into something else altogether, which is the experience of death. Converting the death that arises from within (in the body without organs) into a death that comes from without (on the body without organs)' (Deleuze and Guattari 2004a, p. 362).
91. This is why, as May puts it, 'transformation is a form of death . . . without negativity' (T. G. May, "The Politics of Life in the Thought of Gilles Deleuze," *SubStance* 66, no. 3 [1991]: 24–35, 31).
92. 'The experience of death is the most common of occurrence in the unconscious, precisely because it occurs in life and for life, in every passage or becoming. It is in the very nature of every intensity to invest within itself the zero intensity starting from which it is produced, in one moment, as that which grows or diminishes' (Deleuze and Guattari 2004a, p. 363).
93. 'Intensive emotions' are particularly demonstrative examples of this process in everyday life inasmuch as they are 'closest to the matter whose zero degree they invest in itself' (ibid.).
94. This account is prefigured in Deleuze's *Difference and Repetition* and its syntheses of repulsion/attraction/conjunction (G. Deleuze, *Difference and Repetition*, London: Continuum, 2004d; see J. Williams, *Gilles Deleuze's* Difference and Repetition*: A Critical Introduction and Guide*, Edinburgh: Edinburgh University Press, 2003, p. 48; L. DeBolle, "Deleuze's Passive Syntheses of Time and the Dissolved Self," in *Deleuze and Psychoanalysis: Philosophical Essays on Deleuze's Debate With Psychoanalysis*, ed. L. DeBolle, Leuven: Leuven University Press, 2010). Freud's concept of the death instinct as repetition in organic life presupposed the conservative nature of any organism as the object of any return (K. Ansell-Pearson, *Germinal Life: The Difference and Repetition of Deleuze*, London: Routledge, 1999, p. 113).
95. What has taken place is therefore a fundamental reworking of Freud's death-drive. It is no longer tied to a morbid desire to regress to an earlier, inorganic state of affairs; now, the inorganic is freed from regression and has become transformed into the intensity of germinal life – the point of zero intensity – from which new fluxes and patterns of life emerge. (K. Ansell-Pearson, "Spectropoiesis and Rhizomatics: Learning to Live with Death and Demons," in *Evil Spirits: Nihilism and the Fate of Modernity*, ed. C. Blake and G. Banham, Manchester: Manchester University Press, 2000, p. 12).
96. There is no doubt that in earlier works, Deleuze uses Freud's concept of the death instinct much less critically. See especially G. Deleuze, *Masochism: Coldness and Cruelty* (New York: Zone Books, 1999), but also G. Deleuze, *The Logic of Sense* (London: Continuum, 2004c) and Deleuze 2004d. There is naturally, therefore, some debate over the 'fairness' of Deleuze and Guattari's critique of the death instinct, and their 'true' departure from Freud (N. Land, "Making It with Death: Remarks on Thanatos and Desiring-Production," *British Journal of Phenomenology* 24, no. 1 [1993)] 66–76; Dale, C. (1997). "Falling from the power to die." *Antithesis* **8**(2): 139–153., p. 148; Proust, F. (2000). "The line of resistance." *Hypatia* **15**(4). p. 25). The placement of death 'on the side of life' is clearly indebted to Freud, as recognised in Guattari (2009), but the doubling of death in *Anti-Oedipus* radically reconfigures desire's energetic productivity in a way that would have been shocking to him. F. Guattari, *Chaosophy* (Los Angeles: Semiotext(e), 2009).
97. A particular assemblage on the Body without Organs (BwO). Bergmann (1969) outlines several alternatives to fear of death, Camus facing up to absurdity, Holderlin's aesthetics of self-expenditure and Nietzsche's completion of the artwork of life.
98. Dale 1997.

99. Reterritorialisation is, one might say, an experience of the death of death, a reduction to stability, concretion, stasis. A denial of mortality essentially: thus, paranoia.
100. Deleuze and Guattari 2004b, p. 166.
101. J. Williams, *Gilles Deleuze's Logic of Sense: A Critical Introduction and Guide* (Edinburgh: Edinburgh University Press, 2008), p. 145.
102. See this concern in S. Zizek, *Organs without Bodies: Deleuze and Consequences* (New York: Routledge, 2004).
103. N. Land, "Circuitries," in R. Mackay and A. Avanessian, *#ACCELERATE: The Accelerationist Reader* (Falmouth: Urbanomic, 2014), p. 261.
104. Deleuze and Guattari 2004a, p. 177.
105. We are enjoined to 'unhook ourselves from the hooks of subjectification that secure us, nail us down to a dominant reality . . . tearing the consciousness away from the subject in order to make it a means of exploration' (ibid.).
106. See Williams 2003, p. 48.
107. Deleuze and Guattari 2004a, p. 92.

> The subject as an adjacent part is always a 'one' who conducts the experience, not an I who receives the model, for the model itself is not the I either, but the body without organs. And I does not rejoin the model without the model starting out again in the direction of another experience. Always going from the model to the experience and starting out again, returning from the model to the experience, is what schizophrenizing death amounts to, the exercise of desiring machines . . . the return to repulsion will condition other attractions, other functionings, that setting in motion of other working parts on the body without organs, the putting to work of other adjacent parts on the periphery that have as much a right to say One as we ourselves do. (p. 364)

108. DeBolle 2010.
109. Deleuze and Guattari 2004a, p. 44.
110. As Adkins points out, such a subject can be thought as 'retrospective', like Klossowski's Nietzsche who passes through multiple intensive states, and is gatherable together into a subjective unity only as a deterritorialised whole, a 'circuit of all [his] cycles of desire', but it is not structurally empty (B. Adkins, *Death and Desire in Hegel, Heidegger and Deleuze*, Edinburgh: Edinburgh University Press, 2007, p. 2).
111. Deleuze and Guattari 2004a, p. 363.
112. Some resonance with Heidegger is clear on this point, but for Deleuze and Guattari, deaths relationship to possibility is thought without a sense of projection towards a negative limit; deterritorialisation takes place on the virtual matrix of the BwO; it is a leap into our impossibility, not a contemplation (dread anticipation), but an active embrace.
113. Deleuze and Guattari 2004a, pp. 19–20.
114. Proust 2000, p. 25.
115. Ibid., p. 28.
116. Proust (ibid., p. 34) prefers death to be mobilised on behalf of life as counter-being. Counter-being actively 'thwarts death by tracing and displacing'. Life 'draws out lines' which counter or resist extant structures of power. The Freudian dualism which orientates her argument is clear when she states that 'resistance is another name for the death drive within the distinction between Eros (Desire, sexuality) and Thanatos (destruction).' Deleuze and Guattari abandon this distinction. Natality and death are elements of the same process; the BwO is the immobile motor for a body's deterritorialisation or experience of becoming. There is no death per se to thwart; there is only the death we experience through our creative deterritorialisation on the BwO, or the death we fail to experience through noncreative stratification. For Deleuze, some deaths are better than others. This is why extra-being trumps counter-being as the name of resistance.

117. Deleuze and Guattari 2004b, p. 177.
118. Ibid.
119. Ibid., p. 166.
120. Ibid.
121. Dale 1997, p. 142.
122. Buchanan (1997, p. 88) describes anorexia as swallowing a desiring-machine and trying to make it one with the BwO, turning the BwO itself into an organised body of pure destruction. The matrix becomes a plan of action for emptying, rather than expanding, the body's affects.
123. Dale (1997, p. 145) is concerned by Deleuze and Guattari's account of masochism as 'empty BwO'; 'the masochist body without organs is far more complex than simply failed or empty'; relegating it 'to the sad heap of unusable bodies exhausted by their uncontrollable speeds and affects' seems a cheap oversimplification of the practice. Deleuze and Guattari do see masochism as a flawed operationalisation, not as entirely worthless. Masochism is not inevitably suicidal. As Deleuze demonstrated in *Coldness and Cruelty* (1989), the masochist is defined by a referential concern for parodying juridical forms; this can have liberating connotations: 'That there are other ways, other procedures than masochism, and certainly better ones, is beside the point; it is enough that some find this procedure suitable for them' (Deleuze and Guattari 2004b, p. 172). The limit, however, is self-murderous; an attempt to build a machine identical to the body without organs. Dale's critique is suggestive however; the association of empty bodies with suicide seems to strip actively suicidal bodies of their affects-deterritorialisations.
124. J. Protevi, *Political Physics: Deleuze, Derrida, and the Body Politic* (London: Athlone Press, 2001), p. 192.
125. Deleuze and Guattari 2004b, p. 180. A similar problem to that faced by Badiou; the subject constructed in fidelity must restrict that fidelity if he or she is to avoid naming the void and becoming obscure.
126. Ibid.
127. A. Badiou, *Deleuze: The Clamor of Being* (Minneapolis: University of Minnesota Press, 1999), p. 77.
128. Ibid. His critique, much like Zizek's (2004), are based almost entirely on a reading of *Logic of Sense*, where Deleuze does indeed posit a fundamental relationship between events and death. Badiou's desire to differentiate himself from Deleuze leads him to misrepresent the latter's position. His claim is not simply that death can be an event, but that all events are like death. Indeed, the interpretation of Deleuze and Badiou as radically opposed thinkers should be seen as in doubt (see for example P. Hallward, *Out of This World: Deleuze and the Philosophy of Creation*, London: Verso, 2006; J. Clemens and O. Feltham, "The Thought of Stupefaction," in *Event and Decision*, ed. R. Faber, H. Krips, and D. Pettus, Newcastle Upon Tyne: Cambridge Scholars, 2010; H. Phelps, Absolute Beginnings . . . Almost: Badiou and Deleuze on the Event," in Faber et al. 2010). The *Logic of Sense*'s reading of Maurice Blanchot does, however, prefigure the accounts in both *Anti-Oedipus* and *A Thousand Plateaus*, and so sheds important light on the suicidally risky politics of creation. The *Logic of Sense* (2004) displays far less distance from Freud and his 'silent death instinct' (especially pp. 364–370). The anti-Oedipal break from Freud has not yet occurred, and the 'grand heredity of the crack' is identified with the death instinct as an inexorable force; an epic movement in the work of Zola. This vision of the crack as the 'epic turning back of death upon itself . . . the obstacle to thought, but also the abode and power of thought, its field and agent' is similar to the account in *Capitalism and Schizophrenia* (of deterritorialisation as the univocal experience of death), but much more Freudian (and closer to Zizek) in its terminology (see p. 370). The other core critique levelled by Badiou, that Deleuze is a theorist of One, is correct only to the extent that it is rooted in a conceptual miscommunication. Deleuze has a metaphysics

in the singular: This is not the same as a metaphysics of the singular. Only Badiou's faith that disparate objects can only assemble in numbered sets, as opposed to a whole variety of hybrid and monstrous groupings of part-objects and mixed bodies, enables their collapse into one another. For Deleuze the process is a question of Being's univocity (there are no flows but mortal flows), to read this as a metaphysical decision on the objective unity of Being underpinning the simulacra-multiplicity of beings is a function of Badiou's conceptual project, not Deleuze's. To make everything add up is not something Deleuze worried about.
129. It is here that Badiou finds support for reading Deleuze as a chimerical revolutionary who surrenders to the becoming-finite of mankind under democratic materialism.
130. Hallward 2006.
131. Deleuze 2004c, p. 170.
132. Ibid., pp. 182, 169, 172.
133. Ibid., p. 182.
134. 'Willing the event is, primarily, to release its eternal truth, like a fire on which it is fed, this will would reach the point at which war is waged against war, the wound would be the living trace of all wounds and the scar of all wounds, and death turned on itself would be willed against all deaths. We are faced with a volitional intuition and a transmutation . . . a change of the will, a sort of leaping in place of the whole body which exchanges its organic will for a spiritual will. It wills now not exactly what occurs, but something in that which occurs, something yet to come which would be consistent with what occurs . . . the Event' (see ibid., p. 170).
135. Ibid., p. 173.
136. Ibid., p. 171.
137. See Hallward 2006.
138. Ibid.
139. As Clemens and Feltham (2010) point out, Badiou's vision of absolute breaks versus the Deleuzean continuity of becoming finite is somewhat undermined by his implicit recognition that little modifications are constantly occurring, and indeed fundamental to any (political) institution. The event is

> rendered equivalent to the procedure of change that institutes a new supplemental situation . . . [thus] Badiou's rare and punctual event is rendered equivalent to the coming of being in a new situation . . . uncomfortably close to Deleuze's conception of any state of affairs being also *a host of events*. (p. 39, emphasis added)

140. Badiou 2009b, p. 1.
141. M. Blanchot, *The Space of Literature* (Lincoln: University of Nebraska Press, 1989), p. 95.
142. Ibid., p. 96.
143. 'No one has ever died by his own hand in a real coming to grips, a full and heartfelt grasping of the situation which would make this act an authentic action' (ibid., p. 99).
144. Ibid., p. 100.
145. Ibid., pp. 102–103.
146. Ibid., p. 104.
147. Ibid.
148. Deleuze 2004c, p. 178.
149. Ibid. The same applies to suicide bombers aiming for immortality.
150. Blanchot 1989, p. 105.
151. Deleuze 2004c, p. 178.
152. Blanchot 1989, p. 105.
153. Ibid.
154. Ibid., p. 106.
155. Ibid.

156. Ibid., p. 107.
157. Deleuze 2004c, p. 170.
158. Ibid., p. 172.
159. The event is the name for 'that itch of unreason which stupefies thought', the impossibility (non-sense) which calls forth will (Clemens and Feltham 2010, p. 19).
160. Deleuze 2004c, p. 172.
161. In the words of Graham Livesey, 'creation, as the production of events, is a kind of dance between an individual agent and a universal field of forces' (G. Livesey, "Event Theory and Creative Agency," in Faber et al. 2010, p. 337).
162. Badiou 1999; Badiou 2009b. Phelps (2010) points out that for Badiou the event is always constructed point by point in a sequence and may be resurrected in new situations. This suggests a more complicated relationship with the past and future of events than pure rupture (the ultimate universalism).
163. Deleuze (2004c) argues that the 'univocity of Being signifies that being is Voice that is said, and that it is said in one and the same "sense" of everything about it which is said' (p. 205).
164. A. Badiou, "The Event in Deleuze," *Parrhesia* 2 (2007): 37–44. He argues that his vision of the event as a break from becoming contrasts directly with Deleuze's vision of the event as becoming. See also Phelps 2010, p. 49.
165. As such 'univocity would then be a synthesis without remainder, the synthesis and affirmation of the immanent multiple' (K. Robinson, "Between the Individual, the Relative and the Void," in Faber et al. 2010, p. 119).
166. Deleuze 2004c, p. 173.
167. Against Badiou, who argues that there is no risk in Deleuze, only destiny and surrender to the One. It is not risking for the stellar void of ontological lack (Badiou), but risking our singularity for the revolutionary univocity of our being mortal, and for precisely this reason, cosmic animals (see R. Brassier, "Stellar Void or Cosmic Animal? Badiou and Deleuze on the Dice-Throw," *Pli* 10 [2000]: 200–216).
168. Deleuze 2004c, p. 173.
169. Ibid., p. 172.
170. Ibid., p. 173.
171. The creative event is thus not a mathematical break of discontinuity as such, but a leap into continuity; a voicing of chaotic nascence. Revolutionary events are birthed from the rushing embrace of reemergent becoming: the dice roll of spinning mortal exuberance.
172. Deleuze 2004c:

> If to will is to will the event, how could we not also will its full actualization in a corporeal mixture, subject to this tragic will which presides over all ingestions . . . how is it to be prevented from precipitating destruction, even if this meant losing all accompanying benefits . . . even life itself. (p. 178)

This clearly prefigures the concept of caution in *A Thousand Plateaus* (Deleuze and Guattari 2004b).
173. 'Is it possible to limit ourselves to the counter-actualization of an event . . . while taking care to prevent the full actualization which characterises the victim or the true patient?' (Deleuze 2004c, p. 179).
174. This categorically gives the lie to arguments which see the suicidal line of flight in *A Thousand Plateaus* as a sudden introduction. See for example Land 1993.
175. Deleuze 2004c.
176. Ibid., p. 179.
177. Contra Badiou, who defines revolutionary events by their degree of intensity (2009b, p. 374); events are maximal, and this applies not only to the existent singularities, but also, crucially, to their consequences. An event, in other words, is eventual because it has consequences of sufficient intensity. See Proust 2000.

178. G. Deleuze, F. Guattari et al., *What Is Philosophy?* (London: Verso, 1994).
179. Blanchot 1989, p. 236.
180. Ibid., p. 81.
181. Ibid., p. 52.
182. Ibid., p. 90. For Kafka the experience of writing was as the 'consciousness of unhappiness' (p. 75). He was in no doubt that 'his work require[d] his ruin', yet was compelled to pursue it nevertheless (p. 74).
183. Ibid., p. 89.
184. 'To write is to conjure up spirits, perhaps freeing them against us, but this danger belongs to the essence of the power that liberates' (ibid., p. 73).
185. Ibid., p. 185.
186. Ibid., p. 236.
187. Deleuze and Guattari 2004b, p. 207.
188. Ibid.
189. Ibid., p. 208.
190. Blanchot 1989, p. 220.
191. Deleuze and Guattari 2004b, p. 207.
192. 'In other words, all those real becomings that are not produced only in art, and all those active escapes that do not consist in fleeing into art, taking refuge in art, and all those positive deterritorializations that never reterritorialize on art, but instead sweep it away with them towards the realms of the asignifying, asubjective, and faceless' (ibid., p. 208).
193. Ibid.
194. Deleuze (2004c, pp. 360–363) will term this, discussing Zola, the 'great heredity of the crack' which follows life, making heredity possible, whilst tracing it with the possibility of degeneration and destruction. This is still a very much Freudian conception inasmuch as the transmission of the great crack in that text is utterly silent (the profoundly silent death instinct around which all the other instincts swarm).
195. Deleuze and Guattari 2004b, p. 220.
196. Ibid., pp. 224–225.
197. Ibid., p. 225.
198. Ibid., p. 227.
199. 'There is no problem of application: the lines [Schizoanalysis] brings out could equally be the lines of a life, a work of literature or art, or a society' (see ibid., pp. 225, 227).
200. Ibid., p. 330.
201. Ibid.
202. Ibid., p. 331.
203. Ibid., p. 334.
204. It is worth pointing out that Deleuze and Guattari see contemporary capitalism as uniquely deterritorialised and deterritorialising. Zygmunt Bauman has argued that art has taken on the (autodestructive) essence of capitalism (or rather liquid modernity); its love of transience and disposability, and therefore cannot be thought as revolutionary (see Z. Bauman, "Liquid Arts," *Theory, Culture & Society* 24, no. 1 [2007]: 117–126). It is certainly the case that capitalism's prolific deterritorializations cannot be trusted; but they are, nonetheless, the reason that it is the most immanently revolutionary diagram ever invented.
205. Deleuze and Guattari 2004b, p. 330.
206. J. Suk, "The Rest is Silence," in *Jan Palach* (Prague: Prague House of Photography, 2009); H. G. Skilling, *Czechoslovakia's Interrupted Revolution* (Princeton, NJ: Princeton University Press, 1976).
207. Jan Palach's suicide note, in K. W. Treptow, "The Winter of Despair: Jan Palach and the Collapse of the Prague Spring," in *From Zalmoxis to Jan Palach: Studies in East European History* (New York: Columbia University Press, 1992), pp. 117–136, 126.
208. As Suk's photographic collection visually documents; see Suk 2009.

209. Palach was followed by Jan Zajic's self-immolation on 25 February, Evzen Plocek's on Good Friday, and Michael Leucik's in May (K. Williams, *The Prague Spring and Its Aftermath: Czechoslovak Politics 1968–1970*, Cambridge: Cambridge University Press, 1997, p. 190). These acts were interpreted as the work of individual depressives. The existence of the 'group of others' mentioned in Palach's note is now widely held in doubt (Suk 2009, p. 145).
210. It has more been common tendency to identify the Czech cultural uniqueness of the event, or writing a 'teleologically inspired story of these societies' inevitable adoption of a West European political and socio-economic model' (V.V. Kusin, *The Intellectual Origins of the Prague Spring*, Cambridge: Cambridge University Press, 1971, pp. 27, 136; M. Bracke in L. Cashman, *1948 and 1968: Dramatic Milestones in Czech and Slovak History*, Abingdon: Routledge, 2010, p. 102). Widely interpreted in terms of the rise of (democratic) ideas in the intelligentsia (see especially Kusin 1971, pp. 134, 135; but also A.J. Liehm and J.-P. Sartre, *The Politics of Culture; with Jean Paul Sartre's "The Socialism That Came In from the Cold,"* New York: Grove Press, 1973, p. 44; I. Svitak, *The Unbearable Burden of History: The Sovietization of Czechoslovakia. Vol. 2: Prague Spring Revisited*, Prague: Academia, 1990a; Williams 1997, p. 6). This reading is more in line with that of Antonin J. Liehm, the intellectual reformist and then blacklisted editor of *Literarni Noviny*, who would term the Prague Spring a political conjugation of 'all the manifold creative forces in [the Czechoslovak] nation' (see Liehm and Sartre 1973, pp. 64, 66).
211. Kusin 1971, p. 15.
212. The Czech philosopher Ivan Svitak termed it a bureaucratic dictatorship (Svitak 1990a, p. 75). This was a system in which the ideal was certainty, and the enemy uncertainty – the paragon of a paranoiac system (see Williams 1997). Stalinist faith could bear not one molecule of doubt (Liehm and Sartre 1973, p. 17). Its prefabricated order was overlaid on the Czechoslovak milieu, with the party its guarantor, and each individual repeating the molar line at every point (Skilling 1976, p. 824).
213. Liehm and Sartre 1973, p. 8.
214. 'The basic facts had been known, but people simply refused to believe them' (Putik in Liehm and Sartre 1973, p. 242).
215. Skilling 1976, p. 825.
216. Ibid., p. 824.
217. G. Golan, *The Czechoslovak Reform Movement: Communism in Crisis, 1962–1968* (London: Cambridge University Press, 1971); Kusin 1971; Liehm and Sartre 1973, pp. 21–24; Skilling 1976.
218. The flux set in motion was to find its outlet in various fields. As Kusin (1971, p. 28) outlined in his seminal work; voices for de-Stalinisation initiated criticism first of the political trials in legal critiques of Stalinist nihilism which developed concepts of the lawful state (Kusin 1971, p. 35). Philosophers subjected dogma, obedience, and bureaucratism to fundamental critique, especially Karel Kosik and Ivan Svitak (p. 37; Svitak 1990a). The Fourth Congress of Historians (first prohibited, then delayed to 1966) challenged 'the false belief that everything . . . must serve a single aim, variously formulated as the consolidation of revolutionary power'. Egregious Stalinist distortions in Czech history (especially concerning Gottwald, the founder of Czechoslovak communism) were exposed (Kusin 1971, p. 78). With this the resurrection of sociology lead to a critique of its puerile replacement by historical materialist doctrine.
219. Kusin 1971, p. 60.
220. Whilst distinguishing its creative process from capitalist marketization.
221. Kusin 1973, p. 62.
222. Liehm and Sartre 1973, p. 42.
223. Who says 'I believe government should have one goal; to be in harmony with the strivings of avant-garde writers and artists', and that the work of art is to refuse dogmatism (in Liehm and Sartre 1973, p. 101).

96 Self-burning

224. Who reveals a rather Deleuzean sentiment in arguing that we must be aware not only of the necessity of criticism, but also of its 'destructive potential'; arguing that there are destructive as well as constructive forces in art and that precisely because art is a matter of uncertainty 'the artist must go too far' (ibid., pp. 153–155).
225. 'The poet is a politician' (ibid., p. 255).
226. Particularly Havel (ibid., p. 374).
227. Golan 1971, p. 22. To explain this process, Liehm (1973) affirms the particularly unique position of the intellectual in Czechoslovak culture (something he ties to its historical lack of an aristocracy). It certainly seems clear that these predominantly socialist intellectuals acted with remarkable unity as a collective actor, and were subjected to surveillance by the state accordingly. Yet that common project need not imply that what we are seeing here is evidence that Czechoslovak society had a cultural program or the intelligentsia can be unified as a coherent body. The cultural politics of the time may rather be understood as the expression of a fundamentally univocal process which captured the intellectual desiring-machine.
228. Golan 1971, pp. 232, 239.
229. Kusin 1971, pp. 74–75, see also Golan 1971, p. 249.
230. Golan 1971, p. 259.
231. In serious decline in the early 1960s, voices for reform were rising against economic centralism on pragmatic grounds. Golan 1971; Liehm and Sartre 1973.
232. Golan 1971, p. 278.
233. As well as providing later inspiration for Euro-Marxists.
234. K. Dawisha, *The Kremlin and the Prague Spring* (Berkeley: University of California Press, 1984); Williams 1997; K. Williams, "The Prague Spring: From Elite Liberalisation to Mass Movement," in *Revolution and Resistance in Eastern Europe: Challenges to Communist Rule*, ed. K. McDermott and M. Stibbe (Oxford: Berg, 2006).
235. See Williams 2006. Ideas are, of course, assemblages of desire; it was clear that the paranoiac socialist machine was being deterritorialised.
236. The changes affected 'all aspects of life without exception' (Skilling 1976, pp. 834–836). Skilling argued that it could easily have become a 'permanent revolution . . . in the sense of successive stages of radical change, each leading to the next, over a period of years, even decades'.
237. Treptow 1992, p. 117.
238. Williams 2006, p. 105.
239. Ibid.
240. Dawisha 1984; Williams 1997; Williams 2006.
241. Williams 2006, p. 105.
242. Williams 1997, p. 173.
243. Ibid., p. 182.
244. Svitak, I. (1990b). Volume 3: the Era of Abnormalization. *The unbearable burden of history: the Sovietization of Czechoslovakia*. Prague, Czechoslovakia, Academia: 3 v. Williams 2006.
245. Williams 2006.
246. See M. Heimann in Cashman 2010, p. 74.
247. This is the connotation, in Treptow (1992), when he argues that 'the suicide of Jan Palach represented the beginnings of the protests of despair; acts which lost sight of any positive political purpose, and reflected the frustration which the foreign occupation had created' (p. 132).
248. The Czech model was certainly held up as a model for imitation by Euro-Marxists. Svitak 1990b, p. 15.
249. Svitak 1990a, p. 109.
250. The Marxian interpretation also expressed by Sartre in "The Socialism That Came In from the Cold," in Liehm and Sartre 1973. One can imagine an interpretation following Badiou along these lines.

251. Badiou's reactive subject is defined by his or her negation of the truth-event, an affirmation of an extinguished present, in which the catastrophic potentialities of the event are denied as too awful to risk – the commonly expressed idea that any revolutionary politics is potentially Stalinist (Badiou 2009b, p. 55). This subject, of course, is the voice of reason, of Dubcek and Husak, who called upon the Czechoslovak people not to resist, to embrace normalisation, 'so as not to risk what had been gained already', whilst steadily corroding the very substance of revolutionary movement. The reactive subject is the subject of the counter-revolution. It is Badiou's obscure subject, however, which interests this book most directly. Such subjects have become so consumed by the truth of the event that he or she 'systematically resorts to the invocation of a full and transcendent body, an ahistorical or anti-eventual body (City, God, Race . . .) from which it follows that the trace will be denied' (pp. 59–60). In the name of transcendent authority, this subject refuses all the differences of the body and as such refuses the body itself. The present itself undergoes occultation inasmuch as the void is named. All creativity is shut down by the formalism of absolute faith; far worse than a reactive subject who at least retains the idea of the faithful subject 'as its articulated unconscious', the obscurantist subject seeks to abolish the present and itself in pursuit of the transcendent vision (p. 61). Badiou describes the obscure subject as a full body (p. 67). By this he means something quite different from Deleuze and Guattari's full body; indeed, he seems to be renaming what they term a cancerous body overflowing with its destructive excess. This is because Badiou (p. 470) sees organisation as essential to the efficacy which makes it possible to live in hopeful fidelity to the trace of the event (we must organise to say yes to the event). Deleuze and Guattari's point is quite different, as we have seen; they argue that the event's stoic counter-affirmation is that which disorganises us, gives us our difference, allowing us to become/live/deterritorialise. For Badiou, the full body destroys the body of the present through its excessive resonance, just as the Nazi cancerous body resonates into abolition. As pointed out in chapter 1, the obscure subject, for Badiou, is represented today by political Islamism. Badiou argues that 'political Islamism represents a new instrumentalization of religion – from which it does not derive by any natural (or "rational") lineage – with the purpose of occulting post-socialist present,' and countering 'political experimentation' which might lead to emancipatory ends. The suicide bomber is the paradigm of the obscurantist; in resolute loathing of all difference, transformation, change, and novelty, embracing a descent into a false universality. For Badiou, jihadis pursue an invented past which masquerades as a revolutionary novelty. There is nothing revolutionary about the jihad: they are truth-labourers for a cardboard-cutout eternity. To term jihadist violence a deterritorialisation would, he implies, claim an impulse to novelty where, surely, we should see only the diametric opposite.
252. Ibid., p. 53.
253. Ibid., p. 67.
254. Badiou's occultation certainly cannot adequately capture the politics of Palach's suicide; perhaps also, it falls short of capturing the politics of Islamist suicide-bombing (as 'simply' obscurantist).
255. Badiou 2009b, p. 513.
256. Ibid., p. 514.
257. Badiou 2009a, p. 268.
258. See G. Deleuze, *Foucault* (Paris, Continuum, 1999).
259. Suk 2009, p. 146. Even the 'student leaders hesitated to exploit the tragic situation, and cooperated with the government to keep order' (Treptow 1992, pp. 117–136, 127). Indeed, after the event, a self-defeating quality seemed to infiltrate subsequence acts of protest (Treptow 1992, p. 131). Multiple resignations from the party were followed by disorganised and random popular violence. On the day of Palach's funeral, during a solemn march through Prague, 'the extreme physical power of the crowds remained inward looking' (Suk 2009, p. 146).

260. The quiescence of the population following Palach's act was to mark the next twenty years. A realist segment took over in the party (see Williams 1997). Normalisation rolled back all the reforms. This period was marked by widespread preoccupation with 'material pursuits and light entertainment' and a turn inwards to the nuclear family (Williams 2006, p. 110). Longer holidays, television and other consumerist 'tool[s] of distraction' kept the masses at home, and away from potentially disruptive collective activities (Williams 1997; Williams 2006, p. 111). The regime thus deployed a consumer axiomatic to manage the disruptive flows of the populace, attended by a compensatory re-oedipalization.
261. Treptow 1992, p. 130.
262. Suk 2009, p. 149.
263. For Badiou, this would surely preclude its status as an event, since he sees a suprasituational 'maximality of consequence' as a basic criterion of eventality (Badiou 2009b).
264. J. Derrida, "Autoimmunity: Real and Symbolic Suicides – A Dialogue with Jacques Derrida," in *Philosophy in a Time of Terror: Dialogues with Jürgen Habermas and Jacques Derrida*, ed. G. Borradori (Chicago: University of Chicago Press, 2003), p. 90.
265. 'It consists in that, that I do not comprehend: that which I do not comprehend first of all that I do not comprehend, the fact that I do not comprehend: my incomprehension' (ibid.).
266. Ibid., p. 96.
267. Dawisha 1984.
268. Ibid., p. 374.
269. Sartre 1973, p. 36.
270. Dawisha 1984, p. 374.
271. Svitak 1990b, p. 114.
272. Ibid., p. 201.
273. Ibid., p. 302; Deleuze and Guattari 2004b.
274. Deleuze and Guattari 2004b, p. 465.
275. Ibid.
276. Ibid., p. 516.
277. Ibid., p. 465.
278. Ibid., pp. 515–516.
279. G. Metzger, *Auto-destructive Art* (London: Destruction/Creation, 1965), p. 27 (reprinted with the addition of photographs and manifestos).
280. Ibid., p. 6.
281. Ibid., pp. 11, 19.
282. R. Mackay and A. Avanessian, *#ACCELERATE: The Accelerationist Reader* (Falmouth: Urbanomic, 2014), p. 36.
283. Wherein a living creature works to 'destroy its own protection, to immunise itself against its own immunity' (Derrida 2003, p. 94).
284. See Steve Coll, *Ghost Wars: The Secret History of the CIA, Afghanistan, and Bin Laden, from the Soviet Invasion to September 10, 2001* (London: Penguin, 2004).
285. Derrida 2003, p. 95.
286. Ibid., p. 98.
287. Ibid.
288. Domestic or foreign, an individual, group, class, people, event, or world.
289. 'Unassignable material Saboteur or human Deserter assuming the most diverse forms'. 'The very conditions that make the state or World War machine possible, in other words, constant capital (resources and equipment) and human variable capital, continually recreate unexpected possibilities for counterattack, unforeseen initiatives determining revolutionary, popular, minority, mutant machines. The definition of the Unspecified enemy testifies to this: "multiform, manoeuvring and omnipresent, of the moral, political, subversive or economic order etc."' (Deleuze and Guattari 2004b, p. 465).
290. Ibid.
291. Derrida 2003, p. 99.

3 Hunger striking

Crossing the threshold

Thresholds are everywhere, but for an alcoholic the 'last glass' has particularly vital significance.[1] An alcoholic must make an assessment of the limit of consumption that he or she can tolerate – and then only after a period of rest and recovery continue drinking. The last glass is the line beyond which the alcoholic changes assemblage, where their drinking turns into an absolute movement. This threshold is the defining horizon of alcoholism, the excess which constitutes the full social, political and personal content of the practice. It is precisely not an ending; it marks a new beginning, the crossing of an ontological barrier into a new formation wherein the alcoholic sets out on a line of suicidal flight. The desire to obviate the disturbing creativity released by crossing that threshold is fundamental to modern accounts of addiction. Suicidal subjects, by contrast, are not defined by their appetites; they are therapeutic objects that must be cured of a lamentable lack of appetite for life.

Whilst inverting the logic of consumption in alcoholism, an identical threshold defines the practice of hunger striking. An uncertain distance from the last meal marks a borderline. Beyond it is a deterritorialisation; a breakout carved on the starving body where death enters the realm of possibility or probability. The political content of the act cannot exist without the hunger striker's identification of that threshold and will to go beyond it. Force-feeding has, during the last century, become the standard response to hunger striking, as the attempt to hold the line and exclude from possibility the breakout into a suicidal assemblage. Hunger striking amongst the inmates of Guantanamo Bay has been more or less continuous since 2004, involving between 80 and 100 of the 148 inmates. Voluntary total fasting (VTF), as hunger striking is referred to in the Camp Delta Standard Operating Procedures (CDSOP), is deemed to be occurring only after refusal to eat nine consecutive meals or take fluids for forty-eight hours. Hunger striking at Camp Delta was formally initiated in protest at inhumane conditions, lack of legal representation, and in response to a series of cell searches that were deemed intrusive and degrading. 'Refeeding', in the language of the CDSOP, occurs when the detainee's body mass index drops below 16, they are incapacitated, or simply when it is ordered by a medical officer.[2] Having determined the threshold, the

Guantanamo Bay prison authorities seek to make death by self-starvation impossible by restraining and pumping fluids directly into inmates' stomachs through their nostrils. The Guantanamo prison authorities aim to preclude the threshold into a suicidal political assemblage. This is revealing in itself, as a marker of somatic and biopolitical control in the high-security prison environment, but it also suggests a concern for the consequences of allowing the inmates to die that appears, in this context, to go beyond a concern to shore up legitimacy.

Hunger striking finds its modern political origins with the Russian anarchists of the late nineteenth century.[3] Vera Figner recorded an early anarchist hunger strike in 1889 amongst imprisoned members of the People's Will, the group that had successfully assassinated the tsar in 1881. She provides in her autobiography a very concise theorisation of the hunger strike as a political practice. She records how an inspection, revealing one prisoner reading Mignet's *History of the French Revolution*, led to the removal of all political books from the prison library. A minority decided to respond to this 'moral catastrophe' with a 'fast until death',[4] but the pressures of 'comradeship and sympathy' swiftly drew all others to participate. Figner argues that this participation due to a sense of collective moral obligation meant that the strikers suffered from insufficient resolve.[5] When the prison doctor refused to help a sick hunger striker on the grounds that he had already chosen to die, the majority immediately abandoned the strike. Figner makes clear that a conscious will to die is the unambiguous condition for hunger striking. As she puts it, 'a hunger strike either should not be attempted at all, or else should be undertaken with the serious resolve to carry it through to the end'. The threshold is constitutive – 'the boundary line beyond which the firm will cannot turn back' – and accordingly she would set out 'to finish what she started'.[6] Figner recognised that a suicidal threshold constitutes the politics of hunger striking. She suggests, therefore, that hunger striking, as a prison politics, is never reducible to the often limited aims it declares.[7] Finally, she makes clear that force-feeding was not present at the start. Indeed, medical intervention was initially entirely absent from the tsarist state's responses to the practice; this was a regime willing to witness death.

Force-feeding only emerges with the liberal state, the British response to the suffragette movement. London had been a staging ground for Russian revolutionaries including Vera Figner, who after twenty years in prison spent a decade in Europe. As Grant suggests, this likely introduced the practice to and facilitated its adoption by the suffragettes.[8] In July 1909 Marion Wallace Dunlop went on hunger strike in Holloway prison, following arrest for stencilling a bill of rights to the Palace of Westminster. She did so in explicit imitation of anarchist practice, as the joint editor of the *Votes for Women* journal Frederick Pethick-Lawrence noted when he referred to Dunlop as following 'the Russian method'.[9] Initially, hunger-striking suffragettes seemed to have assumed that the weight of public sympathy, or insufficient prison resources, would preclude force-feeding on a mass scale.[10] Mass artificial feeding was, however, introduced almost immediately, and suffragettes imprisoned in significant numbers just prior to World War I were almost universally force-fed, often on the grounds that they were suffering from hysteria.[11] This labelling of the hunger striker as psychologically abnormal would set the recurrently gendered pattern in the state response, supported by the use of the material artefacts (principally, the nasal catheter) invented in the madhouses. Challenged unsuccessfully in court by Mary Leigh in 1909, force-feeding was widely viewed amongst suffragettes as a rape by the state, and hunger-striking suffragettes came to view force-feeding, rather than the inherent threshold unto death, as the principle element of horror.[12] Hair-raising first-hand accounts of suffragettes caused considerable societal disquiet, and were in large part responsible for the introduction of the 'Cat and Mouse Act' which authorised release when health deteriorated, then rearrest after recovery on the original charges. The timing of the death of Emily Wilding Davison under the hooves of King George V's horse in 1913 is significant here.[13] Davison, having been force-fed forty-nine times, was well positioned to recognise the extant limits of the hunger strike campaign. It seems highly likely that her act at the 1913 Epsom Derby was a considered attempt to cross the threshold by alternative methods in this new juridical context.

Whilst the suffragette's use of hunger striking inspired a wide variety of anti-colonial nationalist groups, notably in India,[14] Ireland[15] and South Africa, the practice has remained predominantly, though not exclusively, bound to the prison environment.[16] Clearly prisons leave few alternative means of resistance, but incarceration also has a diagrammatic function with respect to wider social relations. The body is principally an assemblage of affective capacities. This is what allows power to act on and through it by organising the movement of desire across it and into the wider social milieu. Inscription on the body is the defining principle of the prison as an institution for social ordering. The body is always already the object of power relations, relying on gendered or racial striations of the societal whole, and its significance as a register for these lines is intensified by physical incarceration. Recognising the energetic intensities marked onto the imprisoned body, the hunger strike restages those lines by manipulating the bodily surface upon which there are inscribed, and as such, constitutes an 'ingenious way of playing hierarchical relations' rather than simply 'abnegating their authority'.[17] Here, politics is indissociable from the assemblage of desire. The practice reoperationalises the inscriptions by which the prison allows the diagram of an exclusionary social order to be mapped onto the individual body.

All hunger strikers refuse to allow the regime against which they struggle to inoculate itself from the stigma of their death. As Allen Feldman noted of the Irish hunger strikes (which culminated in the death of Bobby Sands and nine others in 1981, in response to British state propaganda that framed the act as wholly self-inflicted violence), the blanketmen used their bodies to diagrammatically reenact 'the procedures of the state that drove men to abjection'.[18] These hunger strikers did not, however, in the same gesture seek their own inoculation from responsibility for their deaths.[19] It is precisely the willingness to die that provides 'proof' that a hunger striker is motivated by political conviction as opposed to personal gain.[20] As Feldman recounts, 'going to the edge' was the most common phrase used by Sands and his fellows in reference to it. Going to the edge was

> reaching the cusp of history; it was the creation of a new sociotemporal continuum arising out of the biological time of the dying prisoner . . . the

hunger-striker by 'going to the edge' would take his comrades and possibly Irish society to that edge.[21]

As such, Sands 'constantly reiterated the eschatological and fatal consequences of hunger striking'. The dirty protests which had preceded the hunger strikes had not been understood as stages before this desire, but already demonstrating a will to embrace death by disease, infection and dysentery: The blanketmen of Long Kesh were surprised that the dirty protests didn't kill them. Throughout the campaign they framed death as an act of personal choice, and only therefore as a pedagogical event. Only by consciously crossing the threshold would Sands be able to 'pull the other prisoners over that boundary with him'.[22] As an active self-mortification, 'the hunger-strike as a medium of political action was considered analogous to the prison escape'.[23] Leveraging the inscription of the body by the prison, and thus society at large, the body becomes the register for a wider breakout. All hunger striking deploys a will to cross the threshold of the body, beyond which the prisoner will literally depart the prison itself, but also breaking out of the diagram of order in which it and the actor are located. The politics of the act, in this sense, assumes commitment to one's own deterritorialisation, which makes possible the deterritorialisation of the prison and the social order it inscribes.[24] Taking leave from all territoriality, the hunger strike constructs its politics on the flight of desire.[25] This cannot be reduced to the patterns of heroic meaning that may (or may not) circulate in its aftermath,[26] nor to its attempt to make the legitimacy of the incarcerating regime conditional. The politics of the hunger strike are grounded on its offer of an absolute breakout, a line of flight.[27]

Of course, unlike the suffragettes, the hunger strikers in Ireland also explicitly located themselves within a field of (para)military practice.[28] In 1981 some had clearly 'hoped that the dramatic display of the dead hunger striker would transubstantiate into collective and cathartic uprising against the British state' through subsequent memorialisation. Nothing like this occurred after the event.[29] Rather, Sands's breakout seemed to directly reinvigorate the cycle of tit-for-tat sectarian conflict, as well as internecine Republican violence.[30] Only after that violence had accelerated out of control for a decade would conditions emerge for a fragile resolution.[31] The conclusion drawn by Feldman is that the hunger strike, inasmuch as it embodied an absolute excess, always risked giving birth to an uncontrollable mimesis of death in a proliferating variety of forms.[32] This uncontrollable morbid charge suggests a potential answer to why the deaths of hunger strikers in Guantanamo Bay must be so carefully precluded: The bodies of these inmates are already overcoded by anxiety concerning death. Indeed, it is the fear of death's proliferation that organises and justifies this prison, with respect to which the production of suicides bears the incomparable terror of a wish fulfilled.

Bodily inscription

Despite Deleuze's suggestions to the contrary,[33] there are clear differences between the thesis put forward by Pierre Clastres in 1974 and that put forward in *Anti-Oedipus* two years earlier, and reconfirmed in *A Thousand Plateaus*, concerning the question of why the state was eventually victorious over the primitive regime.³⁴ Clastres's insight was that rather than missing a state, primitive societies are defined by their deterrence of the centralised state apparatus.³⁵ To prevent the centralisation of power, prestate societies in Latin America insisted that the chief display a series of personal characteristics – as a peacemaker, a good orator and a generous giver of gifts. His power was ultimately fragile, dependent on his capacity to fulfil these roles satisfactorily and retain the goodwill of the tribe, under constant threat of abandonment. The primitive chieftain is thus placed in a position of social bondage through gifts which are nonreciprocal, most notably the rights of polygyny. The refusal of any form of exchange between chief and society ensures that the political sphere is established as radically external to the group.³⁶ Inasmuch as the chief is made external and thus marginal, his authoritative power is nullified at birth.³⁷ Primitive societies are not deficient or incomplete; they do not lack. Rather they are politically defined by their invention of mechanisms for warding off the state.³⁸

For Clastres, reading *Anti-Oedipus*, it is the state 'warded off or triumphant' which establishes the 'theory of history'.³⁹ Deleuze and Guattari agree that 'being the common horizon for what comes before and what comes after, [the state] conditions universal history,' but then abruptly qualify this claim.⁴⁰ Clastres hoped that 'the follow-up to *Anti-Oedipus* will tell us more' about why the primitive societies fail to prevent the state from arising.⁴¹ The answer to this question is actually already implicit in *Anti-Oedipus*, though *A Thousand Plateaus* will indeed spell it out. For Deleuze and Guattari, despite its role as a horizon of primitive regimes, it is not the Urstaat as such, but the Urstaat as a superior response to a far more threatening nightmare that defines its place in Universal History. It is the nightmare of a fully decoded externality which explains why primitive societies were in the end 'defeated'.⁴² Capitalism, and not the state, establishes the theory of history as a figuration of 'the limit that haunts all societies, the displaced represented that disfigures what all societies dread absolutely as their most profound negative: namely the decoded flows of desire'.⁴³ The absolutely deterritorialised flows of desiring-production 'exist from the very beginning'.⁴⁴ Accordingly, coding desire, so displacing the terror of decoded flows, is the central business of all noncapitalist historical formations.⁴⁵ The most basic task of every social machine prior to capitalism was the prevention of its offer of decoding on all registers.⁴⁶ This is why capitalism, and not the state, is the key to Universal History.⁴⁷

Though capitalism's rise was a question of historical accidents, its ideal form haunts all societies as 'their terrifying nightmare, it is the dread they feel of a flow that would elude their codes'.⁴⁸ The primitive is thus caught between two horizons or thresholds that must be warded off: a deterritorialisation and a reterritorialisation. Each presages the death of its molecular social order. The primitive makes 'use of scission to exorcise fusion, and impede the concentration of power by maintaining the organs of chieftainry in a relation of impotence with the group', but must also steer clear from allowing the flux of disruptive decodings to enter its system:

> *The greatest danger* would be yet another dispersion, a scission such that all the possibilities of coding would be suppressed: decoded flows, flowing on

blind, mute deterritorialized socius – such is the nightmare that the primitive social machine exorcises with all its forces.[49]

To guarantee the deterrence of the state, the primitive regime would have to skirt too close to that absolute decoding it fears above all; thus the 'hysteria' of the primitive, who oscillates between frantic deterrence by inscribing codes upon their own bodies and a strange melancholy derived from an anticipation of a death at the hands of the overcoding state.[50] Such a death is inevitable because the primitive regime must in the end embrace cruel fusion-processes of inscription to combat the endless threat of decoding, which open the door to overcoding by the despotic mechanism.

Deleuze and Guattari assert that unconscious desire 'knows nothing of exchange; *it knows only theft and gift.*'[51] They argue that nonstate societies are defined by 'a socius of inscription where the essential thing is to mark and to be marked . . . There is circulation only if inscription requires or permits it'.[52] Clastres confirms that 'primitive societies are first of all societies that mark' their order on the body.[53] Deleuze and Guattari reference Clastres's early work on primitive rites of passage, pointing out that the carving of tribal markers on the bodies of youths entering adulthood is an invariably torturous process.[54] Clastres argues that 'initiation rituals often constitute a basic axis around which the whole social and religious life of the community is organised.' They involve 'laying hold of the body' so as to make it the site or 'focal point of tribal ethos'.[55] Those black squares on Queequeg's body are representations of an ancestral debt,[56] an inscription of death which ensures desire circulates only according to social precepts.[57] Self-authored violence and torture is the essence of the primitive's social modelling of death. Social inscription must be born in silence, as proof of individual fortitude. Indeed, the method used must be as painful as possible. Deleuze and Guattari quote Clastres's account of the utilisation of jagged stones in Guayaki rituals, which cause the most pain and scarification. The marks, as Clastres[58] put it, leave 'an irrevocable surplus' by which society implants its memory on the body. Deleuze and Guattari are explicit in *Anti-Oedipus* that the role of these 'cruel mnemotechnics' is to anchor the codes of social life. The inscription of a socially determined model of death on the body allocates and distributes surplus value – the marks which remain establish an irrevocable obligation to the ancestral lineage, instituting the primitives' distinctive form of decentralised order.

The primitive regime is a cruel 'recoding, inscribing socius', which operates by 'tattooing, excising, incising, carving, scarifying, mutilating, encircling, and initiating'.[59] In this way, the body is made a repository of collective memory and ancestral law. The inscribed body displays the collective investment in fantasy and myth, and its associated behavioural prescriptions. Each 'knows' on his or her body that they are equal members of an ancestral filiation.[60] Bodily inscription moulds 'men and their organs into the parts and wheels of the social machine'.[61] This inscription thus has nothing to do with exchange.[62] It facilitates a controlled circulation of death in the form of a debt to the ancestral lineage. The ancestor always remains the master of debts which circulates in the form of inscriptions.

The primitive experience of death is thus anchored to the body. Here, all debts are mobile inasmuch as they determine the criterion for socially ordered flows of desire and power, generally in the form of alliance marriages. Bodily inscription predesignates how the capital flows (male or female bodies, depending on which gender is obliged to live with the partner's family) may be allowed to circulate (i.e. join other tribes).[63] All forms of exchange are categorically rejected, since free exchange implies a decoding that is precluded by ensuring the ancestral codes are physically engraved on each tribal body.[64]

Whilst the historical or real limit of primitive societies is the sovereign state, their absolute limit is a schizophrenic decoding.[65] 'Coding pain and death, [primitive society] has foreseen everything,' but because it is so unwilling to skirt too close to the anarchy of a full decoding of flows, the path is laid open for 'a break, a rupture, a leap': the rise of the Urstaat.[66] In *A Thousand Plateaus*, Clastres is accused of retaining an evolutionist problematic.[67] Deleuze and Guattari argue that 'Clastres maintained the autarky of counter-state societies and attributed their workings to an over-mysterious presentiment of what they warded off and did not yet exist.'[68] Clastres cannot explain how and why the state arose given the prevention mechanisms at the disposal of primitive societies.[69] This is because he failed to recognise the common problematic that links despot and primitive together. Deleuze and Guattari argue that states and primitive regimes found various registers of common cause against decoding. The archaeological record reveals how state and primitive regimes existed in combination and together, linked by networks, linguistic or otherwise.[70] Virtual opposition does not, therefore, imply actual historical non-coexistence or linear succession. The state diagram simply seeks to 'ward off capitalism as the threshold of its mode of social production' through a more complete inscription.[71] To do so, it captures the flexible codes of the primitive and overcodes them. The fear of the revolutionary outside of deterritorialised flows (death unbound) is thus the originary reason for the rise of the Urstaat and the fundamental operator of Universal History. The primitive inscribed death on the body only because it knew that it carried the secret of a revolutionary social production; the despot simply seeks an even more definitive organisation of death by overcoding each already coded body. All bodies must be doubly inscribed: scars upon scars.

The marriage between the fields of subjectivity and social structure in Deleuze and Guattari's philosophy is fundamentally a question of the way in which different social structures organise individual desire by collectively organising death through inscriptional practices. The nightmare of a revolutionary experience of death is that which all precapitalist social orders anticipate and seek to prevent from actualising. Capitalism unbridles the revolutionary nightmare of death uninscribed. This is why Deleuze and Guattari state that 'the primitive and the barbarian, with their ways of coding death, are children in comparison with modern man and his axiomatic.'[72] Capitalism, a historical singularity, retrospectively determines the 'conditions and the possibility' of Universal History because it constitutively displaces the limit of all diagrams.[73] The monism of this account (in the pure externality of death as decoded flux) differentiates Deleuze and Guattari from dialectical thinkers.[74] Mortality established the revolutionary limit of any social order; this is why, for Deleuze and Guattari, suicide is *the* political problem of Universal History.

Decoding death

The characteristics of a political body reflect its social organisation of death.[75] The more a diagram seeks to organise death within the societal milieu, so as to manage the flows of desire, the more strongly its presence will be felt. The explosive force of desiring-production constitutes a limit that must be ejected, or at least displaced, if hierarchies or striations in the social order are to remain in place.[76] Systems of representation ensure the desiring flows are restrained in accordance with presanctioned norms. The free flow of desire is the limit of any collectivity, and so precapitalist societies construct a social model and experience of death to code, and in doing so manage the raw process. This means that the death-carrying elements of the social order always mark the openings within a societal assemblage to revolutionary decoding.[77] This is particularly obvious under despotic diagrams,[78] where death is socially elevated as an infinite debt owed to the overlord.[79] Precisely because of this vertical coding of death, a productive dialectic of law and transgression ensures that desire constantly finds escape from the despotic socius. Death retains political potency under the despot, folding into social life an immanent challenge to his law ('so kill me').

In a capitalist society the situation is reversed. Death is contained within each subject, whilst being endlessly reproduced and displaced across the societal milieu.[80] Rather than coding the flows they are now 'directly apprehended in a codeless axiomatic that consigns them to the universe of subjective representation'. Death and desire appear to become a wholly private matter.[81] This formal separation of private desire from public economic activity allows the death instinct to effuse, laying hold of the entire productive apparatus, putting in place 'a mortuary axiomatic'.[82] As the regimes of social and desiring production are apparently cut off from one another, their identity in nature becomes ever more apparent. Capitalism, in seeking to domesticate death as a private instinct, comes to be defined by its operationalisation as productive principle: the urge to creative destruction. Capitalism's unprecedented economic productivity is thus directly consequent to this peculiar instrumentalisation of death.[83]

With death no longer localised (in the objectivities of ancestral myth or under despotic authority), under capitalism 'anti-production [i]s spread throughout all of production'.[84] By contrast with Bataille, for whom antiproduction is essential waste, for Deleuze and Guattari, antiproduction is simply a condition for the possibility of production, understood as pulsing or intensity.[85] Capitalist production is defined as a constrained realisation of the desiring-productive process; a generalised operationalisation of destruction as indispensable. One might say that capitalism seeks to imitate the desiring-productive oscillation. Rather than making the model that from which new pulses emerge, it spreads death throughout the economy as an instinct that regulates its flow. Schumpeter's characterisation is illustrative in this context;[86] 'the fundamental impulse that sets and keeps the capitalist engine in motion comes from new consumer goods, new methods of production or transportation, the new markets, the new forms of industrial organisation that capitalist enterprise creates'; all these processes of creation rely on the decomposition from within of the productive codes which defined them in a 'perennial gale of creative destruction'.[87] It is only this perpetual passing of the old which ensures the famous tendency to the fall in the rate of profit is constantly displaced by innovation.[88] Deleuze and Guattari are clear that it would be a 'serious error to consider *the capitalist flows and the schizophrenic flows as identical*, under the general theme of a decoding of the flows of desire'; but there is clearly an affinity between them.[89]

The difference is that capitalism must immediately arrest any process which promises revolutionary transformation to the arrangement of forces within the social assemblage.[90] Capitalism correctly sees in an unrestrained deterritorialisation 'the image of its own death'.[91] In this sense, capitalist modernity destroys codes – this is its primary function,[92] but it does so only to see them reestablished elsewhere, in an endlessly arrested process of decoding-recoding-decoding. This is the most obvious function of money.[93] Money is an abstract quantity indifferent to the quality of the flow in question. It evacuates stable cultural content, replacing it with the floating image that is the machine-part of the consumer mechanism. Such dissolved codes retain functionalities. Indeed, capitalist societies 'exhibit a marked taste for all codes' but only in an explicitly 'destructive and morbid' fashion.[94] Antiproduction functions as a stimulus for the proliferation of cynical or residual recoding.[95] In this way, we are constantly encouraged to seek meaning amidst the assumption of its impossibility (lack). Capitalism decodes, and whilst this allows us to 'believe in liberated desires', we ground them on codes which 'like cadavers' are already disappearing or melting away.[96] This marks the cynical piety of capitalism; we are enjoined to passionately believe in, say, progress or the liberating qualities of a particular lifestyle, yet acknowledge that belief is residual and external to the functioning of modern existence.[97] In this way, capitalist machines 'regulate the organisation of lack through the market' by offering temporary islands of meaning to rest on before our next insistent dissolution.[98] In this sense, Jacques Camatte's concerns seems worth taking seriously, that the future of capital may not even be the destruction of the humanity, but far worse, the creation of a wholly 'degenerated humanity which lacks the power to destroy it'.[99] The death of meaning is everywhere constitutive of modern life. This is why 'the only modern myth is the myth of zombies'.[100] There is nothing more definitive of capitalism than an operative consciousness of lack.

Exchange

Jean Baudrillard's *Symbolic Exchange and Death* (published in 1976) may be read as a direct response to Deleuze and Guattari's *Anti-Oedipus* (published in 1971).[101] Baudrillard writes a genealogy of death's exclusion from modern society,[102] which paradoxically ensures that, under capitalism, its symptomatic mark is to be found everywhere.[103] Just like Deleuze and Guattari, for Baudrillard all societies are defined by their distinctive thanatopraxes.[104] Where, however, *Anti-Oedipus* saw coding death as a central action of precapitalist societies in the face of the socially revolutionary implications of mortality, Baudrillard's conceives of death as calling up semiurgic practices to escape the loss of signification associated with the putrefying body, which must be coded for any social order to exist.[105] Baudrillard thus reintroduces the lack which Deleuze and Guattari had been careful to excise from the analytic of mortality.[106] Death, for Baudrillard, is a principally an absence of meaning: a pure negation.[107] For Deleuze and Guattari, death is the effusion of sense and affect. As such, whilst for both theories coding death is the foundation of social life, their implications regarding the politics of suicide are very different.

For Baudrillard, primitive society[108] had little fear of death because through rituals of initiation it was fully integrated into social life.[109] For Deleuze and Guattari such initiation rites established codes of communality by marking death on the body of the initiate, forming thereupon a milieu for the circulation of mortal flows now coded in the form of a debt to the ancestors. For Baudrillard, by contrast,

> initiation is the crucial moment, the social nexus, the darkroom where birth and death stop being the terms of life and twist into one another again; not towards some mystical fusion, but in this instance to turn the initiate into a real social being.[110]

The initiatory rite is a symbolic death after which the initiate is able to undergo a second birth as member of the collectivity. This is not about the eclipse of the biological fact of death. The function of the initiation is to conjure away 'the splitting of life and death'. Death for the primitive is recognised as socially defined, as having no natural significance or connotation.[111] Primitive initiation rites thus resolve the separation of life and death in a 'social act of exchange'.[112] Far from entailing a regime of coding that follows from physical rites of inscription to achieve a determinant political function,[113] the symbolic is the primary milieu of the gift/counter-gift exchange, a register within which life and death are able to circulate freely.[114] History has witnessed an inexorable process by which practices of symbolic integration have been ejected from social life.[115] A gradual extradition of the dead now constitutes the modern meaning of life. Life has become the survival of death,[116] as the constitutive boundary dividing the dead from the alive. Modern life assumes this constitutive disjunction; in other words, for we moderns, 'defined as living beings, death is our imaginary'.[117]

Baudrillard argues that the exclusion of the dead underpins all the other binary divisions of modernity, madness being 'only ever the dividing line between mad and sane' and humanity being a constitutive product of inhumanity's exclusion.[118] Foucault's genealogies of discrimination must all be rooted in the primary extradition by which death becomes pure 'delinquency . . . an incurable deviancy'. This supplies the function of all universalising programs as the foundational source of modern exclusionary rationality. Modernity's binaries – mad/sane, human/

inhuman, even man/woman – are all rooted in a primary real/imaginary disjunction of life/death. Death and power are thus intimately related. All power is directly based on 'the management of the imaginary sphere of death'. All power (over life) is at root a management of the imaginary sphere of death.[119] Social control begins with control over the dead, and law originates from that guardianship of real/imaginary distinction.[120] Inasmuch as this process is unidirectional it involves the steady alienation of the dead, a democratisation of access to immortality after death, and a movement towards ever more 'deathless' societies. The 'prohibition of death' in everyday life acts as the 'primary source of social control' today.[121]

It is striking that Baudrillard's account lacks a clear articulation of why modernity is an irreversible evolution defined by this disjunction. Baudrillard seems, at times, to adopt an explanatory conception of modern power defined by the occlusion of the symbolic by the semiotic.[122] Deleuze and Guattari's account of death as the nightmare of decoding haunting all social diagrams from the limit of Universal History is replaced by an evolutionary narrative. For Baudrillard capitalist (semiotic) production is the farthest departure from primitive (symbolic) exchange.[123] Capitalism is defined by its decoding and an axiomatic mode of function.[124] But its reliance on the extradition of death means for Baudrillard that capitalism is uniquely vulnerable. Capitalist economic power is literally 'life taking death hostage'. Labour is the form of a deferred death, a pure gift of capital: 'Labour is not exploitation, it is given by capital.' For this reason, capitalist production is a matter of 'dead labour'.[125] For Baudrillard, 'whoever works has not been put to death . . . labour is first of all the sign of being judged worthy only of life.' As a consequence of his indebtedness to capital, labour is left with no capacity for authentic resistance barring the refusal of work which is both literally and symbolically an act of suicide.[126]

Indeed, for Baudrillard only an act which 'takes the form of death' can challenge the unilateral operation of power as capital; 'only in the sacrifice of death can the slowly administered death that is labour be disrupted or annulled'. The extraordinary positivity of capitalism can call up only one response; a symbolic negation constituting a revolutionary 'trans' politics of suicide:

> To defy the system with a gift to which it cannot respond save by its own collapse and death . . . The system turns on itself, as a scorpion does when encircled by the challenge of death. For it is summoned to answer, if it is not to lose face, to what can only be death. The system must itself commit suicide in response to the multiplied challenge of death and suicide.[127]

Labour, as the gift of life by capital, can only resist by entering into a symbolic exchange whereby a collapse of the regime of pure positivity of the capitalist imaginary/real occurs.[128] The worker must mobilise 'death as rupture, contagious dissolution and negation'.[129] We see here very strong resonances with Walter Benjamin's account of the general strike that, as an articulation of divine violence, acts only through a pure negation. The revolutionary act is a symbolic gift.[130] Revolutionary politics = symbolic suicide.

For Baudrillard, as for Deleuze and Guattari, Freud's theory of the death instinct is a myth which sanctions some of the fundamental processes of our culture.[131] Also like Deleuze and Guattari, Baudrillard seeks to 'retain its radicality' by turning the concept against psychoanalysis whilst identifying the 'insufficiencies of its vision'.[132] But, for Baudrillard, the function of death is 'beyond the unconscious'.[133] Categorically, death's contemporary significance has nothing to do with desire. This is an explicit rejection of Deleuze and Guattari's account in *Anti-Oedipus*. Baudrillard claims that Bataille's account of death 'as the paroxysm of exchanges, superabundance and excess'[134] is a massive improvement on the Freudian account which, for all its radicality, sees death as a function of equilibrium and repetition.[135] Baudrillard reads Bataille's as viewing 'death as excess, always already there', implying that 'life is only defective when death has taken it hostage, that life only exists in bursts and exchanges with death.' Bataille thus apparently counters Freud's account of sexuality and death with the idea that they are 'exchanged in the same cycle'.[136] Bataille's 'luxurious' vision of death as continuity, for Baudrillard, suggest a problematic which 'can never be confused with either the real or with science'.[137] Baudrillard claims that Bataille is in error only inasmuch as he identifies this sphere of excess with reproduction and desire rather than the symbolic. Reproduction is too functional, too naturalistic, it has no real excess; the only example of a truly excessive operation is symbolic sacrifice.[138] Bataille naturalised 'a tendency to discontinuity' leading him to an unfortunate (for Baudrillard) subjectivist metaphysics of prohibition and transgression. Bataille's naturalism can, however, be jettisoned, allowing us to draw on his premonitions to see 'the challenge posed by death to economic organisation'.[139] What Baudrillard critiques in Bataille is precisely what Deleuze and Guattari affirm: the unconscious repetition of difference which relies on positing the natural immanence of death and the productive.

This takes us to the rub of Baudrillard's acerbic critique of Deleuze and Guattari,[140] that what haunts 'schizo-nomadic imaginations' of death is an 'idealism of desire', in the belief that we can

> rediscover some miraculous innocence where the flows of 'desire' roam freely and the primary processes are realised without prohibition . . . In Deleuze and Guattari's *Anti-Oedipus*, [Desire] remains the promise of a savage *naturality*, the phantasm of an objective, liberatory pulsional energy to be liberated – a force of desire inherited from the mobile field of revolutions.[141]

This image of desire as 'purged of all negativity, a network, a rhizome, a contiguity diffracted ad infinitum' strikes Baudrillard as a suspicious collusion with the diffused character of contemporary power.[142] Deleuze and Guattari's unconscious is literally 'the psychic metaphor of capital', which 'glories the axiomatic of desire and the unconscious in its purest form'.[143] Something similar has been suggested by both Zizek[144] and Badiou.[145] In *Forget Foucault*, Baudrillard accuses Deleuze of establishing 'a notion of desire along the lines of future forms of power'.[146] Indeed, power and desire are often indifferentiable in Deleuze and Guattari's work.[147] Deleuze and Guattari simply multiply ad infinitum the real/imaginary bar between life and death 'in cellular and molecular succession' according to the power-dream of the semiotizing capitalist machine.[148]

This is a disturbing critique. Indeed, it is astonishing that it elicited no explicit response.[149] A response can nonetheless be read in Deleuze and Guattari's contrasting articulation of the primitive regime. For Deleuze and Guattari, the melancholic primitive regime cannot deter the nightmare of absolutely decoded flows whilst also deterring a state of overcoding. This is why it is doomed. For Baudrillard the primitive regime is simply defined by symbolic exchange. In this way, the symbolic forms not a structure, category or agency, but a kind of primary social relation which resolves the real/imaginary distinction itself.[150] Why, then, does it increasingly disappear from social life? Unlike Lacan, for whom the symbolic 'plays a balancing act between the demands of a lost imaginary and a lost real', for Baudrillard, the symbolic is precisely a social act of exchange which is irreducible to the imaginary/real distinction, both of which are effects (rather than causes) of consciousness.[151] Very simply, the real, for Baudrillard, is already imaginary, and symbolic exchange unconceals this. Given the primary status of the symbolic, it is therefore curious that Baudrillard provides no answers to why there is such an 'irreversible evolution from savage societies to our own' defined by its loss. This marks what Pawlett terms the 'temporal problem of which comes first, the symbolic order or the real/imaginary opposition?'[152] The symbolic exchange takes on the characteristics of a state of grace prior to modern rationality. For Deleuze and Guattari, by contrast, the cruelty of primitive rites of passage is a 'theft that prevents the gift and the counter-gift from entering into an exchangist relation'; it sets up a register of ancestral debt from which primitive social production derives. For Baudrillard, the gift and counter-gift integrate life and death precisely by accessing a primary milieu of reciprocity between them. Is not, then, the symbolic exchange a semi-transcendent 'real of death in itself' for Baudrillard?[153] It is clear that, for Deleuze and Guattari, primitive inscription is a way of coding death as a primary milieu of revolutionary decoded flows, death understood as contingency and mortal rupture in and of itself. For Baudrillard, primitive initiation accesses not the real as such, but a symbolic-real of gift exchange. Baudrillard's use of the term counter-gift is thus insufficient to ward off the charge that his is a semitranscendental characterisation of the symbolic.[154] Baudrillard refuses Deleuze and Guattari's naturalism, but flirts with a symbolic idealism instead. The exchange of death has to come first, as the ideal displaced origin of all human experience.

For Deleuze and Guattari there is simply no 'question of returning to the pre-signifying and pre-subjective semiotics of primitive peoples'.[155] Baudrillard's error is that of nostalgia; his symbolic exchange is the dream of an 'impossible return' to an imagined condition of ideal symbolic equanimity.[156] Symbolic exchange with their ancestors results from the effort the primitives have gone to code their nightmare; it is not a prior state but a practice. Inasmuch as the symbolic exchange takes on an ideal function, Baudrillard cannot recognise the pragmatic and political function of initiation in primitive societies.[157] The primitive circulation of desire under ancestral debt, in other words, mediated via myth, has discrete functions as part of the primitive anticipation-prevention machine seeking to code death's promise of a revolutionary disorder. Baudrillard moves in the opposite direction, theorising an ideal primitive equilibrium of death as gift exchange beyond the unconscious, which is tragically occluded by the onset of modernity.[158]

This is not to deny that Deleuze and Guattari's account is naturalistic; clearly it is, as Baudrillard claims, rooted in a categorical reading of the relationship between death and creativity. When Baudrillard points out that what bothers him 'about desire is the idea of an energy at the source of all these fluxes',[159] he raises a cogent point: Deleuze and Guattari are engaged in an explicitly vitalist project.[160] For Deleuze and Guattari, desire is the pure continuity of revolutionary deterritorialisation.[161] Desire is neither essentially human nor even biological; the unconscious is a machine of machines breaking the primary disintegrating flow of desires/intensities. Desire is the flux of intensity in the movement between affective states which is assembled or cut into by machines of any type or genus. Not only do animals have revolutionary desires, but so do plants, industrial machines, and ecological processes: Revolutionary desire is simply the deterritorialising movement of matter itself.[162] Desire's deterritorialisation is the expression of the primacy of a vital tendency to creative disintegration in all assemblages.[163] Naturalism defines Deleuze and Guattari's Universal History.[164] For the same reason, revolutionising capitalism is unfolding it to nature. Much as Badiou's work emerges out of fidelity to Cantor's mathematics, Deleuze and Guattari's work operates out of a fidelity to a natural movement that is generically creative: an anarchist materialism.

Terror and production

Baudrillard provides a very clear account of why an inmate starving himself to death in Guantanamo might convey the terror of a revolutionary production. The field of the symbolic exchange is the only place where the entire system of capitalist social production can be put at question:

> The worst error of all our revolutionary strategies is to believe that we can put an end to the system on the plane of reality: this is their imaginary, imposed on them by the system itself . . . We must therefore displace everything into the sphere of the symbolic, where challenge, reversal and overbidding are the law, so that we can respond to death only by an equal or superior death.[165]

The only way to defy the system is to offer it a unilateral gift of death; responding to its gift of life with a terroristic gift of symbolic death.

In *Symbolic Exchange and Death*, Baudrillard describes terrorism, specifically hostage-taking, as a symbolic exchange. The terrorist's demands act as a rupture in the logic of the real; the system can only respond by killing the terrorist which is an insufficient response at the symbolic level. Terrorists place death 'as their stake'; by killing them the 'system has merely impaled itself on its own violence *without really responding to the challenge that was thrown at it*.[166] All the real power and legitimate violence of the state (held in its institutions, police, and army) is revealed to be symbolically ineffective. Having denied the sphere of the symbolic exchange, the system has no means with which to respond to the terrorist's willingness to sacrifice life; its humiliation is absolute. Regardless of inequalities in power, the terrorist is able to mobilise the symbolic; the system can only be 'driven to suicide in return ... manifest in disarray and defeat'.[167] The force of 9/11 as an event, Baudrillard argues, can only be understood in such terms: 'With the attacks on the World Trade Centre in New York, we might even be said to have before us the absolute event, the "mother" of all events, the pure event uniting within itself all the events that have never taken place'.[168] As a system of pure positivity, the reality of globalisation functions by ejecting the event just as much as it ejects death. The concentration of technocratic world power is conditional on its success in 'absorbing and resolving any crisis, any negativity'; ejecting death from its real/imaginary.[169] The fragility of this formation derives from its reliance on an almost perfect exclusion of the negative.[170] September 11th marks the moment at which the opponents of absolute positivity – the structurally excluded, but also the beneficiaries of the system inasmuch as there is a universal 'allergy to definitive order'[171] – intuit this fragility. In wagering their deaths, the 9/11 hijackers gave a counter-gift to the system against which deterrence or counter-destruction was a priori obsolete:

> Here then, it is all about death, not only about the violent irruption of death in real time – live, so to speak – but the irruption of a death ... which is symbolic and sacrificial – that is to say, the absolute, irrevocable event. This is the spirit of Terrorism.[172]

For Baudrillard, then, self-sacrifice of a hunger striker in Camp Delta leverages the hypnotic compulsion to return all gifts. This was equally the essence of the force of the 9/11 event: Through the use of modern technology and organisation (the system's elements mobilised against itself), the emergence of the threat from within the monotonous and privileged life of suburbia (the sleeper-cell), its spectacular dissemination live on 24-hour news all reinforced its charge, the secret of its success as an event was tied its operationalisation of the symbolic as 'pact and sacrificial obligation'.[173] Its images scattered in viral fashion around the world because, through the symbolic mobilisation of death, 'both images and events' were 'resuscitated' in the face of the 'desert' of hyperreal positivity.[174] Baudrillard is absolutely explicit: 9/11's status as a real event has nothing to do with the scale of its violence, or its unimaginability prior to the attack, but with a fascination that derives from its status as a symbolic death.[175] The event *was* death:

> The death of the terrorist ... creates a gigantic suction or void, and enormous convection. Around this tiny point the whole system of the real and of power gathers, transfixed; rallies briefly; then perishes by its own hyper-efficiency.[176]

September 11th was the spectacle of the spectacle, the event of an event – the return of the symbolic exchange to a zero-death system. Its fascination enacts a seductive injunction to complicity in our own destruction. September 11th cannot be understood in terms of ideology or meaning, but as 'the point of paroxysm'.[177] The symbolic stakes of the game invented by the terrorist tip the system into suicide; it reveals in its own nonmeaning the correspondent 'non-meaning and indifference which are at the heart of the system'.[178] The pervasive spread of conspiracy theories about 9/11 are not interesting because they attempt to deny the event its real meaning, rather, conspiracy theory expresses the desperate attempt to safeguard some positivity or reality principle.[179] It is the systems symbolic 'loss of credibility, the collapse of image' that 9/11 effected.[180]

The absolute negativity of 9/11 seduced the system to partake in its own abolition, resulting in the immunitary rise of US unilateralism and paranoia that distinguished the War on Terror. The declaration of unilateral aggressive wars and the scandals of Abu Ghraib and Guantanamo Bay acted to corrode the legitimacy upon which the power of the system relies, resulting in a 'slump in value-system, in the whole ideology of freedom, of free circulation and so on, on which the Western world prided itself'.[181] As the US acted more and more like a police state, uncontrolled and arbitrary in its violence, Baudrillard sees the effectiveness of a symbolic implosion of the real/imaginary.[182] September 11th was maximally evental. This is precisely what Baudrillard called for in the strongest terms in the 1970s: a glorious counter-gift which renders the system literally speechless and suicidal. Whilst it is oversimplistic to view him as an ideologue of 9/11, he certainly sees in here the very essence of evental politics. Suicide is neither the last nor even postpolitical event. Rather, beyond the 'dead point' of the system, the 9/11 Event of Death was 'transpolitical'.[183] Baudrillard's vision rests on the categorical equation: (trans)politics = suicide.[184] For this reason, the hunger striker in Guantanamo Bay is the spectre of an unshakeable nightmare for the system.

The War on Terror, unable to achieve a symbolic retort to death, simply contributed to the systemic collapse:[185] 'a police state globalization, a total control, a terror based on law and order measures'.[186] Diverse vectors of reterritorialisation, defined by a unilateralist US foreign policy, and underpinned by discourses of apparently naked imperial ambition, were certainly an egregious consequence of 9/11. The War on Terror has accordingly been widely interpreted as a reemergence of an authoritarian sovereign power, displacing the more deterritorialised mechanisms of global governance which had emerged in the decade following the end of the Cold War.[187] September 11th, in this context, imposed a self-defeating logic of return, with the US overreaction (as revealed at Abu Ghraib and Guantanamo Bay) radically deconstructing its pretensions to moral authority, and undermining its reach for ontological security. Baudrillard posits the autodestruction of Western moral universality:[188]

> As much as terrorism rests . . . on the despair of the humiliated and insulted, it rests also on the invisible despair of the privileged beneficiaries of globalization, on our submission to an integral technology, to a crushing virtual reality, to the grip of networks and programs.[189]

September 11th tapped into the suicidalism already integral to the modern reality-principle and its exclusion of the dead.

From Baudrillard's point of view, inasmuch as the hunger strikers in Guantanamo offer an unreturnable gift, the system is terrorised by their continuing embodiment of the spectre of symbolic exchange. Baudrillard's idealism is clearly in evidence here. Baudrillard sees in such potential suicides the necessitation of systemic implosion. Whilst there are longstanding empirical grounds to support Baudrillard's claims about the extradition of the dead from everyday life-practices with the rise of modernity,[190] surely capitalism remains a death regime par excellence. Indeed, for Baudrillard in *Symbolic Exchange and Death*, modern societies were deemed cultures of death in direct proportion to their attempt to disjoin life from death. Extraditing the dead is taken to mean that the living city obtains 'all the functions of the cemetery'.[191] This left open the possibility that we might identify the work of death immanent to the functioning of the system. By *The Spirit of Terrorism*,[192] however, the zero-death system of positivity is categorically challenged by the symbolic gift of death because all morbid features of the contemporary regime have disappeared. Death-lacking global power is fundamentally challenged by a suicidal gift. Even more radically than Clastres's evolutionism (from the primitive regime to the state), Baudrillard now assumes an inexorable historical declination from primitive equanimity with their dead to our present state of dizzying positivity which bans death altogether; and whereby capitalist 'desacralized universality' is now so jealous of 'still sacrificial' cultures that it offers itself up to abolition.[193] Suicide is idiomatic to contemporary order, but only in the form of an expression of its lack of a negational matrix.

From Deleuze and Guattari's point of view, such an implication that death is in some way antithetical to modern social order is simply implausible.[194] For all its transformation of death into an instinct at the level of desire, capitalism's propensity to socially advantage the schizophrenic tendency inexorably exposes the continuing functionality of death to its regime of social production. Capitalism has no need for jealousy; it can always find productive uses for death. Baudrillard attributes a wholly negative strategic insight to the terrorists: Terrorism 'inaugurates nothing. It simply carries things to the extreme, to the point of paroxysm', in accordance with a speculative 'principle of uncertainty'.[195] The problem here is that a sense of radicalised uncertainly precisely underpins the legitimacy of global war today. The War on Terror did not presage the retreat of global order as Baudrillard surmised it would. What was reterritorialised on the one hand was deterritorialised on the other in the birth of a globalised war machine binding a multiplicity of states, international organisations, private contractors, aid agencies, technical innovations, and new governmental approaches circulating around the novel problematization risk and uncertainty.[196] Quite apart from expressing a straightforwardly imperialistic gesture, the War on Terror sought principally to construct a smooth space for its own unconstrained operation. The most productive and lasting dimensions of the event are the radically innovative epistemological and ontological conclusions that the proponents of the War on Terror drew from the events spectacular embodiment of the uncertainty principle; the production of a new and radically deterritorialised strategic doctrine of preemption amidst virtualised unknowable danger or inexpungable potentiality.[197]

In Donald Rumsfeld's now iconic commentary on the existence of 'unknown unknowns' the insufficiency of our predictive knowledge about contemporary threats were explicitly recognised as impossible to overcome, and turned into a methodology for global political practice. The epistemological connotations of 9/11 as unexpected event, Rumsfeld suggested, must be taken as simultaneously ontological, as defining an objectively smooth condition of indeterminate global risk potentiality.[198] September 11th's event of death did not simply reveal our structural 'poverty in death-stakes', but revealed the paroxysm that is death as the infinitely displaceable limit of our mode of social production. This is why 'at Ground Zero, in the rubble of global power, we can only, despairingly, find our own image'.[199] It revealed that ours is a society that can now function only through the axiomatic displacement of death. If there is a morbid spirit of political suicide, it is in its dreamlike reach for a proliferating affective production by purely embodying destruction. Suicide, in this sense, defines a uniquely contemporary politics, for which the bodies of the inmates of Camp Delta have become registers. The incarceration of these bodies is warranted on the grounds that we must contain the affective uncertainty associated with their capacity to die. Inscribed with the smooth space of an unalloyed contingency, the inmates' starving body politics can only endorse the risk-logistics that constitute the justification for global war. To let these inmates cross the threshold is, precisely if paradoxically, to run the risk of further terrorist acts. Making live is the only way to contain possibility in this context.

Notes

1. G. Deleuze and F. Guattari, *A Thousand Plateaus* (London: Continuum, 2004b), p. 484.
2. 'The protest may or may not be verbalized. Detainees who eat portions of the meals are not normally considered to be on a VTF [. . .] After a detainee has refused to consume nine consecutive meals, ensure the Delta Clinic begins the VTF Protocol . . . The detainee will be admitted to the Detention Hospital if supplemental feeding is necessary. The JTF Commander is the only person who can authorize forced feeding [. . .] Consult with the Command Judge Advocate before force treatment is initiated. The legal opinion should be noted in the detainee's medical chart' (CDSOP/04, section 19–8).
3. One of the earliest documented episodes relates to a series of hunger strikes in a Siberian prison demanding the transfer of the prison commandant, which culminated in them committing suicide by poison (followed by seventeen male inmates). See K. Grant, "British Suffragettes and the Russian Method of Hunger Strike," *Comparative Studies in Society and History* 53, no. 1 (2011): 113–143.
4. V. Figner, *Memoirs of a Revolutionist* (DeKalb: Northern Illinois University Press, 1991), p. 219.
5. Ibid., p. 220.
6. Having made this determination clear, two fellow prisoners, who had already abandoned the hunger strike, informed her they would commit suicide if she died. Figner reads this as the 'product of a 'masculine vanity [that] would not permit a women should prove herself more consistent and steadfast', a 'moral violence' which forced her to abandon the hunger-strike and resulted in a decision to end all participation in collective action in the prison (ibid., p. 222).

7. Seeking, for example, including access to literature, better food, or appropriate prison uniform.
8. See Grant 2011, pp. 113–143.
9. See ibid.
10. K. Roberts, *Pages from the Diary of a Militant Suffragette* (Letchworth: Garden City Press, 1911), p. 81. See also J. Purvis, "The Prison Experiences of the Suffragettes in Edwardian Britain," *Women's History Review* 4, no. 1 (1995).
11. E.A. Williams, "Gags, Funnel and Tubes: Forced Feeding of the Insane and of Suffragettes," *Endeavour* 32, no. 4 (2008): 134–140.
12. Force feeding was, and remains, a torturous experience, as confirmed by the World Medical Association in 2006 which declared that 'Forcible feeding is never ethically acceptable ... [it] ... is a form of inhuman and degrading treatment'. WMA Declaration of Malta on Hunger-Strikes, Guideline Number 13.
13. Though considerable effort in recent years has gone into claiming that death was not Davison's aim, as is often deduced from the fact that she had retained a return train ticket, it seems likely that she must have recognised death to be a distinct possibility attendant to running out in front of a galloping adult horse. A willing commitment to step over the threshold into self-destruction cannot be excised from the act.
14. Gandhi had moved in suffragette circles in 1909, witnessed their hunger strikes, and explicitly recognised them as inspiration for his own death fasts against British colonialism. Echoing the suffragette literature, Gandhi assumed societal conditions impacted upon its use, specifically; the presence of a liberal bureaucracy. As he put it, 'you cannot fast against a tyrant'.
15. Hunger striking was adopted for example, by both strands of the Indian movement against colonial rule, appearing in the nonviolent Gandhian strand and in the nationalist movement. Hunger striking was of course explicitly theorised by Gandhi himself on several occasions. The concept of the death-fast, he argued, could only work in a democratic context. After the perceived failure of Gandhi's nonviolent movement in the 1920s, the prison camps of the Andaman Islands became a site for anticolonial resistance amongst nationalist convicts sent there to separate them from the wider population, a protest which contributed to reinvigorating resistance back home in India. In Ireland, hunger striking has a long history as part of the anti-British struggle, culminating in Bobby Sands's hunger strike in the early 1980s in Long Kesh Prison.
16. P. Kumar, *Hunger-Strike in Andamans: Repression and Resistance of Transported Prisoners in Cellular Jail, 12 May–26 June 1933* (Lucknow, India: New Royal Book, 2004).
17. M. Ellmann, *The Hunger Artists: Starving, Writing, and Imprisonment* (Cambridge, MA: Harvard University Press, 1993), p. 21.
18. Feldman recorded 'the instrumental staging and commodification of the body by political violence' in Northern Ireland. He conducted his research in Ireland between 1985 and 1986, during which he collected an enormous range of oral histories from actual participants in the Irish conflict. Its theoretical sophistication and complexity combined with its empirical rigour identifies it as the definitive study of the period of conflict leading up to and including the hunger strikes of 1981. See A. Feldman, *Formations of Violence: The Narrative of the Body and Political Terror in Northern Ireland* (Chicago: University of Chicago Press, 1991), p. 8.
19. Contra Karin Fierke, who suggests that hunger strikes cannot and should not be read as political suicides precisely because all responsibility for death is transferred to the state. The prison warden is placed in a distinctive dilemma by the hunger striker only to the extent that the act is not read as a suicide. Hunger striking places the legitimacy of the prison regime (literal or figurative) in question precisely by making it responsible for the death of the hunger striker. Success thus relies on contesting the state's claim that the hunger striker is responsible for her own death. K.M. Fierke, *Political Self-Sacrifice: Agency, Body and Emotion in International Relations*, Vol. 125 (Cambridge: Cambridge University Press, 2012).

20. Feldman 1991, pp. 71, 117.
21. Ibid., p. 225.
22. Ibid., pp. 242–243. Sands's story of the lark encapsulated this pedagogy of the threshold: The caged lark refuses to sing; only when set free does it give voice.
23. 'Mass hunger strike, that undifferentiated rush of the collective body to the "edge" and beyond, indicates the extent to which the hunger-strike as a medium of political action was considered analogous to the prison escape'. See ibid., p. 249.
24. Fierke (2012), in failing to recognise the constitutive function of the threshold unto death, sees hunger striking as a definitive example of a sovereign politics. She argues that the 'act of speech' that flows from the injured or dying flesh and blood body communicates that

> I am sovereign, you have no power over me. You can kill me for my disobedience, but you cannot take away by ability to act as a sovereign agent even if this means my death. In saying 'I am sovereign, you have no power over me,' the self and community to which it belongs is, in one and the same movement, destroyed and reborn, the first as a martyr and the second in its connection to contemporary and past martyrs who suffered on behalf of the nation. The self sacrifice becomes the performance by which sovereignty is enacted. (p. 102)

In other words, what makes a political message is that it embodies a desire for sovereignty. At stake here is how 'the self-sacrifice of the individual body becomes an expression of the loss of collective sovereignty, which materialises the injustice experienced by the community and thereby creates the condition for its restoration' (p. 79). Political desire is an urge to 'the restoration of dignity [which] goes hand in hand with the reconstitution of the community. 'The Martyr is the embodiment of the nation' (p. 53).

25. 'The prisoner who starved himself to death achieved an act of purification that separated him irrevocably from the stigma of criminalization, and as a subtext removed him from the defiling topos of the prison. This conviction on the part of the blanketmen was the strongest motivating force behind the necessity of the Hunger strike. It just about predetermined the death of the hunger-striker, though it was also believed that those who experienced a hunger strike, who had "gone to the edge" and returned, would have achieved a radical act of separation culminating in both political and personal transformation' (Feldman 1991, p. 236).
26. When Fierke (2012) discusses liminality she partly captures this point, only to mistakenly bind it to affective reterritorialisation.
27. When Fierke argues that 'sacrifice . . . delegitimizes dominant power structures in favour of alternative forms of community', she domesticates the revolutionary dimensions of the act, which do not have territories of being but flights of becoming as their symbolic object (ibid., p. 39).
28. As Feldman put it, a 'political technology of the body connected to paramilitary practice both inside and outside the prison' (1991, p. 213). In this sense, then, hunger strikes did not occupy a separate space to the rest of the conflict, as the practitioners made clear:

> When questioned about the functions of the body in the military operation, in the breaking of the interrogation sessions, and in the hunger strike of 1981, when ten Republican prisoners wilfully starved themselves to death, Republican paramilitaries made no essential distinctions between these various political usages of the body. Either the body was extended by the technology of weaponry in the military operation, or it was extended into a weapon in the interrogation centre and the prison. (p. 143)

As Feldman makes clear, 'at each of these sites of political conflict, the paramilitaries saw their bodies as occupying and exploiting a single political and performative continuum' (p. 7).

29. Ibid., p. 256.
30. Feldman (ibid.) notes that the result of these 'sacrificial acts was violence, not sovereignty. This is tied to a radical challenge to Girard's concept of sacrifice. Feldman argues that the search for legitimate violence that 'can precipitate the forging of new social forms that address violence as autonomous, culturally generative, and meaning endowed practice. The search for legitimacy through the search for nonmimetic practice resolves into a new cultural conduction of violence'. Rather than resolving violence the attempt to resymbolise the violence of the republican movement, in erasing criminality, results in a new origin myth. In this sense, for Feldman – the hunger strikes are politicised by their resymbolising force, but what is resymbolised is violence in itself (p. 259). As he explains, 'the central conundrum of sacrificial violence is predetermined by the necessity of posing a structural discontinuity with mimetic violence through a new form of violence' (p. 260). Sacrifice thus creates a new mythically legitimised violence but in doing so 'the sacrificial rite repeats violence and unavoidably confirm the performance of violence as hegemonic and legitimate.' For this reason 'the sacrificial rite is vulnerable to new levels of mimetic appropriation precisely because it establishes a ritualized for of violence and surrogate victimage as hegemonic' (ibid.): In other words, the sacrificial rite itself, in sacralising violence, creates more violence, and the hunger strike, in being part of a singular milieu of violence 'effected the resymbolization of the Republican movement' (p. 264) and was widely seen as therefore legitimatising PIRA violence. This need legitimated violence 'flow[ed] from the self-inflicted sacrificial act as its excess, as the surplus value of a new historical legitimacy'. More violence was therefore not accidentally related to the hunger strikes, but rather their inevitably result: 'the Hunger-strike was condemned to perpetuate political violence' (p. 265). The result was a return to generalised economy of violence: willingness to die 'immediately translatable to the practice of violence against others by the same hardening and enduring body' ('the blanketmen insofar as they were masters of their own bodies, were masters over the bodies of others' (p. 268), something which became very apparent in the spike in prison violence).
31. Fierke makes the somewhat roundabout argument that the hunger strikers laid the foundations for political dialogue a decade later, planting 'a seed that eventually contributed to the possibility of moving beyond conflict' (2012, p. 133). This seems rather speculative given that none of these factors were direct results of the hunger strikes. To argue that peace-building supplies any political meaning of the hunger strikes is not only to ignore the explicit statements of Sands et al., who explicitly saw themselves as contributing to the armed struggle, but also to misunderstand the dynamics which led to the peace process – which were nonviolent, in a way that the hunger strikes manifestly and explicitly were not.
32. Feldman (2012) thus mistakenly refers to this as the mimesis of the sacrificial form. It is not the sacrificial ritual that is reproduced by mimesis, but that which the Girardian ritual is designed to quell: The hypnotic autopoesis of death itself.
33. Deleuze in F. Guattari, *Chaosophy* (Los Angeles: Semiotext(e), 2009), p. 89.
34. Deleuze and Guattari's account of primitive social production is bound up with the work of the political anthropologist Pierre Clastres. The influence went both ways, with Clastres directly referencing *Anti-Oedipus* in his most famous text, *Society against the State: Essays in Political Anthropology*, trans. R. Hurley in collaboration with A. Stein (New York: Zone Books, 1989).
35. Ibid., pp. 189, 22.
36. Ibid., pp. 41–42.
37. In particular, the gift of the rights of polygyny establishes political power whilst simultaneously, and in the same gesture, forbidding and nullifying it.
38. Clastres 1989, pp. 42–44.
39. Clastres quoted in Guattari 2009, p. 86.
40. It is taken to be true 'only provided it is on the outside, but always off to the side' (G. Deleuze and F. Guattari, *Anti-Oedipus*, London: Continuum, 2004a, p. 240).

41. Clastres quoted in Guattari 2009, p. 86.
42. Deleuze and Guattari 2004a, p. 153; Guattari 2009, p. 89.
43. Deleuze and Guattari 2004a, p. 193.
44. For Deleuze and Guattari (ibid.), then, capitalism 'is the thing, the unnameable, the generalised decoding of flows that reveals a contrario the secret in all [prior] formations' (p. 168).
45. Ibid., p. 153.
46. Ibid., p. 156.
47. 'Capitalism is the only social machine that is constructed on the basis of decoded flows, substituting for intrinsic codes an axiomatic of abstract quantities in the form of money. Capitalism therefore liberates the flows of desire, but under the social conditions that define its limit and the possibility of its own dissolution, so that it is constantly opposing with all its exasperated strength the movement that drives it towards this limit. At capitalisms limit the deterritorialised socius gives way to the body without organs. Hence it is correct to retrospectively understand all history in the light of capitalism' (ibid., p. 153).
48. Ibid., p. 154. Deleuze and Guattari are clear that the three virtual diagrams of social production enter into various actual assemblages, with the state's retaining savage codes, and capitalist processes (such as exchange and decoding) being 'found at the heart of . . . empires throughout the whole of Classical antiquity', and in savage orders (F. Guattari, *Chaosmosis: An Ethico-aesthetic Paradigm*, Sydney: Power, 1995, p. 105). All social forms carry a trace of the outside of absolute decoding (Deleuze and Guattari 2004a, p. 267).
49. Deleuze and Guattari 2004a, p. 167 (emphasis added).
50. Ibid., pp. 167, 192.
51. Ibid., p. 203.
52. Ibid., p. 156.
53. Clastres 1989, p. 187.
54. Deleuze and Guattari 2004a, p. 207.
55. Clastres 1989, p. 180.
56. 'Such a face! It was of a dark, purplish, yellow colour, here and there stuck over with large blackish looking squares. Yes, just as I thought, he's a terrible bedfellow; he's been in a fight, got terribly cut, and here he is just from the surgeon. But at that moment he chanced to turn his face so towards the light, that I plainly saw they could not be sticking plasters at all, those clack squares on his cheeks . . . As I live these covered parts of him were chequered with the same squares as his face; his back, too, was all over the same black squares.' H. Melville, *Moby-Dick; or, the Whale* (Evanston, IL: Northwestern University Press, 1988), p. 21.
57. Deleuze and Guattari 2004a, p. 208.
58. Clastres 1989, p. 184.
59. Deleuze and Guattari 2004a, p. 158.
60. Mutilation moulds 'the subjective positions of each individual within age group, sex, function, race' (Guattari 2009, p. 182).
61. Deleuze and Guattari 2004a, p. 159.
62. Ibid., p. 202.
63. Ibid., p. 163. The filiative stock, that is to say, the physical tribal body, produces the 'surface energy of inscription' but ancestral 'debt is the actual direction of movement' (p. 164). Flows and chains of exchange are of (ancestral) debt.
64. In this sense, capitalist exchange is 'well known in the primitive socius – but as that which must be exorcised, encasted, severely restricted' (ibid., p. 302).
65. Ibid., p. 192.
66. Ibid., p. 209.
67. Clastres implies a limited sympathy for a demographic evolutionism in society against the state, suggesting that the rise of the state model may be linked to primitive population density.
68. Deleuze and Guattari 2004b, p. 474.

69. Ibid., p. 396.
70. Ibid., p. 475.
71. Ibid., p. 483.
72. Deleuze and Guattari 2004a, p. 368.
73. G. Lambert, *Who's Afraid of Deleuze and Guattari?* (London: Continuum, 2006), p. 121.
74. For Jameson, this monism endlessly threatens to collapse back into dualism (of the nomad and state/good versus evil). See F. Jameson in I. Buchanan, ed., *A Deleuzean Century?* (Durham, NC: Duke University Press, 1999), p. 24.
75. Deleuze and Guattari 2004a, p. 369.
76. Ibid.
77. Which is why, in precapitalist societies, 'death comes all the more from without as it is coded from within' (ibid., p. 210).
78. The primitive regime's socialisation of death through practices of ritual bodily inscription and initiation institutes a flexible and thus stable coding of desire. Through primitive inscription 'death is [socially] inscribed in the primitive mechanism of surplus value [the primitive model of death] as well as in the movement of the finite blocks of debt [the primitive experience of death]' (ibid., p. 370).
79. Ibid.
80. In this way, the difference in regime between capitalist social-production and desiring-production is increased in a catastrophic fashion.
81. Deleuze and Guattari 2004a, p. 370.
82. Ibid., p. 371.
83. Ibid., p. 369.
84. The relationship between the concept of death (as the model and experience of desiring-production) and the concept of antiproduction is not instantly clear in *Capitalism and Schizophrenia*. On the one hand, antiproduction is used to describe the paranoiac function. Antiproduction is the subtraction of affect, any movement towards a totalitarian model, the closure of any potentially productive experience through guilt and anxiety. On the other hand, antiproduction is framed as integral to all desiring-productive processes. (ibid., p. 371).
85. Antiproduction is thus the concept coined to counter the 'problem of negativity' (T. May, "The Politics of Life in the Thought of Gilles Deleuze," *SubStance* 20, no. 3 [1991]: 24–35, 28). The concept of antiproduction, as the contraction integral to any productive process, implies that production always admits negativity as integral to positivity (as the zero-point from whence all intensities pulse).
86. D. Harvey, *The Enigma of Capital: And the Crises of Capitalism* (London: Profile, 2010); J.A. Schumpeter, *Capitalism, Socialism and Democracy* (New York: Harper and Brothers, 2011).
87. Schumpeter 2011, pp. 83–84.
88. See also M. Foucault and M. Senellart, *The Birth of Biopolitics: Lectures at the Collège de France, 1978–79* (Basingstoke: Palgrave Macmillan, 2008), p. 231.
89. Deleuze and Guattari 2004a, p. 266.
90. See E. W. Holland, *Deleuze and Guattari's* Anti-Oedipus*: Introduction to Schizoanalysis* (London: Routledge, 1999), p. 36.
91. 'Schizophrenia is the exterior limit of capitalism itself or the conclusion of its deepest tendency, but capitalism only functions on condition that it inhibit this tendency, or that it push back or displace this limit . . . it axiomatizes with the one hand what it decodes with the other' (Deleuze and Guattari 2004a, p. 267).
92. For a classical reference on this point, see M. Berman, *All That Is Solid Melts into Air* (London: Verso, 1983).
93. Deleuze and Guattari 2004a, p. 245.
94. 'Whilst decoding undoubtedly means understanding and translating, it also means destroying the code as such, assigning it an archaic, folkloric, or residual function' (ibid., p. 266).
95. Holland 1999, p. 79.

96. Deleuze and Guattari 2004a, p. 371.
97. Holland 1999, p. 80.
98. F. Guattari and S. Nadaud, *The Anti-Oedipus Papers* (New York: Semiotext(e), 2006), p. 166.
99. J. Camatte, "Decline of the Capitalist Mode of Production or Decline of Humanity," 1973, in R. Mackay and A. Avanessian, *#ACCELERATE: The Accelerationist Reader* (Falmouth: Urbanomic, 2014), p. 133.
100. Deleuze and Guattari 2004a, p. 368. See also B. Adkins, *Death and Desire in Hegel, Heidegger and Deleuze* (Edinburgh: Edinburgh University Press, 2007), p. 1.
101. See D. Kellner, *Jean Baudrillard: From Marxism to Postmodernism and Beyond* (Cambridge: Polity Press, 1989); M. Gane, *Baudrillard's Bestiary* (London: Routledge, 1991); P. Hegarty, *Jean Baudrillard: Live Theory* (London: Continuum, 2004); W. Pawlett, *Jean Baudrillard* (London: Routledge, 2007); R. J. Lane, *Baudrillard* (London: Routledge, 2009).
102. Following Philippe Aries (*Western Attitudes toward Death: From the Middle Ages to the Present*, London: Marion Boyars, 1976).
103. Gane 1991, p. 112.
104. As opposed to assuming a 'strong constructivist or culturally relative position on death' (Pawlett 2007, p. 61).
105. Ibid.
106. Ibid.
107. Baudrillard thus denies Deleuze and Guattari's contention that death has a model and experience in the unconscious; for Baudrillard, the unconscious has nothing to do with it.
108. Baudrillard, like Deleuze and Guattari, roots his genealogical analysis in primitive or savage societies. Lane critiques him for developing an 'idealized and romanticised' vision of the primitive as other of the Western self. See Lane 2009, p. 59. A kind of primitive idealism certainly seems present in Baudrillard which Deleuze and Guattari, in their more foregrounded recognition of – and explanation for – primitive cruelty, avoid.
109. Kellner 1989, p. 103.
110. J. Baudrillard and I. H. Grant, *Symbolic Exchange and Death* (London: Sage, 1993), p. 132.
111. Ibid., p. 131.
112. Ibid., p. 132.
113. Dispelling decodings whilst deterring the formation of a state apparatus.
114. In the Middle Ages the symbolic exchange, exemplified by the evocative images of the scythe, clock and apocalyptic horsemen represented in macabre plays, was central to social life.
115. Gane 1991, p. 114.
116. A 'surplus value after death subtracted from it' (see Baudrillard and Grant 1993, p. 127).
117. Ibid., p. 133.
118. Ibid., pp. 126, 127.
119. Kellner 1989, p. 106.
120. See Gane 1991, p. 116. Related to this claim, Baudrillard points out that in the Pharaonic states of Egypt only the supreme leader had an immortal soul. In hierarchical systems, immortality is the right of particular classes. Baudrillard argues that historically speaking a 'sort of social conquest' takes place whereby gradually 'everyone accedes to immortality' (Baudrillard and Grant 1993, p. 128). From being a right of the despot, immortality is redistributed democratically. Immortality spreads in sync with the identification of what counts as a real human in the spread of colonialism. In this sense the basic logic has not 'changed greatly since Egypt' (see also Gane 1991, p. 115; Baudrillard and Grant 1993, p. 129).
121. Baudrillard and Grant 1993, p. 129.

122. Ibid., p. xii.
123. Though similarly to Deleuze and Guattari, there is no great capital which acts for Baudrillard (ibid., p. 33).
124. Looking 'strictly to political economy and its critique for its alibis, and lives through its own denunciation from within itself' (ibid., p. 31).
125. This seems to correspond with Deleuze and Guattari's claim that capitalist production establishes a mortuary axiomatic for an undead labour force.
126. Baudrillard and Grant 1993.
127. Ibid., pp. 38–39.
128. Ibid., p. 176.
129. Baudrillard's argument is that labour strikes and such can symbolically challenge the unilateral gift of labour (ibid.).
130. 'Only death can put an end to political economy' (ibid., pp. 186–187).
131. Ibid., pp. 149–152.
132. Ibid., pp. 153–154.
133. Ibid., p. 154.
134. Ibid.
135. Deleuze, of course, reworked Freud's theory in terms of difference and repetition; a reading which underpins the account of death in *Capitalism and Schizophrenia* (G. Deleuze, *Masochism: Coldness and Cruelty*, New York: Zone Books, 1989; G. Deleuze, *Difference and Repetition*, London: Continuum, 2004d; G. Deleuze, *The Logic of Sense*, London: Continuum, 2004c).
136. Baudrillard and Grant 1993, p. 155.
137. Ibid., p. 157.
138. 'Sacrificial death is anti-productive and anti-reproductive' (ibid.).
139. Ibid., p. 158.
140. Ibid., p. 137.
141. Ibid. (emphasis added).
142. J. Baudrillard, *Forget Foucault* (Los Angeles: Semiotext(e), 2007), p. 35.
143. Ibid., p. 40, and footnote on p. 41.
144. S. Zizek, *Organs without Bodies: On Deleuze and Consequences* (London: Routledge, 2004).
145. A. Badiou, *Logics of Worlds* (London: Continuum, 2009b).
146. Baudrillard 2007, pp. 30, 36.
147. Accordingly, Baudrillard enjoins us to 'beware of the molecular' (ibid., p. 47).
148. Ibid.
149. As Douglas Kellner notes (1989, p. 152).
150. Baudrillard and Grant 1993, p. 133.
151. B. Butterfield, "The Baudrillardian Symbolic, 9/11, and the War of Good and Evil," *Postmodern Culture* 13, no. 1 (2002), p. 7.
152. Pawlett 2007, p. 61.
153. A question raised by Hegarty 2004, pp. 37–38.
154. Ibid., pp. 38–39.
155. Deleuze and Guattari 2004b, pp. 209–210.
156. For Deleuze and Guattari, the primitive symbolic or 'presignifying regime' is simply one in which 'enunciation is collective', and statements are 'polyvocal', so that deterritorialisation remains relativized according to the flexible operation of language, ritual and belief under the shared ancestral memory (ibid., p. 149).
157. See Clastres 1989.
158. Baudrillard and Grant 1993, p. 237.
159. In Baudrillard's opinion, desire 'has nothing to do with it' (G. Genosko, *The Uncollected Baudrillard*, London: Sage, 2001, p. 126).
160. It is clear, however, that Baudrillard's alternative is at least as problematically foundationalist (Baudrillard 2007, p. 77).

161. There is thus a vague essentialism at work here, as Connolly implies (W. E. Connolly, *Capitalism and Christianity, American Style*, Durham, NC: Duke University Press, 2008, p. 81).
162. Badiou's claim that Deleuze develops a metaphysics of finitude which amounts to little more than a submission to the animalistic becoming-finite of any body, remarks on exactly this issue.
163. Baudrillard's comments in this context are essentially descriptive. He correctly identifies that the concept of revolutionary desire in Deleuze and Guattari is naturalistic in a strong sense.
164. As evidenced by the claim that capitalism integrally opens onto revolutionary schizophrenia.
165. Baudrillard and Grant 1993, p. 36.
166. Ibid., p. 37.
167. Ibid.
168. J. Baudrillard, *The Spirit of Terrorism and Other Essays* (London: Verso, 2003), pp. 3–4.
169. Ibid., p. 15.
170. Ibid., p. 16.
171. On this note, Baudrillard argues that the ascendency of the positivity system calls up a kind of perverse pleasure, even in America, in the act; spelt out in the popularity of disaster movies for example. The events on 9/11 were seductive because, ironically given Baudrillard's antipathy to the problem of desiring-production in Deleuze and Guattari, they tapped into a deep vein of repressed desire.
172. Baudrillard 2003, pp. 16–17.
173. Ibid., p. 22.
174. S. Zizek, *Welcome to the Desert of the Real: Five Essays on September 11 and Related Dates* (London: Verso, 2002); Baudrillard 2003, pp. 23, 75.
175. Baudrillard 2003, pp. 28–29.
176. Ibid., p. 18.
177. Ibid., p. 58.
178. Ibid., p. 73.
179. Ibid., pp. 80–81.
180. Ibid., p. 82.
181. Ibid., p. 32.
182. Baudrillard argues it was germane to the force of the act that it was the World Trade Center and not the White House which collapsed – affirming that it was the pillars of global capitalism which were the target, not simply the American nation-state. The Twin Towers are symbols in what he terms a weak sense, of deathless positivity of the capitalist real. This distinction between strong and weak senses of the symbolic is curious. The Twin Towers apparently act as the perfect visual nexus, or nerve centre, for the symbolic strike of the terrorists to have the maximal effect, but this has little to do with the true force of the event. For Baudrillard, these weakly symbolic features are only a sideshow to the 'symbolic in the strong sense' connotations: 9/11 was evental because it remobilised death in a system that thought it had comprehensively ejected it.
183. See Gane 1991, p. 133.
184. Lotringer (in Baudrillard 2007, p. 110) asks if, for Baudrillard, the political is simply 'the art of not occupying a position yourself, but creating a void for others to rush into'. Baudrillard responds that politics is always an optical illusion the secret is a mobilisation of ambiguity and duplicity (following Machiavelli) so as to 'throw the others into space'. The symbolic exchange of death is precisely this gesture, whereby the terrorist forces the state to work as its partner, causing the implosion of the social (p. 113). Baudrillard's theory, if we could say it has a politics, operates on this field; seeking to rigorously 'cut itself off from any system of reference' (p. 121). This is

theory understood as a political suicide game (p. 118), in which theory attempts to make itself disappear and drag hyperreality down with it. Baudrillard sees himself as a master of the art of theoretical disappearance, to implode hyperreality with the suicide of pure theory (pp. 119–120). Baudrillard never, however, departs from the field of theory to enter political reality. He rejects categorically any idea of judging theory, as Deleuze and Guattari do, on criterion of 'What can you do with that?'; his work is pure antiproduction as transpolitics (p. 123). It is here, naturally, that Deleuze and Guattari's account, and its fidelity to a politically productive concept of death and desire, gleams with continuing (surplus-transversal) value. Baudrillard simply pays insufficient attention to questions of political creativity.

185. Baudrillard 2003, p. 34.
186. Ibid., p. 32.
187. M. Hardt and A. Negri, *Empire*. Cambridge, MA: Harvard University Press, 2001.
188. See J. Baudrillard, "The Violence of the Global," in *The Spirit of Terrorism and Other Essays* (London: Verso, 2003).
189. Baudrillard 2007, p. 104.
190. The argument of Aries 1976.
191. Baudrillard and Grant 1993, p. 127.
192. Baudrillard 2003.
193. Baudrillard 1993, p. 98.
194. In their terms, mistaking the contemporary difference in regime between capitalist social-production and desiring-production for their nonidentity in nature.
195. Baudrillard 2003, p. 58.
196. J. Reid, *The Biopolitics of the War on Terror: Life Struggles, Liberal Modernity and the Defence of Logistical Societies* (Manchester: Manchester University Press, 2006).
197. B. Massumi, "Potential Politics and the Primacy of Pre-emption," *Theory & Event* 10, no. 2 (2007), p. 14.
198. 'The situation is objectively one in which the only certainty is that threat will emerge where it is least expected. This is because what is ever-present is not a particular threat or set of threats, but the potential for still more threats to emerge without warning. The global situation is not so much threatening as threat generating: threat-o-genic . . . Objective uncertainty is as directly an ontological category as an epistemological one. The threat is known to have the ontological status of indeterminate potentiality' (ibid., p. 13).
199. Baudrillard 2003, p. 59.

4 Terror

Human bomb

The consciousness of political struggle as integrally prone to suicidal commitment is antithetical to the liberal imagination. Its most cherished assumptions regarding human individuals' pursuit of self-interest are nonetheless disturbed by the human bomb.[1] By identifying organisational logics standing behind it, this practice can become one amongst a plethora of violent means by which collectives pursue rational ends.[2] Suicide bombing is certainly a highly effective tool from this point of view: self-guiding, uncomplicated, inexpensive, and uncompromising.[3] The willingness to die combined with the broaching of taboos on targeting goes some way to countering any advantage held by an opponent.[4] Tactical utility is matched by strategic functionality.[5] Suicide bombings clearly often occur in organised campaigns as part of a coercive strategy of national liberation.[6] Its propaganda value, in this context, can be impressive, setting off affective cascades amongst diverse audiences, but it is clear that retrospective political payoffs are highly uncertain.[7] This uncertainly follows from the presence of multiple audiences, mirrored by a multiplicity of organisational aims,[8] often operating simultaneously; from retaliation, revenge, and frustration, to intergroup competition, or rivalry between family groups and individual.[9] The complex social networks in which all political organisations are embedded overdetermines any decision to deploy a human bomb.[10] In other words, even at the organisational level, suicide bombings occur in a 'complex cauldron' of calculation and affect.[11]

Utilitarian explanations of suicide bombing clearly reach their limit with the question of why individuals might desire participation. Grooming, indoctrination or brainwashing are common concepts deployed in this context to recognise the ways in which organisations construct the pool of candidates.[12] Organisations often do carefully select participants, train them, and provide economically for their families. They ensure social capital is ascribed to the martyred individual, praising them on posters and websites, and ensure families accrue these incorporeal benefits. In some cases organisations play a role in creating 'martyrdom videos', a function of which is to render it difficult for volunteers to back out.[13] Leadership worship[14] is also important in other cases.[15] It is implicit that organisations must, however, find fertile grounds in which to work. A leader's charisma may be an aid to encouraging participation, but it is implausible to posit this as the only actant driving participation. Political scientists thus commonly assume that nonrational and as such, nonpolitical vulnerabilities are required to explain why an individual might kill themselves; no matter how politically rational the act is deemed to be from the organisation's point of view. Consequently, accounts affirming the rationality of the practice implicitly or explicitly lean on accounts of the underlying individual, ideological and social structural conditions which make the suicide in suicide bombing possible.

One approach has been to map psychological 'risk factors that predict suicidal behaviour' onto human bombers.[16] Clearly in many cases personal tragedy has influenced decision-making.[17] But understanding the 'why' of suicide bombing requires appreciation of a wide variety of possible individual motivations, from loss of home in Palestine,[18] to rape at checkpoints in Sri Lanka or the torture and killing of a husband or brother in Chechnya by the security services.[19] Inasmuch as trauma clearly does not necessarily lead to suicide bombing, this could never lead to a predictable profile. In openness to trauma, as in all else, individual suicide bombers seem psychologically indistinguishable from society at large.[20] This is mirrored by the results of studies which test for structural determinants like low education[21] or poverty.[22] On a global scale the individual specificity of suicide bombers is even more striking.[23] In the face of this variance, research has turned to wider structures for explanation of the phenomenon. Suicide bombing has increasingly come to be seen as a social syndrome as much as an organisational tool.[24] For sociologists examining Palestine, Chechnya, Sri Lanka or Turkey, where sustained campaigns of human bombing have occurred, collective frustration and humiliation, deriving from the experience of regular and long-lasting occupation by what is perceived to be external power clearly play an important role. The desperate social situation, collective trauma, and a sense of helplessness establish conditions under which human bombers can appear.[25] Amongst other things, they are assumed to render a religious account of life after death more appealing. What is emphasised in these literatures is the manner in which suicide bombing occurs as a sociopolitical symptom of conditions that the society as a whole suffers,[26] as an expression of latent frustration built up under occupation.[27] Repeated humiliating experiences at checkpoints, for example, create fertile conditions for the emergence of suicide bombing within a social formation.[28] Socially entrenched patterns of loyalty directed at the community or 'fictive kin'[29] also play a role, as they do in all sacrificial forms.[30] Grievance experienced vicariously and a sense of solidarity with the community allow suicide bombings to be interpreted, as they often are by their enactors, as an assertion of will to resist the sense of a community under assault or suffering sustained humiliation.[31] In this turn to a repressive or violent context suffered by the community at large, the suicide bomber is framed in symptomatic terms as emerging from conditions of extreme repression or violence. In such a case, any suicidal desire in suicide bombing cannot be conceptualised as political in any but a radically proscribed fashion, as a structural product of extant conditions. Clearly, however, not every instance can be satisfactorily linked to a sustained experience of colonial or postcolonial occupation.[32]

In search of alternative explanations, authors chart the genealogy of martyrdom within the history of particular faiths, explaining suicide bombing by reference to its ideational context. Islam certainly has a tradition of martyrdom as deep as Christianity's, derived, in the Shia tradition, from the death of Hussein, which may be drawn on to construct the legitimacy of suicide bombings.[33] The inevitable next step has been allocating Islam itself with an explanatory value, in carrying 'murder-by-suicide script' exclusive to the Islamic world.[34] Rapoport's distinction between sacred and political terrorism has been influential in this context. Suicidal violence is, Rapoport famously argued, peculiar to sacred terror. What is crucial is the "transcendent source of holy terror."[35] Unlike the utilitarian character of political terrorism, for sacred terror aims and means are set in advance. This means sacred terrorism tends to put a far "lower premium on the assailants risk."[36] Rapoport does note, somewhat curiously given the thrust of his argument, that this does not preclude the use of what might be termed suicidal-like methods by modern political terrorists, like the Russian anarchist group *Narodnaya Volya* – whose preferred method, a hand-thrown bomb, required such intimacy as to almost guarantee death or capture. This, of course, suggests that whilst it is clearly impossible to deny the religious dimensions of many suicide-bombings, exclusive focus on that religious aspect serves to efface the intrinsic cross-over between "Holy Terror" and the political.[37] Profound commitment to some kind of 'transcendent' belief, whether nationalist or/and religious in content, is central to much, if not all, political violence; the question which remains to be addressed is precisely how such profound belief goes 'suicidal' and how it can be thought politically once it has done so.

The concept of Islamofascist ideology has emerged in this context.[38] The assumption implicit to this concept is that the willingness to commit murder while killing oneself is necessarily found only within totalitarian formulations of any ideational structure, mirroring the patterns of ideological topology underpinning twentieth-century state totalitarianisms. The global jihad is characterised by such an ideology, and as such is like the movements of the last century, fascism and Stalinism, which displayed similarly suicidal lines.[39] Clearly the referent Islam cannot account for why a suicidal line emerges within particular assemblages, given suicide bombing appears in non-Islamic and nonreligious groups like the Sri Lankan Liberation Tigers of Tamil Eelam (LTTE) and the Kurdish Kurdistan Workers' Party (PKK).[40] Indeed, a multiplicity of ideas and beliefs, both religious and secular or nationalist, seem to go into the justification and motivation of suicide missions.[41] It seems logical to infer that any belief or combination of beliefs, sufficiently passionately held, can motivate suicide bombing. The problem is mapping how such passions emerge.[42]

Studies thus turn to sociomimetic processes. In this context the idea of a 'cult of martyrdom'[43] seeks to explain how, in Palestine for example, the practice spread to the nationalist out of the religious groups by taking on a curiously independent social significance: What must be identified, in this approach, is not a set of structural predeterminants, but precisely how 'suicide-bombings . . . gather their own apocalyptic momentum' within a particular social formation.[44] Suicide bombing clearly imprints on social forms and practices, with teens idolising martyrs in

Palestine rather than sportsmen, and children playing games imitating them.⁴⁵ The community thus immanently legitimates the grounds upon which suicide can be utilised as a weapon. Martyrdom is a social construct; the community must be willing to make this construction if it is to have any legitimacy.⁴⁶ This is to say, suicide bombing only has content in relation to the architecture of meaningfulness within in which its agents are embedded.⁴⁷ When Hage describes the practice as bound into a desire to 'generate meanings for life', he is mapping the construction of a suicidal line in Palestine: a trajectory of fulfilment pinned to self-abolition.⁴⁸ Such social machines precisely have a life of their own, for the addition of a suicidal charge supplies its own intensity to their motion across the social and cultural milieu.⁴⁹ Suicide bombings are thus often interpreted as a social disease spreading in its host. The practice has displayed a powerful ability to capture and redeploy shared meanings.⁵⁰

The social scientific literature on the causes of suicide bombing is increasingly characterised by recognition of a high level of complexity or multidimensionality.⁵¹ Works assemble the multiplicity of variables into a complex 'mosaic', to incorporating organisational, individual, ideological-religious, social and historical factors.⁵² Suicide bombing clearly has multiple causal dimensions which interact and assemble and are not equally relevant in different cases. Heterogenesis applies here, given different combinations of factors may be implicated in suicide bombing at different geographical or temporal locations – such that a suicide bombing in Sri Lanka might be explained by reference to individual trauma, signalling to resist occupation, leadership-worship and organisational-grooming, whilst a suicide bombing in Palestine involves the input of a socially disseminated cult of martyrdom and religious motivation more or less absent from the Sri Lankan case. To posit that the 'anti-essentialist current' in contemporary social scientific thinking has yet to penetrate terrorism analysis would be to neglect the evident complexity of much of the literature dealing with the causes of suicide bombing.⁵³ Essentialist reduction is certainly to be found, but it is hardly universal or determinant.⁵⁴ Suicide bombing is viewed as far from a 'uniform' phenomenon, and most authors identify the contingent dynamics of its dispersion.⁵⁵ The practice is recognised to have spilled over to neighbouring areas, as within Lebanon or between Lebanon and Palestine directly through training camps or indirectly through emulation.⁵⁶ Actualisation in specific contexts is dependent on a number of contingently present factors, varying from location to location, as it 'taps into latent angers', for example.⁵⁷ Multidimensional approaches thus tend to remain symptomatological in their approach to the constitutive suicidal dimension of the practice.⁵⁸ Political calculation may define the utility of suicide bombing to an organisation, but its particular suicidal actualisations will be dependent on specific vulnerabilities which are understood in explicitly nonpolitical terms. Given the flexible utility of the practice to organisations, and its links to multiple overlapping rationales, authors increasingly conclude that the symptomatic conditions are the real drivers for suicide.

The likelihood is that there are an unlimited number of potential combinations of organisational rationalisations for suicide bombing if sufficient facilitatory conditions are given (say the existence of extreme repression, a socially pervasive cult of martyrdom, and an adjacent group that is already utilising the practice).[59] This seems a classic example of overdetermination. Suicide is evidently the symptom of multiple causes. As such, the danger is that Talal Asad's claim that 'the uniqueness of suicide bombing resides . . . not in its essence but in its contingent circumstance' is increasingly recognised as accurate, but this insight is purchased at the price of a politics.[60] The dichotomy of local symptom (structure) and organisational rationality (agency) within accounts from complexity displaces political theorisation of the act itself. Given the variety in its sufficient conditions, the emergence of suicide bombing in so many different contexts for so many reasons, the opposite hypothesis is surely as compelling; desires which reach all the way to their nihilation are integral to the nature of the political as such.

The despot

If the primitive is rendered prone to 'hysteria' by the double bind in which he finds himself, the despotic regime is a 'manic depressive'. The despot's singular nightmare is a schizophrenic decoding,[61] so it aims to preclude 'once and for all, the prospect of a final discharge'.[62] Despotism is intrinsically counter-revolutionary: it seeks to close off all avenues for desires' deterritorialisation.[63] In pursuit of surety, all debts are rendered infinite. A single line of credit now runs from every point to the apex of the pyramid.[64] Where death was inscribed on individual bodies prior to the state, debts could flow between tribes under the guidance of a deceased ancestral authority; now the debts are inscribed in stone.[65] This new inscription is no less morbid, as a 'debt of the existence of the subjects themselves'. Death is overcoded, so as to be given a singular meaning.[66] Monotheism is always on the horizon of despotism. The political theologies of Schmitt and Kantorowicz suffered from a tremendous shortness of sight. They placed monotheistic religion at the source of all modern political concepts, where of course the despotic state is the origin and source of monotheism as an idea.[67] Monotheisms are creatures of the despotic diagram, of its authoritative overcoding of death as a universal debt. All religions are simply chapters in the history of the political assemblage of death and desire.[68] Politics is logically and historically prior to theology.

The primitives had every reason to always be on guard against the rise of a despot, who would overcode all debts and suck all surplus value up in to a machine of horrific transcendent unity.[69] Indeed, their reliance on a filiative coding of death prefigures the nightmare of a singular deity.[70] The Urstaat sets up the first centralised structure of governance. Residence, both physical and psychic, is fixed under threat of murder and damnation.[71] Despotism replaces the full body of the primitive with a paranoiac emptiness; a machine of antiproduction demanding tribute up to and including life itself.[72] The reason for its absolutism is that the despot lives in terror of any escape whatsoever.[73] The despotic regime is thus the definitive regime of terror – its model of law hinges on a double coding of death.[74] Punishment according to despotic law is always a form of vengeance enacted upon that terror itself. Vengeance is 'the juridical form assumed by the infinite debt', a rage 'exercised in advance' upon a passive citizenry in terror that it might become active.[75] Despotism functions by categorically transforming death from principle of flux into principle of stability and order. This is an extraordinary achievement; the creation of a death = lack principle. It is in this sense that the despot is the death instinct personified by Deleuze and Guattari.[76] The despot codes death under an authoritarian instinct, so as to preclude the consciousness of mortality as permanent revolution; fear of death becomes the means to order all things.

For Michel Foucault, 'sovereign power', that definitive possession of the despot, is a 'right of the sword', founded on the right of the despot to kill, or to allow individuals to live, according to its will.[77] Under sovereign orders, Foucault argued, the citizen is always neutral and passive with regards to his or her life and death. It is the sovereign who makes the juridical decision with regards to his status as one or the other; by exercising, or not, his right to kill.[78] He speaks and citizens die (or stays silent and they are allowed to live). At least potentially this means that for Foucault self-destruction offers a limited strategy of resistance to sovereign power.[79] Foucault showed some interest on this subject, commenting on the individual and collective self-sacrifices mobilised in historical struggles against sovereign power in Tunisia and Iran, asking 'What on earth is it that can set off in an individual the desire, the capacity, and the possibility of an absolute sacrifice without our being able to recognize or suspect the slightest ambition or desire for power and profit?'[80] In later works, Foucault developed this problematic by suggesting that in a condition of complete sovereign control (an occupation or extreme despotism) 'power can be exercised only insofar as the other has the option of killing himself, or of killing the other person'.[81] This offers suicide as a kind of political antithesis to sovereignty's murderous order-word. The politics of suicide seem to engage a potentially *anti*sovereign endeavour in as much as it challenges sovereignty's monopolistic right over the decision on death; a brute rejection of sovereign authority over death and affirmation of an alternative sovereignty in death. The implication is that if a monopoly on death is where power is rooted then chosen, death is how it might be challenged. The problem here is that of course one can always commit suicide and escape the despotic order, but this can do no more than confirm his authority: a debt called in. As Esposito points out, there is no juridical mechanism for simply taking back individual autonomy from a sovereign that commands death in the name of life's immunisation from it.[82]

In *A Thousand Plateaus*, the relationship between politics, death and resistance under the despot is clarified through the concept of the 'order-word'. The order-word is the operator which defines a language as either major or minor, as releasing becomings (flights) or operating as a mechanism of antiproductive domination (enantiomorphism). The order-word is the despotic signifier (this is this and that is that; disagree and you are finished). It is death transmuted from principle of revolutionary productivity into a principle of obedience:

> The order-word... always implies a death sentence, even if it has been considerably softened, becoming symbolic, initiatory, temporary, etc. Order-words

bring immediate death to those who receive the order, or potential death if they do not obey, or a death they must themselves inflict, take elsewhere. A fathers orders to his son, 'you will do this,' 'you will not do that,' cannot be separated from the little death sentence the son experiences on the point of his person.[83]

That this is the definitive despotic function is visible in the tendency for languages to coalesce into dominant modes. 'The unity of language is fundamentally political . . . [as in] a power takeover by a dominant language that at times advances along a broad front, and at times swoops down on diverse centres simultaneously.'[84] The Urstaat model principally reproduces itself in grammar and syntax. The function of the Urstaat model at the linguistic level is as a power of constants, of homogenisation, centralisation. Overcoding through linguistic centralisation is common in actual despotic systems, whereby minor languages are displaced, effaced, left untaught, and a major language disseminated, enforced and programmed into public education.

Resistance to the domination (*pouvoir*) of a major language is never a matter of simple opposition. Rather, the power (*puissance*) of the minor language is indissociable from the major form it seeks to resist. No major language is unattended by, or mixed with, multiple processes of variation at its edges.[85] There is a necessary becoming-minoritarian which operates at the fringes of any dominant language form which is the key to understanding the resistance that is associated with death. Rather than viewing the major/minor distinction as dividing languages from each other, there are major and minor processes to be discovered in any language or system of coding. Likewise, no minority language can function without vectors of centralisation, order and coherence upon which shared meaningfulness is based. The order-word, as definitive function of the Urstaat model, is the constant rule of encoding which allow language to exist as opposed to 'continuous variation'.[86] Yet this encoding operates only by opposition to the processes of variation which preexist it. Within any language we have usages or functions which may be major or minor, which move towards enclosure and unification, and which open to variation and deviance.[87] What is in question here is a creative autodestruction; submitting a language to minor usage involves making oneself stammer and thereby proliferate.[88] One submits a major language to a minor usage by destabilising its referents. A minor usage is the deterritorialisation of the major. The implication here is that resistance never takes the form of binary opposition, but of unfolding the major.[89] Deleuze and Guattari make clear that a 'majority assumes a state of power and domination, not the other way around'.[90] Linguistic unification is a marker of state processes which enclose, whereas 'all becoming is minoritarian'.[91] The order-word is thus the source of a minoritarian consciousness, and all creativity.[92] Becoming-revolutionary is becoming-minor; what we see here is a nondialectical ontology of liberation understood as deterritorialising the major. Even a sovereign language is always subject to a double movement; becoming minor, producing continuous variation (deterritorialisation) and becoming major, so extracting a constant (reterritorialisation).

The order-word is this 'double direction'.⁹³ The first aspect of the order-word is its despotic function. The order-word enacts what Elias Canetti called enantiomorphosis. Enantiomorphosis refers to the use of death to prohibit transformation. The Urstaat is

> a regime that involves a hieratic and immutable master who at every moment legislates by constants, prohibiting or strictly limiting metamorphosis, giving figure clear and stable contours, setting forms in opposition two by two and requiring subjects to die in order to pass from one form to the other.⁹⁴

The despotic regime is thus enantiomorphic par excellence; death is transmuted from principle of danger and variation into principle of control through prohibition. This is the major function in language – 'death as the expressed of the statement'. Death becomes

> a pure act, a pure transformation that enunciation fuses with the statement, the sentence. That man is dead . . . You are already dead when you receive the order-word . . . in effect, death is everywhere, as that ideal, uncrossable boundary separating bodies, their forms, and states, and as the condition, even initiatory, even symbolic, through which a subject must pass in order to change its form or state.⁹⁵

The major function of language is directly correlated with the way death is utilised in the despotic regime to give shape to the body in space and time. Deleuze and Guattari quote Canetti as saying that 'death itself, the strictest of all boundaries, is what is interposed between classes'.⁹⁶ This is the way in which death is harnessed by despotic order-words as a certifier of form, stability and identity. Taking command of death, a major language hopes to quell its vectors of transformation.

The despot dictates what can and must, and what cannot and must not be said if there is to be meaning.

> But, the order-word is also something else, inseparably connected: it is like a warning cry or a message to flee. It would be an oversimplification to say that flight is a reaction against the order-word; rather, it is included in it, as its other face in a complex assemblage, its other component.⁹⁷

This other aspect of the order-word is its line of flight. This is that aspect of the order-word which allows a revolutionary unfolding; releasing variables 'in a new state, that of continuous variation'. This is not, however, a matter of 'eliminating death'. Rather, death must be made into 'a variation of itself' by way of a 'passage to the limit'. In this way the variables of a language are set free in a movement of metamorphosis, which causes 'them to reach or overstep the limits of their figures'.⁹⁸ Death is the marker of transformation; a vector of absolute deterritorialisation in the sovereign language itself. This other aspect of the order-word is the capacity for a 'movement that pushes language to its own limits'.[99] Becoming-minor is the order-word being swept up by its own use of death, reclaiming death from the sovereign in the form of his transformation, mutation and destabilisation. Becoming-minor is thus directly linked to death:

> the question was not how to elude the order-word but how to elude the death sentence it envelops, how to develop its power of escape ... how to maintain or draw out the revolutionary potentiality of the order-word.[100]

The duality of the order-word is central to the revolutionary potential of language, but it is equally central to any concrete political act against despotic power. The major or Urstaat model, even at the linguistic level, is crossed by the forces of morbid creativity, lines of flight, of becoming-minor: 'In the order-word, life must answer the answer of death, not by fleeing, but by making flight act and create'.[101] To respond to the enantiomorphic function, death must be returned to its creative function. Resistance is mortality become a means-of-passage. Any revolutionary-becoming must work to 'put the system to flight', and it can do so only by taking flight itself – turning the despotic order-word into a pass word: 'There are pass words beneath order-words.'[102] Resistance to despotism is making death take flight.[103] The fact that death is the essence of sovereign power means it is crucially limited – precisely by the fact that all that can be demanded in the end is death. One may posit suicide as the blunt subversion of the order-word ('I die when I choose'), but more than the structural antithesis of the despotic mode is clearly necessary for a nonsovereign politics.[104] A revolutionary politics cannot simply offer death against death. Such an opposition is too easily a form of tribute. Becoming-revolutionary, qua becoming minoritarian, requires setting the order-word to flight as a pass word: Resistance is deterritorialisation.

Liberal suicides

Liberal state capitalisms explicitly locate their authority in the determinant value or priority furnished to individual life and human rights. Whilst we may certainly find traces of archaic sovereign discourses within today's liberal states, such bodies claim legitimacy in relation to their maximisation and support for the life of their populations through democracy, welfare and technological progress. Does this mean that a despotic order-word no longer organises contemporary states?

Michel Foucault famously argued that we live in a political order governed by the liberal logics of biopower rather than sovereignty.[105] Biopower signifies an approach to the problematic of government or governmentality which stands in direct contrast to the early modern discourse of order based on the coercive killing power or decisional authority of the sovereign.[106] Biopower is a diagram for 'the acquisition of power over man insofar as man is a living being';[107] an assemblage of discourses, practices, architectural forms, subjectivities, institutions, statements and propositions. It is a configuration, in other words, of heterogeneous elements which institutes a power-knowledge formation, resulting in a new approach to government centred on the administration and management of the life of populations.¹⁰⁸ It regulates and attempts to perfect the healthy circulation of individual bodies, economic flows and rhythms of reproduction and disease in the population. The population is thus understood as a living mass to be regularized, monitored and supervised, so that the causes of imbalance that enter into it can be controlled.¹⁰⁹ Biopolitics thus entails a fundamentally numerical representation of mankind, the life of which is understood via measurable norms and averages, public health and risk. These technologies of representation allow the life of the population to be administered to ensure its most ideal and full manifestation, compensating for the dangers that are natural and internal to its constitutive processes, so as to pursue an 'overall equilibrium'.¹¹⁰

The central mechanism of government shifts from the sovereign capacity to deal out death to those it chooses and to allow others to live accordingly, onto the capacity to 'to make live and to let die': to give life to its population through constant regulation and securing practices, or to leave a segment of the population to its natural fate by withholding its attention.¹¹¹ What follows is the 'famous gradual disqualification of death'.¹¹² Under sovereign rule, death had been at the centre of power, its very authorisation, not only as the moment of powers activity but also as the moment of a transmission from sovereign authority to divine authority.¹¹³ Under biopolitical modes of governance, death is the end of life, and the end, therefore, of power's reach. Death is when 'the individual escapes all power'.¹¹⁴ As Foucault puts it in his lectures: 'Power no longer recognises death, Power ignores death.' Death is literally 'outside the power relationship'.¹¹⁵

Liberal government is expected to take responsibility for the becoming of the life of its population. The liberal concept of a right to life explicitly renders illegitimate any right to demand the death of individuals, except under highly restricted criteria. This seems to distinguish liberal biopower fundamentally from the collectivising sacrificial coding of death that reveals sovereignty as a political theology. Authors drawing from Foucault have argued that biopolitical or liberal modes of governance are increasingly globalised. The functioning of biopolitical rationales are found in the administrations 'for life' of the World Health Organization, attempts at regulation of the increasingly globalised labour market, or even in the military reproduction of liberal democratic states advocated by the neoconservative project, and in logics of development.¹¹⁶ Biopower and its identification of life as the central concern of global governance find particularly clear enunciation in the peculiarities of liberal state security policy.¹¹⁷ Suicide bombing, for example, is understood as a contagion in the population that needs surgical attention through various strategies for affecting its complex sociohistorical facilitators.¹¹⁸ This calls up administration of the populations in question. In the counter-insurgency campaigns of Iraq and Afghanistan, a similar rationale leads to emphasis on infrastructure building, as the 'infrastructure of life' and population protection.¹¹⁹

The philosopher John Seery suggested that Foucault can be taken to imply that 'suicide might be viewed as a promising strategy of *individual* resistance against biopower' inasmuch as it offers a private means of escape from its regulatory reach, but because biopower has definitively relegated death to the margins of its diagram, such an individual act of liberation falls short of even an antithetical politics.[120] Death is irrelevant to political power in an age dominated by biopolitical governmentalities, leaving us in what Seery terms a dead end for political theorisation.[121] It is argued that sovereignty and biopower are thus essentially incommensurable diagrams; the former roots its authority in the coding of death, the other in seeking to approach a zero-death regime. Biopolitics would then place any subversive (nonsovereign) politics of suicide in question. This correlates with the suggestion that suicide bombings must be seen as the enactment of a fundamentally outmoded politics.[122] The fundamental character of contemporary (bio) power suggests that we might view suicide bombing as the definitive archaism, a residuum of a passé politics fruitlessly seeking to negate the inexorable progression of life-affirming modernity.[123]

Challenging any claim to the contemporary apolitics of suicide Foucault famously charted the hideous combination of life politics with death politics during the historical constitution of modern order. Refusing any simple dichotomy between an increasingly global administrative life politics and a passé sovereign death politics, Foucault argued that despite being a zero-death power in essence, biopower retains some morbid features in practice. Biopolitical states evidently do not refuse the right to kill. In fact, biopolitical modes of governance radicalise the art of killing to previously unimaginable levels, through the development of the technological capacity to kill life itself with nuclear or biological weapons of mass destruction.[124] The power of death is thus smuggled back into the regime of biopower. At a certain point in history, Foucault argued, racism intervenes to justify the killings that modern nation-states engage in.[125] War is made to serve the becoming of life by ensuring that the enemy is understood in terms of an encroaching threat to species health. His death becomes essential to maintaining the health of the home population. The death of the 'bad race' is understood to 'make life in general healthier'.[126] Such logics come to their radical extreme with the totalitarianisms of the twentieth century, but are embedded in the genealogy of all biopolitical (and thus liberal) governance: 'Once the state functions in the biopower mode, racism alone can justify the murderous function of the state'.[127] Whilst biopower seeks primarily to regulate and maintain the health of its own population, it constantly engages in murderous war against those it deems enemies. As such, the new right of power over life 'does not erase the old right . . . [of power over death] . . . but does penetrate it, permeate it'. Biopower does not follow sovereignty; rather the two discourses or governmentalities overlap and interplay.[128]

Giorgio Agamben,[129] developing and radicalising this point, argued that the conception of life administrative biopower as a separate discourse entering into, or overlapping with, death-dealing sovereignty is deeply problematic. His widely discussed argument is that Foucault failed to sufficiently develop the fundamental relationship between the two that circulates around a decision on where death, and life, should be. The 'thanatopolitical' decision on death remains, for Agamben, the ontotheological heart of political praxis.[130] Agamben argued, following Schmitt, that politics has always functioned through making an exception – deciding who is under the law and who lies outside of it – but that this juridical exception has always been intimately bound to the designation of life itself. The 'bios' of the political community, where life is pursued and administered, is predicated on the construction of thanatopolitical spaces which lie outside the bios. Indeed it is, ironically given that discourses of human rights are so often mobilised in opposition to the morbid logics of sovereign power, precisely in these marginal spaces that the concept of life itself, as a life that is fundamentally exposed to death, is first established.[131] This reaffirms the sacrificial institution of political sovereignty, inasmuch as the included-exclusion of those thrown out of the juridical order defines the bounds of political community, and constitutes subjects as political by drawing their living limits under sovereignty. For Agamben 'inclusion of bare life in the political real' is the concealed nucleus of sovereignty; the production of a biopolitical body thus constitutes 'the original activity of sovereign power'.[132] The politics of life and the politics of death occur in spaces that are necessarily mutually delineated. The sacrificial terms of political theology are integral to the operation of biopower.

In a totalitarian state biopolitics collapses into what Agamben terms a full thanatopolitics. Death follows closely at the heels of any life form under biopolitical totalitarianism – any digression from the norm is a step into thanatopolitical space. The death camps represent the absolute expression of this 'pure space of exception', constituting a life that was a living death.[133] Yet, Agamben argues, the globalisation of biopolitical governmentality also clearly entails an obscured thanatopolitics. Indeed, the line 'marking the point at which the decision on life becomes a decision on death, and biopolitics can turn into thanatopolitics . . . no longer appears today as a stable border dividing two clearly distinct zones'.[134] In our liberal age this 'line is in motion' opening multiple moments for the global political production of bare lives and death spaces. He observes that today the exception increasingly 'becomes the norm'; as the possibility of being constitutively excluded from the bios spreads throughout and inhabits every corner of the global order.[135] As a consequence, all over the world, 'politics is now literally the decision concerning the unpolitical' which forms thanatopolitics.[136] Spaces of 'letting die', such as refugee camps, failed states, and migrant holding centres, can certainly be just as horrific as the direct activity of killing.[137] Liberalism does not refuse the right to kill, but rather justifies killing by identifying certain (diseased/unpolitical) bodies in the global space as integrally threatening to population health. In this sense, for Agamben, the death camp is the 'hidden paradigm' of liberal late-modernity, where 'the absolute capacity of the subjects' bodies to be killed forms the new political body of the west'.[138] Humanity is the liberal order-word, its limits voiced under an often occluded but nonetheless brutal death sentence. Life must be protected from, and by way of, its outliers – the human garbage or collateral damage of the politics of life which may be let-die.[139] Despite liberalism's promise of a global order rooted in the protection of human life, spaces spring up everywhere where life is reduced to a living death of relentless precarity.

Agamben also argued that the exposure of populations to death sows the seeds of a political life that radically escapes the grasp of power.[140] In the death camps, inhabitants were deprived of such basic humanity that they no longer registered any difference between fact and law, the SS and the cold. This represents a 'silent form of resistance of sorts', founded in *zoē*, or life itself, to the horrors enacted. In the closure of sense, an absolute rejection takes place that forces us to reassess life itself as carrying an innate ethicopolitical force.[141] Inasmuch as spaces of juridical exception circulate the globe – in refugee camps, asylum centres, and failed states, where life and death are brought together in the bare life of their inhabitants – for Agamben, a new register of the political begins to emerge, a 'bios that is its own zoē', a politics rooted in the very being of life in the face of death.[142]

Explicitly following Agamben, Elizabeth Dauphinee argues that under regimes of biopower '[d]eath is depoliticised. . . . [and] . . . [k]illing takes place without responsibility, celebration or remorse'. This functions to hide killing by the sovereign from view, despite being the constant and obscene underbelly of sovereignty.[143] In late-modernity, desubjectization, through reducing individuals to bare life, characterises this work of biopower at its definitive margins. On rare occasions, Dauphinee argues, such biopolitical exclusions may be resisted by suicide, which subverts power by rendering death explicit as its consequence.[144] In certain circumstances, Dauphinee argues, suicide can form 'the limit condition of resistance' by exposing the politics of death at the core of biopower.[145] Achille Mbembe brings this same point to bear on Palestinian suicide bombing.[146] Mbembe argues that the idea of an acceptable death is historically conditioned by racial differentiation, as is most clearly manifest in the colonial context. Because of the triple loss of home, body and political rights, colonial situations produce a form of slave life. 'Slave life, in many ways, is a form of death-in-life', closely mirroring Agamben's account of the individual reduced to bare life in the death camps.[147] Indeed, Mbembe argues, with Arendt, that the biopolitical exceptions identified by Foucault and Agamben in European totalitarianism are in fact examples of the colonial logic returning home to roost.[148] Conditions of colonial occupation are locations of what Mbembe terms necropower and necropolitics.[149] The half-life and madness of colonial occupation leaves an opening into what Mbembe calls, following Bataille, an ecstatic politics, in which 'death in the present is the mediator of redemption . . . it is experienced as a release from terror and bondage'.[150] Because death is all that is left to the colonised, it becomes the final representation of living freedom, and a means to subvert the regime which dominates them. For Mbembe, Palestine is a true 'death world' in which the 'lines between resistance and suicide, sacrifice and redemption, martyrdom and freedom are blurred'.[151] Palestinian suicide bombings express the synonymy of 'resistance and self-destruction' under necropower.[152] Death here becomes the very expression of Agamben's resistant politics of life itself. The bare life of the body becomes no more than a weapon, and survival in the traditional sense is completely effaced from concern, or rather displaced into an eternal or imagined future.[153]

Within the spaces created by biopower's exclusions, death is the only option available to agents seeking the political. In such conditions they must choose death and invest it with political meaning – making it a sacrificial register for indicting their exclusion. Suicide bombing is a gesture immanent to biopower, an act that reaches the political by bringing biopower to autocritique, revealing the sovereign exclusion that constitutes its politics of life. The Palestinian camp space is justified in explicitly biopolitical terms as essential to maintaining the security of the Israeli population; self-sacrifice witnesses the necropolitical exclusion underpinning the biopolitics of Israeli life. One may easily extend such an analysis to address exclusionary racial biopolitics in Sri Lanka or Turkey. Tamil or Kurdish nationalist campaigns of suicide bombing may be understood to derive political intelligibility from their exposure of the morbid exclusions underpinning Sinhalese or Turkish political life.

Diane Enns similarly argues, following Agamben, that the extreme limit of vulnerability has a strange power, and that under conditions of absolute occupation this comes to the fore. Under these conditions in Palestine the suicide bomber became the 'force that drives resistance'.[154] Enns is wary of romanticising the suicide bomber, but argues that when there is no other option, self-sacrifice is the only meaning available with which to resist, albeit in a crucially limited fashion. Self-sacrificial acts in Palestine, and elsewhere, represent the momentary empowerment of people under occupation, projecting out of their condition of utter domination. For Enns, the suicide bomber cannot be understood without reference to the urge of the colonised to regain dignity from within excluded space.[155] In this sense, for Enns, it is a limited political action, perhaps not a real resistance, but simply a refusal of the attribution of bare life. Enns argues that whilst suicide bombing can and should be ethically condemned, we must recognise the conditions of colonisation which allow such a figure to emerge, and as such the 'complicity of opponents' in their production.[156]

These accounts suggest that suicidal practices like suicide bombings have a politics inasmuch as the practice subjects the liberal prioritisation of life to critique by exposing its structural violence. Registers of suicidal resistance are politically intelligible inasmuch as biopower pretends to the refusal of a politics of death whilst covertly smuggling a morbid political theology back in. This suggests that it is liberalism's construction of a constitutive dichotomy between spaces where life is protected, and spaces where life may and indeed must be killed, which renders suicide bombing intelligible as a political practice. Necropolitics is the concrete signature of a sovereign political theology still in operation. The implication is that suicide bombing is a structural reaction to exclusion by liberal biopower, or rather, an inevitable product of the exception that it covertly maintains.[157] One may infer that the more liberal and or life-affirming a society claims to be, the more effective the political critique consciously or unconsciously embodied by the suicide bomber. Given Robert Pape's observation that the majority of suicide bombings are targeted at liberal democracies, this seems to have some empirical purchase.[158] Suicide bombings reveal the contradiction entailed in a liberal sovereign exclusion. Suicide bombing, irrupting out of radically excluded spaces, truly belong to liberal hypocrisy.[159] In this context, the contradiction entailed in claims, by liberal states, to locate their legitimacy in taking every reasonable precaution to protect life, whilst rendering open to death entire populations in Afghanistan and Pakistan from drone strikes, may be understood as spectacularly displayed by suicidal violence. This suggests that it is liberalism's construction of a constitutive dichotomy between spaces where life is protected and spaces where life may and indeed must be killed, which renders suicide bombing intelligible as a political practice.[160] By expressing, publically and violently, the murderous function of liberalism, suicide bombings act as political indictments of its hypocrisy. For such thinkers, suicide bombing is the reply to a biopower which reduces humans to the living dead – a zombie politics, declaiming political agency though reclaiming death from undeath. The scapegoat of power locates in his or her scapegoating the very capacity to resist. Given this idiomatic relationship, there must be some question as to how the practice could ever go beyond a structural capitulation or submission to the liberal order-word.

This is a point explicitly developed by Michael Hardt and Antonio Negri in reference to the insurgent use of suicide bombings against coalition troops in Iraq and Afghanistan. Challenging accounts that cast suicide bombing as 'the ultimate weapon against a system of total control', they situate suicidal methods within the biopolitical revolution in military affairs (RMA) that increasingly defines late modern global warfare.[161] In contrast to the preceding accounts, for Hardt and Negri, suicide bombing can only express the sovereign limit of liberal biopolitical governmentalities. Suicide bombing does not form any kind of substantive resistance, silent or otherwise, to contemporary biopower, precisely because it is the direct projection of the sovereign necropolitics inherent to that diagram.

Liberal soldiers are expected not only to fight but to transform the invaded population in places like Iraq and Afghanistan. Nation-building is the central, biopolitical justification for modern war. Soldiers are the highly trained agents of biopower at war. 'The body and brain of such a soldier, who incorporates the range of activities of biopower, must be preserved at all cost'.[162] The result is that war become decorporealised, at least on the side of a global liberal-capitalist 'empire'. The soldier is not supposed to die but to 'procreate' Western societies in the target population.[163] Troop casualty numbers becomes one of the most important factors to be minimised. This bodiless form of biopolitical war-making comes to be contradicted by suicide bombing?

> The suicide bomber is the dark opposite, the gory doppelganger of the safe bodiless soldier. Just when the body seemed to have disappeared from the battlefield with the no-soldiers-lost policy of the high technology military strategy, it comes back in all its gruesome, tragic reality. Both the RMA and the suicide bomber deny the body at risk that traditionally defines combat, the one guaranteeing its life and the other its death.[164]

Hardt and Negri situate the suicide bomber entirely within the problematic of the biopolitics of asymmetric warfare. The suicide bomber responds to biopower's attempt to make war into the production of liberal populations whilst devaluing the life being assimilated. This productive devaluation of the target populations lives calls up the suicide bomber as a kind of structural by-product of current military practice. The radically dichotomised life and death spaces created by the

RMA call up suicide bombing, but the practice is therefore purely negative or reactive, and therefore must be interpreted as limited in its political potentialities:

> The suicide bomber appears here once again as a symbol of the inevitable limitation and vulnerability of sovereign power; refusing to accept a life of submission, the suicide bomber turns life itself into a horrible weapon. This is the ontological limit of biopower in its most tragic and revolting form. Such destruction only grasps the passive, negative limit of sovereign power.[165]

This redirects us away from the possibility that suicide bombing truly obstructs power, by suggesting that suicide really is simply the limit of biopower, not its opposition. Such acts can only affirm the constitutive dichotomy of life (biopolitical) and death (necropolitical) spaces at the limit of 'humanitarian' power's operation. The order-word speaks, but it is not set to flight.

Hardt and Negri concur, therefore, with authors like Enns and Mbembe, that it is the particularly liberal claim to have abandoned the politics of death, whilst covertly smuggling it back in, that idiomatically supplies suicide bombing with their political intelligibility today. They argue, however, that this ensures that such acts can have no political productivity, or carry agency, beyond the structural expression of exclusion. Suicide bombing becomes political only in the most reactive and proscribed of senses. The suicide bomber responds to the precise methods of liberal warfare, but in this way simply constitutes biopower's 'gory doppelganger'[166] – a definitively nonproductive creature of the sovereign order-word still immanent to liberal governmentality. In this sense, the Agambenian frame leaves no possibility for a suicidal flight.

Terror and liberalism

Mohammad Siddique Khan, one of the British citizens who conducted the 7/7 suicide bombings in London, declared in his video suicide note a wish to speak in 'a language that you will understand'. There seems little reason to doubt that he aimed to reciprocate the gifts of liberal war, but we need not assume, with Agamben, that this is the last word on liberal antiproduction. Foucault never fully completed his interrogation of biopolitics; the concept contains ambiguities, particularly around its relationship to death, which require interpretation.[167] Foucault argued that an understanding of death 'as the end of life' is 'ignored' by biopower, but was no less clear that the life in question is seized as definitively mortal.[168] Liberal order entails an analytic of human finitude that is specific to it, a distinctive concern for the immanent government of the human qua mortal.[169] The political intelligibility and agency of suicide bombings like those in London is necessarily entangled with this definitively liberal necropolitics.

Liberal biopower entails a reproblematization of mortality that may be linked to, but is clearly distinct from, the sacrificial biopolitics of the sovereign exception. Foucault was clear that individual death as the end of life is ignored by biopower because it cannot be controlled or administered.[170] He also suggested, however, that an analytic of human finitude is integral to biopolitical governmentality. Foucault argued that biopower no longer views death in terms of a sudden or abrupt transformation; 'no longer something that suddenly swooped down on life – as in an epidemic. Death is increasingly understood as something permanent, something that slips into life, perpetually gnaws at it, diminishes it and weakens it'.[171] Death is no longer viewed through the lens of the plagues and catastrophes that 'haunted political powers ever since the middle ages'. Rather, death is reworked in terms of 'endemics, or in other words the form, nature, extension, duration and intensity of the illnesses prevalent in a population'.[172] Whilst ignoring death as the final end of discrete political subjects, which must be sacrificially redeemed, biopower remains operationally focused on the flows of mortality inherent to 'the biosociological processes characteristic of human masses'.[173] Mortality is understood as a constitutive force immanent to the life of those masses, and as such, precisely that which must be governed.[174] As Deleuze points out in his reading of Foucault, under biopower 'death becomes multiplied and differentiated in order to bestow on life the particular features and consequentially the truths, which life believes arise from resisting death.'[175] In other words, whilst death as the final horizon of individual life is certainly ignored as unadministrable and uncontrollable, the pressures of human mortality, viewed as a natural flow that power can measure, mathematize, coordinate and work against, so as to secure and in the process define the life of the population, remains the fundamental referent of biopower. The ontotheological concern for collective immortality, which defined religious and sovereign sacrifices, is thus displaced by an alternative political-theology of death in life, characterised by concern for fostering resilience to the immanent flows of morbidity abiding within human populations.

Death's supposed occlusion under biopower marks the birth of a logistics of mortality. The population is viewed as containing multiple registers of finitude, which call up management and administration for life. Of course, by pursuing liberty through 'organizing its conditions', liberalism always risks frustrating, even 'destroying what it says it wants to create'.[176] At issue here is that the population is opened to biopolitical administration inasmuch as its constitutive mortal flows are identified and managed as such. Flow cannot stop. Accordingly, we must recognise the emergence of a globalised biopolitical project for 'making life live' which smuggles in the necessity of killing.[177] Yet, rather than viewing liberalism as simply retaining an archaic sovereign necropolitics, Dillon and Reid explore the radical novelty of the liberal 'analytics of the finite and the infinite' in this context.[178] What they view as liberalism's operative subject, the 'biohuman', is certainly defined by identifying the elements of that 'biohumanity' which are 'hostile and dangerous to it'.[179] Biohumanity secures itself by removing the dangerous elements of its own body, but must hold short of complete self-destruction. 'The proper nature of the biohuman has become the infinite re-assignability of the very pluripotency of which it is now said to be comprised, against the threat of that very pluripotency itself'.[180] Biopower is thus engaged in a delicate, even paradoxical, balancing act between the pursuance of security and the promotion of its own dangerous pluripotency. This is because biohumanity's integral morbidity determines the parameters and possibilities of the life of its population. The biohuman is defined by its own chaotic and irruptive mortality. Liberalism is concerned not simply to deter but also to harness the productive value that derives from life's immanent morbidity.[181] Death is governmentalized in life, according to the registers of flux which cross living populations. Biopower must promote the pluripotency of human life, recognising that pluripotency is indissociable from immanent vectors of morbidity.

This liberal politics of human finitude is what calls up biopolitical management and administration. One aspect of this is the formation of a kind of refashioned protection racket wherein biopolitical government increasingly finds its 'nihilistic rationale and ultimate test in the operational competence it displays as a service provider of emergency relief'.[182] Vis-à-vis disastrous natural events, liberal biopower does find legitimacy as an administrative buffer against the risks which mortality endows. Biopolitical theorists, however, aver Beck's descriptive master narrative on risk,[183] understanding risk governmentalization as a technological function of the liberal analytic. Risk certainly is a 'technology for governing social problems' biopolitically.[184] It establishes a numerical optic whereby life's integral contingency, in terms of the threatening flows of morbidity inherent to populations (i.e. radicalisation), morbidity originating outside populations (i.e. earthquakes) and potential productivities (qua opportunities for populational growth or development), can be numerically quantified and administered.

Foucault observed that 'the motto of Liberalism is: "Live Dangerously" . . . individuals are constantly exposed to danger, or rather, they are conditioned to experience their situation, their life, their present, and their future as containing danger.'[185] Foucault goes on to argue that the idea of danger as productive stimulus is liberalism's major implication. Liberalism recognises the productivity of life's integral uncertainty; indeed, one might say that uncertainty is the essence of a productive liberal life. Life's mortality, indissociable from its riskiness, is now taken to be its productive ontological characteristic. Liberalism seeks to promote certain forms of life; possessed of foresight, enterprise and self-reliance, which live more productively with mortality or evental contingency. The central principle of liberal rule over life becomes an analytic of exposure: 'only life that is exposed to . . . uncertainty can properly develop the[se] desirable (Liberal) attributes'.[186] Stoic abandonment to the contingencies of mortal life is central to liberalism's approach to securing that same life. Indeed, the central article of faith which secures liberal government is that of the economies of self-organisation through crisis.[187] We see here the clear terms of a uniquely liberal politics of mortality of the human qua mortal. This is suggestive of what Agamben has recently referred to as the economic 'paradigm of providential government' under a logic of immanence, which no less than the sovereign sacrificial-ceremonial paradigm carries the signature of Christian theology.[188]

In relation to the immanent mortal risks which trace it, the biohuman subject of liberalism is enjoined to become resilient. Flexibility and adaptability are the terms of reference for ascertaining productivity which modulate rather than blockade life's contingency. Biopolitics views mortality as a register of opportunities for making life flourish, under a logic which assumes perpetual exposure to mortal risk.[189] The sovereign politics of collective exclusion and ontotheological redemption is thus largely displaced by a liberal logistics of death's immanence to the life of the population. This logistics of life's integral mortality/contingency is precisely what Agamben insufficiently acknowledges in *Homo Sacer* when framing late modern necropolitics purely in terms of the sovereign exception, but gestures towards in his more recent *The Kingdom and the Glory*, suggestively subtitled *Homo Sacer II*.[190] The liberal analytic of finitude reworks the necropolitical problematic in terms of the government of immanent mortal risk. The sovereign necropolitics of sacrificial exclusion and extermination is replaced by concern for the immanent flows or forces of mortality which must be administered and regulated so that the pluripotency of that life may be maximised. Liberal life is the administration of its mortal flows; an ethos of mobility. Liberal 'civil religion' is organised around humanity's immanent mortality in this sense.[191] Liberal governmentality assumes an immanent necropolitics which is quite distinct from the transcendent necropolitics of sovereign political theology. In his analysis of jihadi discourse Faisal Devji identifies a desire to politically surpass liberal humanism.[192] His argument may be read as suggesting that suicide bombing is closely bound up with the distinctly liberal necropolitics of the human. Suicide bombing is certainly intelligible as a reaction to liberal exclusion, but also may be understood to draw political intelligibility from investment in the liberal governmental necropolitics of human finitude. This is particularly evident in the case of home-grown bombers such Siddique Khan, but the implications reach beyond this specific case inasmuch as our attention is drawn to a register for a political agency emerging only at the intersection or imbrication of suicide bombing and liberalism.[193]

For Devji, global jihadi militancy emerges from and functions in the context of the perceived 'ruins of our political institutions'.[194] A perception of liberal failure is manifest in the often violent discontent of those populations who are excluded from the global order. Global forms of protests, like those of Muslims around the world over cartoons denigrating the Prophet Mohammed, may thus be understood as seeking an equal political recognition felt to be lacking. Such protests are, Devji argues, an indictment of the lack of political institutions to facilitate a global collective politics. In an important sense, therefore, discourses of global militancy emerge only by adopting and diverting the cosmopolitan terms that they problematize. Al Qaeda is certainly anything but a local, antimodern or parochial assemblage. It depends not only on English as its main global language of transmission, but on a characteristically late modern form of networked, information-centric organisation. Bin Laden himself drew on Western anticapitalist or antiestablishment figures and arguments; he is firmly a 'part of the West he criticises'.[195] According to Devji, liberal globalisation is the very substance of jihadi militancy.[196] Its discourse is similarly tied into that of the liberal humanism it purports to challenge. Devji argues that it is precisely through engagement with a liberal concept of the politics of human life that jihadis seek to legitimate their suicidal violence. He notes that liberalism thus articulates human life in a fundamentally numerical or statistical manner. This mathematical grasp of humanity underpins a logistical problematization of that life form. Liberal order is 'a global political order based upon the management of lives rather than the guarantee of freedoms'.[197] In liberal discourse the figure of humanity is most regularly voiced or discussed in the context of its immanent morbidity, represented by the deprived and suffering of the developing world. This image of generic suffering has become liberalism's image of humanity itself. Devji suggests that such an immanently suffering-life cannot be a political subject, only the object of a politics: a location for sympathy, aid and securitisation. It is this 'subordination of citizenship to biological needs' that in jihadi discourse is expressively felt to be insufficient to the task of achieving global justice.[198]

Liberalism's logistics of human life is predicated on a distinctive problematization of the risks or morbidities integral to that life. This suggests we might progress Devji's claim: the liberal vision of humanity is bare of all but a logistical function precisely as a life that must be endlessly secured against and through its own integral becoming-finite. The immanent mortality of this suffering-life is constructed as necessitating liberal government, ensuring that the abstract human object of aid is bereft of independent political agency. Islamist suicide bombing queries the numerical formulation of liberal humanity. When suicide bombers attack anonymous human beings en masse in a random manner on trains, on planes or in crowds, the depersonalised aspect of such systems of mass transportation is counterposed to the intensely personal character of suicide bombers. 'In the suicide bombing an abstracted [and thus apolitical] humanity is destroyed at the same time as the infrastructure that makes it possible'. In this way, it is the biopolitical conception of an abstracted population that is forced to commit suicide.[199] Devji argues that 'the martyr produced by the suicide bombing is human precisely in his non-equivalence'; he is individual not numerical. Such acts therefore explicitly aim to manifest a humanity founded in individual 'courage and sacrifice', as opposed to biological existence.[200] The political signification that suicide bombings seek to construct is one of fearlessness in facing mortality, which thus seeks to witness an alternative political humanity rooted in individual faith and courage. Devji's sharp insight here is only limited by his failure to recognise that liberalism's logistics of human life is predicted on its immanent necropolitics, and as such, a misrecognition of the political content inherent in the actions of suicide bombers. Here, the declaration of nonequivalence constitutes the interruption of humanity understood as a flow of finitudes.

Devji reads the home-grown London bomber Shehzad Tanweer's statement that 'we love death the way that you love life' as implying a direct critique of the prioritisation of life over death under liberal understandings of humanity.[201] For Devji, then, jihadi suicide bombers are an individual voice for death against the logistics of a death-free order. If, however, human life is rendered amenable to technical manipulation only as a consequence of liberalism's immanent necropolitics, Tanweer's statement acquires a subversive connotation. In rejecting the logistics of mass humanity, Tanweer's suicidal violence placed liberalism's distinctive analytic of finitude in contradistinction to the affirmed, and thus repoliticised, mortality of an individual human subjectivity under God. The field of contestation between the suicide bomber and liberalism is that of the human qua mortal and the political possibilities implied thereupon. In other words, in both Islamist suicide bombing and in liberal order, a political mandate is derived in common from an affirmation of human life as definitively mortal. The ironic challenge implied by Tanweer's suicide bombing is that liberalism's mass politics of mortality is deficient: This model of death is botched! Mohammad Sidique Khan's claim to speak in 'a language that you will understand' explicitly aimed to reciprocate the killing of Muslims he saw as structural to liberalism, but it also indicated that his and Tanweer's act emerges from a position internal to a liberal society.[202] His reach for a shared language in death is suggestive of a radical immanence. These actors are politically intelligible not simply in their exterior will to give liberal life its due, but in their curious regard for the problematization of the human qua mortal which stands at the heart of liberal biopolitics. Khan's commentary on the collective injustice of liberal killing is tied to an embodied assertion of the integrally political content of individual human mortality. In this sense the language in question is precisely, if ironically, shared. These home-grown London bombers possessed no position outside liberal discourse.

Here we can identify a register upon which the suicidal political content of such acts must be thought in lieu or the logic of categorical opposition. Suicide bombing, inasmuch as it operates here through the valorisation of the possibilities of the human qua mortal, constitutes an act precisely fitted to the liberal politics of human finitude. The political significance of suicide bombing is not a question of being (or not) a structural reaction to liberal necropolitics as it is of being its hybrid and interlocutor. The liberal attempt to manage death's circulation is their condition of possibility. For this reason we must assent to Devji's claim that suicide bombings more broadly signify liberalism being challenged not by its negative exteriority but by an interior limit.[203] Whilst Khan and Tanweer's suicide terrorism explicitly sought to indict and reciprocate liberal killing, their acts are politically intelligible, and construct their agency by seeking the redefinition of human life as political by reference to its integral mortality. At issue here is not simply the rejection of a politics of life. Here cross-contamination and contestation upon a shared field, rather than the posing of a fundamental opposition, governs the political logic. Suicide bombings, in this context, do not simply affirm a sovereign or religious 'idealism of transcendent justifications for a community' in contrast with a liberalism that purports to have gone beyond such logics: Jihadist suicide bombings instantiate on a field of contestation regarding the possibilities of the human qua mortal.[204] Suicide bombing's ontological entanglement with liberalism is clear: These deaths interrupt the population flow by bringing its integral morbidity to the point of excess.

Life's openness to the morbid event is the source of its pluripotency. Liberalism, in recognising this, seeks to promote certain forms of life, possessed of foresight, enterprise and self-reliance, which live more productively with that mortality or contingency. The central principle of liberal rule over life is an analytic of exposure.[205] Stoic abandonment to the contingencies of human life is central to liberalism's approach to securing that same life. Inasmuch as liberal life is defined by the necessity of its own emergency, emergencies endlessly proliferate.

What is axiomatized by liberal capitalism is the flux as such: life's unlimited finity, its emergent capacity to become-different. In seeing becoming as the definite threat to, and simultaneously the definitive characteristic of, life, liberal capitalism assumes it must be allowed a free register of auto-endangerment for life to function efficiently or productively. By the same gesture, threat is now 'indistinguishable from the general environment, now one with a restless climate of agitation.'[206] It is clear that the central condition that allows the liberal state to create its smoothly totalising war machine is not its impressive material resources and equipment, but rather its definition of human variable capital according to the pluripotency of its mortality.

This definition also sets out the conditions for, indeed demands, the emergence of an idiomatic counter-figure: 'The Unspecified enemy . . . , the unassignable material Saboteur or human Deserter assuming the most diverse forms.'[207] Modern securitisation invents its own idiomatically embodied critical subject in the human bomb: the saboteur of humanity's pluripotent flows. The axiomatization of mortal-production is central to all distinctly liberal social orders. The suicide bomber draws not only on the technological resources and equipment of liberal globalisation, but emerges as if from the nightmares of liberalism's "resilient life."[208] There is, however, no specific liberal denial of death, which might render it particularly vulnerable to death's symbolic force. Liberalism already assumes mortality is the central criterion of life's productivity. Suicide bombing sets liberalism to flight because it builds itself directly on its idioms – realising, in the process, an embodiment of pure contingency that feeds and feeds off, in a undecidable cycle, the contemporary ontology of generic life-as-threat due to its productive mortality. The suicide bomber interrupts the flow of death in one place; metastasis is the consistent result.

A politics from the outside

Embodiments of suicidal excess voice the liberal humanist problematic of life as pregnant with its own impossibility. As a counter-conduct idiomatic to liberal governmentality,[209] suicide bombing interrupts and invests its resilient life. The politics of suicide cannot, however, by the same gesture, be reduced entirely to the peculiarities of the liberal governmental diagram, any more than they can be reduced to an urge to sovereign ipseity.[210] Attempting to think what is produced by suicide bombings beyond its interaction with power, Murray[211] argues that suicide bombings call up an 'ambivalent spectre of death that remains inassimilable and incomprehensible' to *any* order. A curious externality seems to trace the politicality of the human bomb.[212]

The inassimilable remainder which defines the act of suicide, for Deleuze and Guattari, is the marker of the fact that our capacity to deterritorialise is constitutively disastrous. Where Foucault attempted to do history 'without universals',[213] Deleuze and Guattari suggest that the act of political suicide is irrevocably an engagement with something transdiagrammatic, an outside which is irreducible to any particular diagram, yet which every diagram seeks to negotiate. Foucault argues that Blanchot's articulation of literature as an 'absolute opening', unveiled always as a radical breakthrough, marks out

> a thought that stands outside subjectivity, setting its limits as though from without, articulating its end, making its dispersion shine forth, taking in only its invincible absence; and that at the same time stands as the threshold of all positivity, not in order to grasp its foundations or justifications but in order to regain the space of its unfolding . . . a thought that, in relation to the interiority of our philosophical reflection and the positivity of our knowledge, constitutes what in a word we might call 'the thought from the outside'.[214]

Foucault praised Blanchot for locating the 'non-discourse of all language', for finding language itself speaking as 'the murmur that is forever taking it apart'.[215] For Blanchot language is a gaze which dies in its extension, as 'courageously negligent solicitude' which attracts the pure outside and the inevitable dispersion which follows from it.[216] As Deleuze does, Foucault recognises that Blanchot's understanding of metamorphosis is 'never-ending death'.[217] Death and its opposite are voiced simultaneously in our inability to die which proclaims the presence of the outside. The necessary attraction to death is the origin of that murmuring space in which the speaker is effaced in speaking the word itself.[218] The origin of literature is the outside where 'death opens interminably onto the repetition of the beginning.' For Foucault reading Blanchot, 'language is revealed to be the shared transparency of the origin and death', and to speak the new is therefore necessarily to promise disappearances with appearances.[219]

Deleuze[220] reads the concept of the outside as central to the political implications of Foucault's work. This is no lazy invention, but it is nonetheless an activist reading on Deleuze's part, which demonstrates very precisely how he believed their oeuvres could be brought into productive relation.[221] As Palladino recognises, there is an implicit critique in Deleuze's reading that Foucault failed to fully purse the implications of his own thoughts on the problem of death and finitude in *The Order of Things*.[222] Deleuze, arguing that the problem of the outside power runs throughout Foucault's work, implies that something akin to the primacy of desire (as mortal-production) is latent in Foucault; and concludes, rather controversially, that Foucault's work must therefore can be read as resulting in a revolutionary vitalism.[223] Foucault, Deleuze argues, mapped diagrams and assemblages of power. For Deleuze reading Foucault, the assemblages of which he wrote his genealogies are mapped by (virtual) diagrams which always include 'free and unbound points. Points of creativity, change and resistance'. Because of these transdiagrammatic points,

> each diagram testifies to the twisting line of the outside . . . without beginning or end, an oceanic line that passes through all points of resistance, pitches diagrams against one and other, and operates always as the most recent.[224]

Between the assembled strata and the great murmur of language, there is a line of the outside which traverses these points as a third agency. This, for Deleuze, is the spirit of evental contingency.[225]

Accordingly, for Deleuze, the outside (as the third agency) is essential to any understanding of Foucault's concept of power as a function which passes through both master and mastered. Deleuze points out that 'the list [of diagrams] is endless.' What is important, in a transdiagrammatic sense, is simply that diagrams represent forces 'in a perpetual state of evolution; there is an emergence of forces that doubles history, or rather envelopes it'.[226] A diagram is therefore, Deleuze argues, 'a non-place: it is the place only of mutation', defined by its relationship to primary forces from the outside. Diagrams are defined by their relationship to an outside which is absolutely nonhistorical. The history of diagrams is history testifying to the primacy of the event. What this ensures is that there is no question of inevitability or teleology in the Universal History of diagrams. The line of the outside is the contact a diagram has with its source and direction of contingent mutation or evolution.[227] The outside crosses and infiltrates all diagrams as the 'points, knots or focuses' by which particular assemblages open to novelty and transformation. For Deleuze this is how we know that 'resistance comes first.'[228] The point is that 'power relations operate completely within the diagram, while resistances necessarily operate in a direct relation with the outside from which the diagrams emerge'.[229] For Deleuze reading Foucault, 'the thought of the outside is a thought of resistance'.[230] Thinking the outside is thinking which is oriented towards a univocal escape – the pure politics of the contingent event.

Deleuze assents to Foucault's general refusal of the universal (in the form of ideas such as the rights of man) as no more than the play of or shadow of the historical stratum, but he argues that towards the end of his works, Foucault's thought opened, through the concept of biopower, to a vision of the living being that resists by univocally unfolding the evental outside. Deleuze argues that, for Foucault:

> When power takes life as it aim or object, then resistance to power already puts itself on the side of life, and turns life against power: Life as a political object was in a sense taken at face value and turned against the system that was bent on destroying it.[231]

In Deleuze's reading, this sets the terms for liberating a 'life become resistance to power when power takes life as its object' not as a (dialectical) condition internal to the contemporary biopolitical diagram, but as univocally testifying to the line of the outside as it is appears in any diagram. Resistance comes from outside, as a politics which is prior to any and all diagrams; 'a vital power that cannot be confined with species, environment or the parts of a singular diagram'. Deleuze argues, therefore, that 'the force that comes from outside' defines a revolutionary 'idea of Life, a certain vitalism, in which Foucault's thought culminates'.[232] A resistant and antisovereign politics is primary politics from the outside, it is also a politics of mortal life itself; a vital politics.

The problem of revolutionary naturalism raised by Baudrillard thus takes on greater clarity. Deleuze is suggesting that the univocality of deterritorialisation is essentially rooted in a concept of the vital as mortal. Disorganisation is creativity, only 'illegitimately' organised into forms which are deemed to be alive precisely to the extent that they oscillate endlessly back to becoming on their death model. Deleuze remarks that, for Foucault, whilst life is certainly at its most intense when its clashes with power, such clashes can take place only at diffuse points in the diagram which mark the 'points of resistance that are in some way primary'. If power takes life as its object and gives rise 'to a life that resists power', this does not imply that the politics of the vital is simply a product of biopolitics.[233] Rather, biopower involves a unique problematization (a superfold) of the outside, seeking to governmentalize an unlimited finity. Liberal states are schizophrenic, and innately revolutionary, inasmuch as the evental outside or right of the untimely is comprehended as the very fabric of life itself. That Deleuze and Guattari's vision of naturally revolutionary desire precisely maps with the central problematic of contemporary biopower is the unavoidable implication of the place of (liberal) capitalism in their Universal History (as displacing the schizophrenic limit of social production). Deleuze points out that whilst for Foucault, 'to think means to be embedded in the present time stratum that serves as a limit,' trying to climb out of the strata and become-revolutionary is unfolding the limit to locate the savage line of the outside crossing all diagrams:

> This is a terrible line that shuffles all the diagrams, above the very raging storms . . . but however terrible this line may be, it is a line of life that can no longer be gauged by relations between forces, one that carries man beyond terror . . . [the] . . . place of the fissure . . . [is where] . . . life exists par excellence.[234]

Deleuze claim is that, following Bichat, Foucault saw death 'as something coextensive with life . . . as something made up of a multiplicity of partial and particular deaths'.[235] For Deleuze, the resistant 'force of life that belonged to Foucault was always thought through and lived out as a multiple death'. As a consequence, Deleuze's central conclusion is that Foucault's work is defined by exactly the problematic which is the central concern of this book. Deleuze thus points out that it is all too easy to conclude that all that remains for a resistant agency is 'to pass through all these deaths preceding the great limit of death itself, death which even afterwards continues'. Under a biopolitical diagram, he asks, must life 'consist [. . .] only in taking ones place, or every place, in the cortège of a "One dies"'?[236] Might, in other words, the question of politics increasingly find itself indissociable from a question of self-destruction? Deleuze states that this is precisely the problem which faces us: The fundamental question is how we can ensure that the life from the outside is 'caught up in a movement that would snatch it away from the void and pull it back from death'. The problem of political resistance is identical with suicide.[237]

Such a revolutionary politics from the outside, Deleuze argues, cannot be 'recklessly searching for death', but it is a matter of 'undo[ing] the doubling and pull[ing] away the folds'.[238] Resistant life, he suggests, is inseparable from death – that is to say, revolutionary politics is unfolding the vital univocity of the outside as desiring-productive deterritorialisation which raises an inevitable risk of suicidal excess. Foucault's vision of biopower raises a question of an integrally suicidal yet vital politics from the outside. A pure politics of the untimely, which gleans its potent capacity to deterritorialise desire today from the fact that the evental outside is already the central problem of the liberal biopolitics of life's eruptive mortal productivity? Deleuze thus reads *The Order of Things* into his Universal History. For Deleuze and Guattari, all diagrams anticipate and seek to prevent the full flux of an absolute deterritorialisation. Deleuze and Guattari's revolutionary naturalism assumes that mortal flux is absolutely primary, but not in the sense of a prior historical state. As Deleuze confirms in *Many Politics*, the primacy of lines of flight 'must not be understood chronologically, or in a sense of an eternal generality. It is rather the fact and the right of the untimely'.[239] Mortality is openness to events which come from the outside, a concept of primary evental contingency.[240] The outside is, for Deleuze and Guattari, not simply the source of revolutionary agency; rather, it is revolutionary agency. Agency is counter-actualising the event to release a univocal deterritorialisation. Counter-actualising the event is a matter of affirming the revolutionary univocity of becoming: To become is be swept away on the terrifying line of the outside.[241]

Foucault evocatively stated that 'as the archaeology of our thought easily shows, man is an invention of recent date. And one perhaps nearing its end'.[242] He goes on to observe that, if the assemblages which composed man were to 'crumble, as the ground of Classical thought did, at the end of the eighteenth century, then one can certainly wager that man would be erased, like a face drawn in sand at the edge of the sea'.[243] Deleuze reads this as suggesting, with Nietzsche, that having already killed God, the death of the man-form is rapidly approaching as the limit of the contemporary biopolitical diagram. He suggests that a new subjective form is inevitably emerging which 'no longer involves raising to infinity[244] or finitude[245] but an unlimited finity, thereby invoking every situation of force in which a finite number of components yields a practically unlimited diversity of combinations'.[246] This marks precisely the problem of the infinitely contingent life of populations to which biopolitics is a specific axiomatic response. Biopower attempts to governmentalize the unpredictably productive becomings of life itself.[247] It is, in this sense, the limit of the 'obligation to work backwards – or downwards – to an analytic of finitude, in which man's being will be able to provide a foundation in their own positivity' which Foucault observed as the heart of modern empiricity in *The Order of Things*.[248] This, Deleuze suggests, leads us inevitably to the conditions for the emergence of something which comes after man (and is therefore no longer conditioned by finitudinal lack):

> The question [Foucault] continually returns to is therefore the following: if the forces within man compose a form only by entering into a relation with forms from the outside, with what new forms do they now risk entering into relation, and what new form will emerge that is neither God nor Man?[249]

For Deleuze reading Foucault, the man-form of finitudinal lack is observably being displaced, particularly through the interaction of cybernetic and biological knowledges. In Deleuze's reading, a determinant unfolding of the human to its unlimited finity is implicit to biopower's axiomatic internalisation and displacement of the outside. Liberal capitalism marks the uniquely axiomatic response to the limit condition of Universal History identified in *Capitalism and Schizophrenia*. Deleuze suggests, in *Foucault*, that we must hope that the subjective forms which emerge from this reproblematization of death do not prove worse than the two forms which preceded it. But there seems little doubt that, for Deleuze and Guattari, liberal capitalism's unfolding of the outside unleashes a potential for our becoming-revolutionary. This futurology is no doubt bound to a 'cyborg fantasy of the man-machine'.[250] The rise of a biopolitical superfold of unlimited finity calls up a new kind of politics at the capitalist displaced limit of Universal History, rooted in a cosmic vitalism which assumes the extravagant abolition of man: The promise of vitalism beyond the human.[251] The worry, the other side of hope, which must surely follow is that these new forms will always be as integrally suicidal as they are potentially revolutionary. This is the central problematic of a politics from the outside. Beyond god, and beyond man, modern biopoliticians find themselves bereft, adrift in a sea of overabundant decoding; possibilities are endless and yet curiously, for the same reason, final. Michael Dillon describes this problem as the 'Eschaton' of biopower.[252] For Deleuze it is the end of Foucault's thought, and indeed his and Guattari's, as well. Once politics takes the infinite finity of life itself as its object, via the axiomatization of mortal flux, we find ourselves in a condition overdetermined by excess. This is why Dillon terms the liberal project a war for a particular eschatological understanding of time regulated by the (un)limit condition represented by the recombinatory possibilities of all finite multiplicities.[253] Liberalism is centrally concerned with securing an uninterrupted dangerousness.

It is the liminal threshold of liberal politics which the human bomb evokes, and this is the source of its capacity to cast us into horror. The suicide bomber embodies the untimeliness of humankind, revealing its contemporary openness to inhuman cyberpositive forms.[254] The practice reveals the politicised humanity promised by liberalism as already insufficient, a summons to something else. The War on Terror recognised in the human bomb this mastery of the strategy of the outside. In literally sabotaging the population flows, at the constitutive limit of the contemporary axiomatic, the human bomb calls up the chaotic proliferation of new axioms to recapture and recode the experience of death as a nightmare unconscionable to liberal order. This flurry of recoding activity seeks to prohibit our recognition of this explosive body-machine as an expression of the death of man; a deserter from liberal humanity.

Notes

1. Suicide bombing bluntly contradicts the founding rationalist assumption of self-interest defined by fear of death. See C. Reuter, *My Life Is a Weapon: A Modern History of Suicide Bombing* (Princeton, NJ: Princeton University Press, 2006).
2. A. Kruglanski and S. Fishman, "The Psychology of Terrorism; 'Syndrome' versus 'Tool' Perspectives," *Terrorism and Political Violence* 18, no. 2 (2006): 193–215.

3. Hoffman argues that the 'fundamental characteristics of suicide bombing and its attraction for the terrorist organisation behind it are universal.' B. Hoffman, "The Logic of Suicide-Terrorism," *Atlantic Monthly*, June 2003, p. 5; see also B. Hoffman and G. McCormick (2004), "Terrorism, Signalling and Suicide Attack," *Studies in Conflict and Terrorism* 27, no. 4 (2004): 243–281.
4. In technology, size of military force or strength of position (R. A. Pape, *Dying to Win: The Strategic Logic of Suicide Terrorism*, London: Gibson Square, 2006). Gupta and Mundra argue that the tactic is used to narrow the casualty ratio between two unequal sides in Palestine (see D. Gupta and K. Mundra, "Suicide Bombing as a Strategic Weapon: An Empirical Investigation of Hamas and Islamic Jihad," *Terrorism and Political Violence* 17 [2005]: 573–598, 574).
5. Pape (2006) argues suicide terrorism is a signal particularly to occupying democracies to compel them 'to withdraw military forces from territory that terrorists considered to be their homeland' (p. 4).
6. Democracies are claimed to be a particularly vulnerable target, it is argued, because they are idiosyncratically vulnerable to coercion through horror, and to be more measured in response. Successes for organisations in the past, in deterring or coercing democracies through suicide bombings, by Hezbollah in Lebanon for example, are deemed to have encouraged this interpretation. Researchers have remarked that the democratic states which Pape deems to attract suicide missions because of their unwillingness to hurt civilians and inclination towards less extreme responses regularly do not respond as he assumes. Russia, Israel, Turkey and Sri Lanka have been willing to respond extremely harshly to attacks, often targeting civilian populations. Escalation may thus also been seen to forms part of the strategy of suicide bombing. D. Reiter and S. J. Wade, "Does Democracy Matter? Regime Type and Suicide-Terrorism," *Journal of Conflict Resolution* 51 (2007).
7. R. J. Brym and B. Araj, "Suicide Bombing as Strategy and Interaction: The Case of the Second Intifada," *Social Forces* 84, no. 4 (2006); A. Moghadam, "Suicide Terrorism, Occupation, and the Globalization of Martyrdom: A Critique of Dying to Win," *Studies in Conflict and Terrorism* 29, no. 8 (2006): 707–729; Pape 2006. Suicide terrorism is observably more successful at achieving short-term than long-term goals. See also G. Michael and J. Scolnick, "The Strategic Limits of Suicide Terrorism in Iraq," *Small War and Insurgencies* 17, no. 2 (2006): 113–125. Bruce Hoffman argues that suicide bombing acts as a 'signalling game'; it is thus an act designed to tell the opposition something. Of course, the problem, as we have seen, is that retrospective semiosis is uncertain, and the audience may receive highly divergent messages (see Hoffman and McCormick 2004, p. 272).
8. Gupta and Mundra 2005, p. 575.
9. In this context, interorganisational competition may be an equally salient rationale behind its adoption. Various groups often rely on the same community for legitimation, support and recruiting; inter-group competition can lead to escalation and suicide bombing. Bloom argues that one key factor is the process by which terrorist groups may engage in outbidding for popular support against domestic rivals. See M. Bloom, *Dying to Kill* (New York: Columbia University Press, 2005), p. 96.
10. A. Pedahzur and A. Perlinger, "The Changing Nature of Suicide Attacks: A Social Network Perspective." *Social Forces* 84, no. 4 (2006): 1987–2008.
11. If there are multiple reasons for suicide terrorism, there are also various direct precipitators for specific attacks, from assassinations and house demolishment to political events and holidays. See Brym and Araj 2006, p. 1982.
12. W. Laqueur, *No End to War: Terrorism in the Twenty-First Century* (London: Continuum, 2003).
13. See also Bloom 2005, p. 53.
14. Such as the cult surrounding Vittupellai Prabakaran – the deceased leader of the Liberation Tigers of Tamil Elam.

15. Prabakaran, it is claimed, had a photo taken with every suicide cadre, adding to the mystique or glamour of participation (Bloom 2005).
16. D. Lester, B. Yang et al., "Suicide Bombers: Are Psychological Profiles Possible?," *Studies in Conflict and Terrorism* 27, no. 4 (2004): 283–295.
17. J. Stern, *Terror in the Name of God: Why Religious Militants Kill* (New York: HarperCollins, 2004).
18. E. E. Sarraj and L. Butler, "Suicide Bombers: Dignity, Despair, and the Need for Hope: An Interview with Eyad El Sarraj," *Journal of Palestinian Studies* 31, no. 4 (2002): 71–76.
19. Bloom 2005, p. 90; A. Speckhard and K. Ahkmedova, "The Making of a Martyr: Chechen Suicide Terrorism," *Studies in Conflict and Terrorism* 29, no. 5 (2006): 429–492.
20. As Pape (2006) puts it, 'few suicide bombers are social misfits, criminally insane, or professional losers ... typically they are psychologically normal' (p. 23).
21. H. Khashan, "Collective Palestinian Frustration and Suicide Bombings," *Third World Quarterly* 24, no. 6 (2003): 1046–1067. Indeed, studies have suggested that high education may be linked to greater support for violence in Lebanon and Palestine, where suicide bombings have at times been endemic. See also S. Atran, "Genesis of Suicide Terrorism," *Science* 299, no. 5612 (2003): 1534–1539.
22. For an international terrorist attack (such as 9/11), enacted by a group like Al Qaeda, only the more educated can fit unnoticed into wider society; consequentially the ill-educated are vetted and excluded from participation. Indeed, Krueger and Maleckova argue that high education has become a factor in ascertaining commitment to go through with the act in Palestine. A. B. Krueger and J. Maleckova, "The Economic and the Education of Suicide Bombers: Does Poverty Cause Terrorism?," *New Republic Online* (2002). They also assess the question of whether absolute poverty causes people to commit suicide bombings, finding that suicide bombers are more likely to be just above the average, middle or upper class than especially impoverished. There have been two millionaires among Palestinian suicide bombers. More studies are supportive of a role for 'relative deprivation' (Krueger and Maleckova 2002; see also Hoffman, B. (2006). *Inside Terrorism*. New York, Colombia University Press. 165). This simply suggests the presence of a politics without providing tools for its analysis.
23. The explanatory limits of individual profiling are exemplified in the Israeli experience. Initially Palestinian suicide bombers seemed to follow a type; young single religious men, and counter-terrorist operatives acted accordingly. Perhaps in response to targeting of those who 'fit the profile', by the Second Intifada, suicide bombers could be 'middle aged or young, married or unmarried, have children or not, be a woman or child', be very religious or relatively unreligious, and be comparatively rich or poor. Hoffman and McCormick 2004, p. 2; see also Stern 2004; A. Pedahzur, ed., *Suicide Terrorism*, Cambridge: Polity Press, 2005; Hoffman 2006; Bloom 2005. Indeed, Atran argues that approaches which focus on the individual are a 'fundamental attribution error ... a tendency for people to explain behaviour in terms of individual personality traits, even when significant situational factors in the larger society are at work' (Atran 2003; see also Gupta and Mundra 2005).
24. Kruglanski and Fishman 2006.
25. As practicing psychiatrist in Palestine puts it: 'Suicide bombings and all these forms of violence – I'm talking as a doctor here – are only the symptoms, the reaction to this chronic and systematic process of humiliating people in effort to destroy their hope and dignity. That is the illness, and unless it is resolved and treated, there will be more and more symptoms of the pathology' (Sarraj and Butler 2002, p. 73).
26. Ibid., p. 74.
27. Khashan 2003.
28. For Hage, suicide bombing can only be understood as a 'tendency emanating from within ... society, and as such has to be explained not as an individual psychological

aberration but as the product of specific social conditions' of occupation and repression in Palestine. G. Hage, " 'Comes a Time We Are All Enthusiasm': Understanding Palestinian Suicide Bombers in Times of Exighophobia," *Public Culture* 15, no. 2 (2003): 65–89, 69.
29. Atran 2003, p. 6.
30. Robert Pape (2006) argued, following Durkheim, that suicide bombing is an example of altruistic suicide, that is, suicide enacted for the community.
31. Stephen Dale's study of jihadist suicide in Islamic Asia provides historical background to such arguments, noting that European expansion into and forcible conquest of the rich and previously Muslim dominated trade routes of the Indian Ocean, first by Portugal and Spain and then by Holland, America and Britain, from the 1400s onwards, was the main driver for the emergence of suicidal Jihads in Atjeh, Calikut and Sulu. Muslim authors at the time reveal the birth of a jihadist narrative response to colonisation, hinging on the development of a discourse of martyrdom amongst those fighting the Christian invaders. Dale argues that once it had become certain that victory against the colonial invaders was impossible, martyrdom attacks aiming simply to terrorise the European settlements emerged as a last gesture in desperation. When victory became accepted as unattainable, individuals turned to a despairing private Jihad, murdering unbelievers in the hope of gaining paradise, 'defending the integrity of their community and intimidating colonial rulers or their native allies' (S. F. Dale, "Religious Suicide in Islamic Asia Anticolonial Terrorism in India, Indonesia, and the Philippines," *Journal of Conflict Resolution* 32, no. 1 [1988]: 37–59, 48).
32. Moghadam, critiquing Pape, suggests that 'the occupation theory' is a less satisfactory model for 'explaining suicide attacks conducted by Al Qaeda or its affiliates, where religion plays a larger role'. The transnational character and aims of contemporary Islamism, including the reinstitution of the Caliphate and Shari'a, he argues, cannot be dismissed as irrelevant. Moghadam 2006, p. 724.
33. D. C. Rapoport, "Fear and Trembling: Terrorism in Three Religious Traditions," *American Political Science Review* 78, no. 3 (1984): 658–677; B. Hoffman, "Holy Terror: The Implications of Terrorism Motivated by Religious Imperative," *Studies in Conflict and Terrorism* 18, no. 4 (1995): 271–284.
34. K. Andriolo, "Murder by Suicide: Episodes from Muslim History," *American Anthropologist* 104, no. 3 (2002): 736–742, 741.
35. Rapoport 1984, p. 674.
36. Ibid., p. 675.
37. Laqueur 2003; T. Eagleton, *Holy Terror* (New York: Oxford University Press, 2005); Pape 2006).
38. F. Fukuyama, "Has History Started Again?," *Policy* 18, no. 2 (2002); I. W. Charney, *Fighting Suicide Bombing: A Worldwide Campaign for Life* (Westport, CT: Praeger, 2007).
39. P. Berman, *Terror and Liberalism* (New York: W. W. Norton, 2004).
40. Pedahzur 2005, p. 24.
41. In seeking to avoid the accusation that they are reducing the practice to its ideological source, writers generally frame the religious or ideological vector as a contextual enabler or facilitator of suicidal praxis. Pedahzur argues that some groups clearly reject suicide bombing out of hand and, as such, that preexisting belief structures must therefore play a crucial supportive role. Pape argues that whilst the primary function of suicide terrorism is secular and nationalist, in situations where religious difference is present in a conflict, it plays a key enabling role in the construction of martyrdom. Michael and Scolnick similarly argue that religion or ideology is a force multiplier when it is present. For most, therefore, suicide terrorism is not caused by religion or ideology, but it serves in a supportive role.
42. In this context, Laqueur turns to the closed societies in which, he argues, an 'emphasis on obeisance' and lack of the 'critical attitude, so dear to the west in modern times',

allows individuals to opt for spiritual or ideological certainties of whatever variety. For Laqueur, such closed societies facilitate the 'psychology of the closed mind' necessary for participation in suicide bombing. That only certain types of (non-Western) societies establish the necessary psychological predispositions for the enactment of suicidal violence is not an uncommon assertion in popular debates. It barely needs stating that the existence of extreme political belief in Western liberal capitalist states (i.e., the Red Brigades in Germany during the 1960s or white supremacist groups in the United States today) gives the lie to such a convenient assumption. Political commitment may indeed often be tied to a closure of mind, a single-mindedness that borders on the fanatical – the pertinent question in this context should be how we can think a political desire which descends on such a line without reducing it either the religion/ideology in question or a crudely framed closed contextual society. Laqueur 2003, p. 93.

43. A. M. Oliver and P. F. Steinberg, *The Road to Martyrs' Square: A Journey into the World of the Suicide Bomber* (New York: Oxford University Press, 2005), p. 8.
44. Ibid., p. xxii.
45. Stern 2004, p. 35.
46. Pape 2006, p. 82.
47. Hage 2003, p. 85.
48. Ibid.
49. Reuter (2006) refers to a mimetic 'culture of death'. He associates the progression of suicide bombings in Palestine with what he terms the 'Werther effect', referring to the suicidal character from Goethe's novel (p. 13). Durkheim famously argued that there is no social fact 'more readily transmissible by contagion than suicide', it follows that suicide bombing is mimetic, like normal suicide, carried throughout a society by social identification processes. E. Durkheim, *Suicide: A Study in Sociology*, ed. G. Simpson, trans. J.A. Spaulding and G. Simpson (London: Routledge & Kegan Paul, 1970).
50. See P. Marsden and S. Attia, "A Deadly Contagion?," *Psychologist* 18, no. 3 (2005).
51. See for example Pedahzur 2005; Pape 2006; Speckhard and Ahkmedova 2006; P. Gill, "A Multidimensional Approach to Suicide Bombing," *International Journal of Conflict and Violence* 1, no. 2 (2007): 142–159; Bloom 2005; Pedahzur and Perlinger 2006.
52. See for example Gill 2007, Pedahzur 2005. Group psychology has not, for reasons of space, been addressed here; for a good recent discussion in the context of jihadi radicalisation see M. Sageman, *Understanding Terror Networks* (Philadelphia: University of Pennsylvania Press, 2004); M. Sageman, *Leaderless Jihad* (Philadelphia: University of Pennsylvania Press, 2008).
53. L. Jarvis, "The Spaces and Faces of Critical Terrorism Studies," *Security Dialogue* 40, no. 1 (2009): 5–27, 14.
54. E. Said, *Orientalism* (New York: Random House, 1979).
55. Bloom 2005, p. 76.
56. Bloom 2005.
57. Ibid.
58. As Bloom (ibid.) makes explicit.
59. That is the instrumentalist assumption that the practice's political status is derived from its mobilisation by political organisations is undercut if such groups necessarily, whether consciously or unconsciously, tap into an extant suicidal propensity (individual, collective, cultural, social, historical, religious, etc.).
60. T. Asad, *On Suicide Bombing* (New York: Columbia University Press, 2007), p. 64. Given overdetermination, it is perhaps unsurprising that the Islamofascist referent has retained such potency as an operator in popular discourse on the subject, since it allows the seemingly senseless assemblage of factors to be reorganised as an ideological contagion passing through the open geography of globalisation.
61. 'The despotic machine holds the following in common with the primitive machine, it conforms the latter in this respect: the dread of decoded flows – flows of production, but also mercantile flows of exchange and commerce that might escape the state

monopoly, with its tight restrictions and its plugging of flows' (G. Deleuze and F. Guattari, *Anti-Oedipus* (London: Continuum, 2004a), p. 214.
62. Ibid., p. 210.
63. Ibid., p. 212.
64. As such, there is a 'remarkable widening of the regime of debts' under the despot, making him the 'the infinite creditor' (ibid., p. 215).
65. The Urstaat as an abstraction, like the primitive regime, seeks to 'ward off capitalism' as the limit threshold of its mode of social production, but just as the Urstaat adopted the codes of the primitive within its regime of social-production, the capitalist regime will adopt and develop the death-instinct from the state form, and reutilises the state apparatus as a utile residuum (G. Deleuze and F. Guattari, *A Thousand Plateaus*, London: Continuum, 2004b, p. 483). There are no pure states or pure capitalisms, only the slippage of one coding of death into the other.
66. There are, of course, many actual variations of state form; feudalism, empires, and so on. 'The despotic state is an abstraction that is realised' in various ways; variously actualised as a impure virtuality (Deleuze and Guattari 2004a, p. 240). From the point of view of Universal History the central paradox is that states are not simply 'transcendental paradigms of an overcoding', but later come to constitute 'models of realization for an axiomatic of decoded forms' (Deleuze and Guattari 2004b, p. 503).
67. The Christian god is a God of infinite debt, a creditor who sacrifices himself for the debtor – and was born of the Urstaat model (Deleuze and Guattari 2004a, p. 236; see footnote on Nietzsche). Logocentric ontotheology is a state logic, not vice versa – the state first puts in place the belief in its truth, before becoming incorporated, itself, as a function of that belief. Christianity, expresses an urge to 'a becoming of the state', in making debt infinite through internalising in physical territory the field of decoded flows whilst simultaneously spiritualising a supraterrestrial field (p. 242).
68. Contra J. Gray, *Black Mass: Apocalyptic Religion and the Death of Utopia* (New York: Macmillan, 2007).
69. Deleuze and Guattari 2004a, p. 213.
70. In historical actuality, the purest state forms arose out of the breakup of larger empires, whether military or religious – the question is impossible to resolve whether primitive societies are prior to states in actuality, for, as virtual forms, the two are equally primordial.
71. The source of social identity; caste, class, and faithful believer.
72. Deleuze and Guattari 2004a, p. 212.
73. The despot is haunted by 'the danger that a single organ might flow outside the despotic body, that it might break away or escape': the schizophrenic threshold of death's decoding (ibid., p. 229).
74. 'Overcoding is the essence of the law' (ibid., p. 231).
75. Ibid., p. 232.
76. The 'new inscription . . . makes desire into the property of the sovereign, even though he be the death-instinct itself'. 'The ancestor – the master of mobile and finite debts – finds himself dismissed by the deity, the immobile organiser', to whom the despot is now viewed as in direct filiation (ibid., p. 217). The rights of incest mark the realisation of this monotheistic seal of rule, the representation of the despot's transcendent domination of desiring-production (p. 219). This doubling of inscription, under an explicit threat of death, is the 'signifier's imperial origin' (p. 225). It is for this reason that in *A Thousand Plateaus* Deleuze and Guattari term the despotic system the signifying regime.
77. M. Foucault, *Society Must Be Defended* (London: Penguin Books, 2004), p. 240.
78. Ibid.
79. As noted by Seery 1996.
80. Foucault quoted in D. Enns, "Bare Life and the Occupied Body," *Theory & Event* 7, no. 3 (2004): 6.
81. Ibid.

82. R. Esposito, *Bios, Biopolitics and Philosophy* (Minneapolis: University of Minnesota Press, 2008), pp. 60–61.
83. Deleuze and Guattari 2004b, p. 118.
84. Ibid., p. 112.
85. Ibid., pp. 113–114.
86. Ibid., p. 114.
87. Franz Kafka, 'a Czechoslovakian Jew writing in German, submits German to creative treatment as a minor language' (ibid., p. 115).
88. Ibid.
89. See G. Deleuze and F. Guattari, *Kafka: Toward a Minor Literature* (Minneapolis: University of Minnesota Press, 1986).
90. Deleuze and Guattari 2004b, p. 116.
91. Ibid., p. 117.
92. Animated by 'powers (puissances) or becomings that belong to a different realm from that of Power (pouvoir) and Domination . . . becoming-minoritarian as the universal figure of consciousness is called autonomy' (ibid., p. 118).
93. This is why the order-word is meta-language (ibid.).
94. Ibid., p. 119.
95. Ibid.
96. Ibid.
97. Ibid., p. 118.
98. Ibid., p. 120.
99. Ibid., p. 121.
100. Ibid.
101. Ibid., p. 122.
102. Ibid.
103. See E. Holland, "Indefinite Subjective Representation and the Perversion of Death," *Angeliki* 5, no. 2 (2000): 85–91, 87. For Foucault in *Discipline and Punish*, the public display of the right to kill is at the very foundations of sovereign order (M. Foucault, *Discipline and Punish: The Birth of the Prison*, New York: Vintage Books, 1995).
104. In other words, more than an antistructure or counter-power.
105. M. Foucault, *The History of Sexuality. Vol. 1: An Introduction* (New York: Vintage, 1990); Foucault 2004; M. Foucault and M. Senellart, *The Birth of Biopolitics: Lectures at the Collège de France, 1978–79* (Basingstoke: Palgrave Macmillan, 2008).
106. Foucault 2004.
107. Ibid., pp. 239–240.
108. G. Deleuze, "Postscript on the Societies of Control," *October* 59 (1992): 3–7.
109. Foucault 2004, p. 249.
110. Ibid.
111. Ibid., p. 241.
112. Ibid., p. 247.
113. Ibid.
114. Ibid., p. 248.
115. Ibid.
116. M. Duffield, *Development, Security and Unending War: Governing the World of Peoples* (Cambridge: Polity, 2007); M. Duffield and V.M. Hewitt, *Empire, Development & Colonialism: The Past in the Present* (Oxford: James Currey, 2009); S. Elbe, "AIDS, Security, Biopolitics," *International Relations* 19, no. 4 (2005): 403–419; L. Medovoi, "Global Society Must Be Defended: Biopolitics without Boundaries," *Social Text* 25, no. 2 91 (2007): 53–79; J. Reid, "Conclusion: The Biopolitics of Critical Infrastructure Protection," in *Securing "the Homeland": Critical Infrastructure, Risk and (in)Security*, ed. M.D. Cavelty and K.S. Kristensen (London: Routledge, 2008).
117. M. Hardt and A. Negri, *Multitude: War and Democracy in the Age of Empire* (London: Hamish Hamilton, 2004); J. Reid, *The Biopolitics of the War on Terror: Life*

Struggles, Liberal Modernity and the Defence of Logistical Societies (Manchester: Manchester University Press, 2006); M. Dillon and J. Reid, *The Liberal Way of War: Killing to Make Life Live* (Oxford: Routledge, 2009).
118. Bloom 2005.
119. Reid 2008.
120. J. E. Seery, *Political Theory for Mortals: Shades of Justice, Images of Death* (Ithaca, NY: Cornell University Press, 1996), pp. 19–20.
121. Ibid., p. 20.
122. See also J. Baudrillard, *The Spirit of Terrorism and Other Essays* (London: Verso, 2003), p. 21; Z. Bauman, *Liquid Life* (Cambridge: Polity Press, 2005), p. 46.
123. See Z. Bauman, *Liquid Modernity* (Cambridge: Polity Press: 2000); Bauman 2005; Z. Bauman, *Liquid Fear* (Cambridge, Polity Press, 2006).
124. Foucault 2004; Foucault 1990.
125. Foucault 2004, p. 254.
126. Ibid.
127. Ibid.
128. Ibid.
129. G. Agamben, *Homo Sacer: Sovereign Power and Bare Life* (Stanford: Stanford University Press, 1995).
130. In his most recent work, *The Kingdom and the Glory*, Agamben retreats from this categorical position, reasserting the distinction between the logic of providential government/biopolitics and the logic of sovereign power/glory. G. Agamben, *The Kingdom and the Glory: For a Theological Genealogy of Economy and Government (Homo Sacer II, 2)* (Stanford: Stanford University Press, 2011).
131. Agamben 1995, p. 83.
132. Ibid., p. 6.
133. Ibid.
134. Ibid., p. 122.
135. Ibid.
136. Ibid., p. 173.
137. See S. J. Murray, "Thanatopolitics: On the Use of Death for the Mobilisation of Political Life," *Polygraph* 18 (2006): 191–215; J. Derrida, "Autoimmunity: Real and Symbolic Suicides – A Dialogue with Jacques Derrida," in *Philosophy in a Time of Terror: Dialogues with Jürgen Habermas and Jacques Derrida*, ed. G. Borradori (Chicago: University of Chicago Press, 2003).
138. Agamben 1995, p. 125.
139. Z. Bauman, *Collateral Damage: Social Inequalities in a Global Age* (Cambridge: Polity, 2011).
140. Agamben 1995, p. 185.
141. Ibid.
142. Ibid.
143. E. Dauphinee and C. Masters, *The Logics of Biopower and the War on Terror: Living, Dying, Surviving* (New York: Palgrave Macmillan, 2007), p. xiii.
144. Ibid., p. 237.
145. Ibid.
146. J.-A. Mbembe, "Necropolitics," *Public Culture* 15, no. 1 (2003): 11–40.
147. Ibid., p. 21.
148. See also Foucault 2004, p. 257.
149. Mbembe 2003, p. 27.
150. Ibid., p. 39.
151. Ibid.
152. Ibid.
153. Ibid., p. 35.
154. Enns 2004, p. 27.

155. Ibid.
156. Ibid., p. 43.
157. Enns 2004.
158. Pape 2006.
159. See Asad 2007.
160. Enns 2004.
161. Hardt and Negri 2004, p. 45.
162. Ibid., p. 44.
163. Ibid., p. 45.
164. Ibid.
165. Ibid., p. 54.
166. Ibid.
167. Dillon and Reid 2009, p. 36.
168. Foucault 2004, p. 248.
169. Agamben (2011) distinguishes between two political theologies in the Christian tradition: that of sovereignty – associated with the sacrificial exception, and that of the 'divine *oikonomia*' – concerned with biopolitical government and effective management of man.
170. Foucault 2004, p. 248.
171. Ibid., p. 244.
172. Ibid., p. 243.
173. Ibid., p. 248.
174. Ibid., p. 250.
175. Gilles Deleuze, *Foucault* (Paris: Continuum, 1999), p. 79.
176. Esposito 2008, p. 74.
177. Reid points out that 'humanitarian organizations have become complicit in practices of "letting die" lives' inasmuch as 'liberalism refuses to recognize the suffering of the lives which fail to live up to . . . [its particular] . . . criteria. There is, in other words, a necropolitics implicit in the design [of contemporary humanitarianism]' (J. Reid, "The Biopoliticization of Humanitarianism: From Saving Bare Life to Securing the Biohuman in Post-Interventionary Societies," *Journal of Intervention and Statebuilding* 4, no. 4 [2011]: 391–411, 394). Note the difference between popular humanitarian responses to the 2010 earthquake in Haiti, an island which has already been subject to multiple lamentable interventions from interested external powers (see P. Hallward, *Damming the Flood: Haiti, Aristide, and the Politics of Containment*, London: Verso, 2007), and Western donor responses to the floods in Pakistan during the same year (a 'dangerous' source of terror).
178. Dillon and Reid 2009, p. 32.
179. Ibid., p. 31.
180. Ibid., p. 33.
181. See J.A. Schumpeter, *Capitalism, Socialism and Democracy* (New York: Harper and Brothers, 2011).
182. Dillon 2007, p. 19.
183. See U. Beck, *World Risk Society* (Cambridge: Polity, 1999); U. Beck and M. Ritter, *Risk Society: Towards a New Modernity* (London: Sage, 1992).
184. C. Aradau and R. Van Munster, "Governing Terrorism through Risk: Taking Precautions, (un)Knowing the Future," *European Journal of International Relations* 13, no. 1 (2007): 89.
185. Foucault and Senellart 2008, p. 66.
186. M. Duffield, "Total War as Environmental Terror: Linking Liberalism, Resilience, and the Bunker," *South Atlantic Quarterly* 110, no. 3 (2011): 763.
187. Schumpeter 2011.
188. See Agamben 2011, pp. 266, 284. Agamben argues here that the ceremonial-sacrificial diagram of the sovereign exception and economic-managerial diagram of biopolitical

governmentality constitute two distinct if historically imbricated theological lineages. This implies a move away from the Schmittian claim in *Homo Sacer* that unites sovereignty with biopolitics at an originary level, since it implies an independent theological root for the biopolitical tradition of providential government through immanence. The significance of this shift is that it reemphasises the contingent assemblage of immanence and transcendence in contemporary political theology, and brings Agamben closer to Foucault's claims, in *Society Must Be Defended* (2004), with respect to the contingency of the assemblage of sovereignty and biopolitics.
189. See M. Dillon and L. Lobo-Guerrero, "The Biopolitical Imaginary of Species-Being," *Theory Culture Society* 26, no. 1 (2009): 1–23; Dillon and Reid 2009; B. Evans and J. Reid, "Dangerously Exposed: The Life and Death of the Resilient Subject," *Resilience* 1, no. 2 (2013): 83–98; B. Evans and J. Reid, *Resilient Life: The Art of Living Dangerously* (Hoboken, NJ: John Wiley & Sons, 2014).
190. Agamben 1995, 2011.
191. This is the essence of Badiou's critique of democratic materialism. See A. Badiou, *Logics of Worlds* (London: Continuum, 2009b).
192. F. Devji, *The Terrorist in Search of Humanity: Militant Islam and Global Politics* (London: Hurst, 2008).
193. This is a register for political agency inasmuch as it is not derived from a structural opposition to liberalism. This does not purport to be an exhaustive account of agency in suicide bombing. Such an account would need to involve a more systematic analysis of terms of jihadi discourse independent of liberalism, as well as deal more substantively with the politics of killing.
194. Devji 2008, p. 163.
195. Ibid., p. 204.
196. Ibid.
197. Ibid.
198. This seems to firmly locate Devji with respect to the biopolitical tradition of thought. See ibid., p. 55.
199. Ibid.
200. Ibid.
201. Ibid., p. 201.
202. Khan and Tanweer were, after all, born in and of a liberal state.
203. Devji 2008, p. 10.
204. A. Houen, "Sacrificial Militancy and the Wars against Terror," in *Terror and the Postcolonial*, ed. E. Boehmer and S. Morton (Malden: Wiley-Blackwell, 2010), p. 115.
205. For 'only life that is exposed to . . . uncertainty can properly develop the desirable (Liberal) attributes' (Duffield 2011, p. 763).
206. B. Massumi, "National Enterprise Emergency: Steps Toward an Ecology of Powers," *Theory Culture & Society* 26, no. 153 (2009), p. 154.
207. Deleuze and Guattari 2004b, p. 465.
208. Evans and Reid 2014.
209. C. Death, "Counter-Conducts: A Foucauldian Analytics of Protest," *Social Movement Studies* 9, no. 3 (2010): 235–251.
210. Stuart Murray (2006) raises a comparable question. He argues that suicide bombing cannot be thought without relation to the contemporary biopolitical diagram, but that something else must be included in our political analysis: the gesture towards unrestricted, absolute freedom which is inescapably integral to the meaning of suicide bombing.
211. Ibid., p. 195.
212. Ibid.
213. Foucault and Senellart 2008, p. 3.
214. M. Foucault and M. Blanchot, *Foucault-Blanchot* (New York: Zone Books, 1987), p. 16.

215. Ibid., p. 26.
216. Ibid., p. 31.
217. G. Deleuze, *The Logic of Sense* (London and New York, Continuum, 2004c); Foucault and Blanchot 1987, p. 39.
218. Foucault and Blanchot 1987, pp. 54–55.
219. Ibid., p. 58.
220. Deleuze 1999.
221. Essentially, by inserting the event into Foucault.
222. P. Palladino, "Revisiting Franco's Death," in *Foucault on Politics, Security and War*, ed. M. Dillon and A. Neal (London: Palgrave Macmillan, 2008); M. Foucault, *The Order of Things. An Archaeology of the Human Sciences, Etc.* (London: Tavistock, 1970).
223. This point is stated explicitly; it is 'certain idea of Life, a certain vitalism, in which Foucault's thought culminates' (Deleuze 1999, p. 77). The accuracy of Deleuze's reading of Foucault is less important here than what it can do for our understanding of Deleuze and Guattari on the subject of politics and suicide as determined by a naturalistic understanding of revolutionary desire (from the outside).
224. Ibid., p. 38.
225. Ibid., pp. 51, 58.
226. Ibid., p. 71.
227. Ibid., p. 73.
228. Ibid., p. 74.
229. Ibid.
230. Ibid.
231. Ibid., p. 76.
232. Ibid., p. 77.
233. Ibid., p. 78.
234. Ibid., p. 100.
235. Ibid., p. 79.
236. Ibid.
237. Ibid.; see also G. Deleuze and C. Parnet, "Many Politics," in *Dialogues II* (London: Continuum, 2002).
238. Deleuze 1999, p. 82.
239. Deleuze 2002, p. 136.
240. Contrasting with Duffield (2011), who argues that there is no such thing as pure contingency, there are only contingencies as constructed by particular administrative rationalities.
241. 'The place of the fissure where life exists par excellence' (Deleuze 1999, p. 100).
242. Foucault 1970, p. 387.
243. Ibid., p. 442.
244. The god-form.
245. The man-form.
246. Deleuze 1999, p. 109.
247. Through what Deleuze terms a superfold.
248. Foucault 1970, p. 315.
249. Deleuze 1999, p. 109.
250. B. Noys, *Malign Velocities: Accelerationism and Capitalism* (London: Zero Books, 2014), p. 33. See also R. Mackay and A. Avanessian, *#ACCELERATE: The Accelerationist Reader* (Falmouth: Urbanomic, 2014).
251. Deleuze 1999, p. 77.
252. M. Dillon, "Specters of Biopolitics: Finitude, Eschaton, and Katechon," *South Atlantic Quarterly* 210, no. 3 (2011).
253. Ibid.
254. S. Plant and N. Land, "Cyberpositive," in *#Accelerate: The Accelerationist Reader*, ed. R. Mackay and A. Avanessian (Falmouth: Urbanomic, 2014), reprint.

5 Cult and revolution

Revolutionary suicide

Revolutionary politics has become indissociable from the panic of raw creativity. Here Deleuze and Guattari identify themselves within the broad milieu of political thought that recognises making and breaking as intimate bedfellows.[1] This autodestructive line runs through the canon of radical emancipation. Challenging readings of an urge to sovereignty running through all radical activism; those writing on this line suggest that it is only by the possibility of suicide that a nonsovereign politics is made possible.

The doctrine of revolutionary suicide, developed by the cofounder of the Black Panthers, Huey Newton, is the condensation of this insight.[2] Newton's text is a manifesto of violent racial liberation. Marking the incremental rise in black suicides in 1970s America, Newton distinguishes a revolutionary suicide from

> reactionary suicide: the reaction of a man who takes his own life in response to social conditions that overwhelm him and condemn him to helplessness ... bereft of self-respect, immobilised by fear and despair, he sinks into self-murder.[3]

Newton argued that this reactionary suicide

> is a spiritual death that has been the experience of millions of Black people in the United States. This death is found everywhere today in the Black community. Its victims have ceased to fight the forms of oppression that drink their blood. The common attitude has been: what's the use? If a man rises up against a power as great as the United States, he will not survive: Believing this, many Blacks have been driven to a death of the spirit rather than of the flesh, lapsing into lives of quiet desperation.[4]

Any hope for a better world, Newton argued, required a complete 'assault on the establishment', that assault could only take the form of revolutionary suicide.[5] He reasons that 'it is better to oppose the forces that would drive me to self murder than to endure them. Although I risk the likelihood of death, there is at least the possibility, if not probability of changing intolerable conditions.'[6] Indeed, he goes on 'we are all – Black and white alike – ill in the same way, mortally ill'; the only critical question is to decide how to live. 'I say with hope and dignity; and if premature death is the result, then that death has a meaning reactionary suicide can never have. It is the price of self respect'.[7] As the price of self-respect, suicide becomes revolutionary. This involves no death wish, rather its opposite: to fight the forces of reaction to the point of death is the only real act of affirmation.

Newton finds support in Nechayev's *Catechism*, which he attributes incorrectly to Michael Bakunin.[8] Bakunin certainly himself prioritised intensity of individual dedication and fullness of consciousness over the breadth of a revolutionary alliance, and planned to wage 'savage, unrelenting war – if necessary to the death'.[9] Only such a potentially suicidal commitment, he argued, could establish conditions 'favourable to the awakening of popular initiative . . . and shake the masses out of their sheepish state'.[10] Destruction itself can awaken the 'spirit of revolt, the source of all moral and material emancipation', by translating a universal but blind instinct to rejection of hierarchy and despotism into conscious popular revolutionary will.[11] For Bakunin, then, suicidal violence can unleash the deterritorialising urge already immanent to the masses, but the claim to an intrinsically revolutionary potency in suicidal violence was brought to its violent apogee by Sergie Nechayev. The self would now be fully folded under the wings of negation.[12] Now 'the revolutionist is a doomed man . . . everything in him is absorbed by one exclusive interest, one thought, one passion – the revolution.'[13] Nechayev exhorted revolutionaries to break all bonds with the social order, reject all established laws, conventions, doctrines and moralities, and to devote themselves wholly and fully to the task of the destruction of society root and branch. Nechayev thus extends a vision of the revolutionary as suicide, rejecting all codes and identities; 'ready to die at any moment'. This suicide is not the autonomic act of an individual but the expression of a revolutionary passion constructed on an impersonal line: all cold calculation with no more personal impulses.[14] A line into the absolute becomes here the principle of all revolutionary practice. Its energy comes from the outside. Refusing social bonds, comrades and the self are simply energy to be spent on the line as necessary.[15] The self is dissolved into the action; assassination, manipulation, conspiracy and violence, liberating the self with the masses through ensuring their relentless mutual exposure to abolition. All constructive organisation is 'the business of future generations. [The revolutionary's] business is destruction, terrible, complete, universal and merciless'.[16] Suicide, for Nechayev, was the only revolutionary principle. Only self-negation can spark new consciousness.

Ernesto 'Che' Guevara argued that 'the guerrilla fighter, who is general of himself, need not die in every battle', but he must always be 'ready to give his life'. For Guevara, what supplies the '*positive* quality of this guerrilla warfare is precisely that each one of the guerrilla fighters is ready to die, not to defend an ideal, but rather to convert it into reality'.[17] Indeed, as the embodiment of this positive principle in the establishment of revolutionary focos, he advocates the forming of a 'suicide-platoon' of volunteers who can strike at the most dangerous locations: 'Entrance to this platoon should be regarded as almost a prize for merit'. Guevara was careful to distinguish, however, the willingness to die from the will to die. Unnecessary self-exposure to 'defeat or annihilation' is simply the marker of bad strategy. Death and destruction carry no integral charge. Death is revolutionary only as a code of practice; suffering 'formidable privations' up to the point of death is essential to the pedagogy of the revolutionary.[18] Guevara's contemporary Regis Debray was no less explicit; for the focoist, death is a principle of conduct.[19] To be a revolutionary is to risk all, and through such a commitment, to be able to turn any failure into a springboard to later success.[20] 'To conquer is to accept as a matter of principle that life, for the revolutionary, is not the supreme good'.[21] Only commitment unto death can prevent the taming of the revolution under reformism. A pragmatics of revolutionary suicide was similarly central for Mao Tse-Tung. Mao shared with Bakunin and Nechayev the view that violent action must spark a revolutionary moment.[22] Unlike Nechayev, however, he distinguished between worthy and unworthy suicides.[23] He recognised death is a common occurrence whenever there is revolutionary struggle. An indomitable spirit, willing to 'fight the enemy to the last drop of our blood' is always critical.[24] But the revolutionary must avoid unnecessary sacrifices. Mao stated in a classical excerpt that the meaning of weight of death varies widely in accordance with the place of our self-expenditure: 'it may be heavier than Mount Tai or lighter than a feather'.[25] Not all deaths are equal.

Newton references both Guevara and Mao as grounds for his thesis, arguing that revolutionaries are often simply not prepared to accept the morbid actualities of revolutionary practice identified by both.[26] The Black Panthers would not 'romanticise the consequences of revolution in our life time'. There is, Newton argues, little chance of participating in a revolution and then dying of old age, and he claimed to have no expectation of seeing the revolution fulfilled in his lifetime, only that 'the revolution will grow in my life time ... I do not expect to enjoy its fruits'.[27] You cannot, he implies, be a revolutionary and expect to survive.[28] This fact had been borne out, he argued, in every example of resistance – from the American colonists to the French of the late eighteenth century, the Russians of 1917, the Jews of Warsaw, the Cubans, the National Liberation Front and the North Vietnamese: 'any people who struggle against a brutal and powerful force – are suicidal'.[29] Newton's prison experience confirmed this insight to him: His constant defiance resulted in Newton receiving far worse treatment than his peers. Indeed, he claims that his actions were such that the guards thought he was suicidal. They assumed he would crack under the disciplinary pressure, but instead, he became ever stronger: 'If I had submitted to their exploitation and done their will, it would have killed my spirit and condemned me to a living death. To cooperate in prison meant a reactionary suicide to me'.[30]

As such, only because his actions carried the risk of death and mental destruction could they be a means of propagandising to and radicalising the other inmates and thus promoting the revolution against passive or reactionary suicide. In this sense, for Newton,

> the concept of revolutionary suicide was not defeatist or fatalistic. On the contrary, it conveyed an awareness of reality in combination with the possibility

of hope – reality because the revolutionary must always be prepared to face death, and hope because it symbolises a resolute determination to bring about change ... above all, it demands that the revolutionary sees his death and his life as one piece.[31]

Newton's text imputes eschatological connotations, because of a 'greater, more immediate danger ... the survival of the entire world'. Newton argues that 'If the world does not change, all its people will be threatened ... The handwriting is on the wall'. Only by adopting a strategy of revolutionary suicide, can the Black Panthers 'establish ... the means for creative work'.[32] Only with suicide can they challenge the suicide machine of the racist Urstaat.[33]

There can be little surprise that the Panthers were to be deemed such a fundamental threat to the US state formation. A startling claim is explicitly being developed by Newton. He suggests that revolutionary politics is a game which makes self-murder the currency of every decision. In doing so, it presents an active death against a reactive death, with no dialectical resolution on offer in this meeting. Newton posited an antiracist and antisovereign politics that emerges in making pass words out of the morbid order words of sovereignty; the deterritorialisation of the death that an inherently racist power decrees. Such a deterritorialised and deterritorialising death simply has no relation to the autonomic suicides implicated in Western notions of sovereign individuality. It is revolutionary because it explodes the self in the declaration of its finitudes. Far from suicide being posited as the ideologeme of pure identity, it is claimed here to embody the passing of every sovereign.

Jonestown

Revolution is an urge, not a meaning. This appears to be the implication of the Jonestown event. After the enthusiasm of 1968, the Jonestown mass suicide marks the apogee that accompanied the historical closure of that era's deterritorialising tendencies.[34] Jonestown may be viewed, in this sense, as exemplifying the fatal trajectory that resides on all lines of flight: the risk of becoming caught up in a celebrant movement into a black hole.[35] The Peoples Temple began its life as a radical experiment in constructing a racially integrated church in an era when congregations remained largely segregated. Jim Jones, a white preacher, drew on traditions of faith healing and motifs of worship after the mould of Father Divine.[36] Jones was a very different creature, explicitly binding from the start his religious doctrine to a revolutionary politics. In the era before McCarthy, Jim Jones's church received widespread opprobrium for its radical political claims, but it was only following departures from the church by a group of younger members who deemed it insufficiently radical that Jones took flight across the plains to California, moving the Temple into San Francisco in 1973. This was the first exodus in the face of diverse pressures which would culminate in an unparalleled act of collective abolition.[37]

In San Francisco, Jim Jones's congregation grew exponentially, along with the standing and heft of the Peoples Temple. The Temple expanded involvement in the provision of social housing, treatment of drug addiction, alcoholism, and poverty alleviation under government contracts. It became wealthy, but maintained a communalistic ethos, collecting and redistributing money amongst its members, living in shared accommodation, and directing a voting bloc. Jones was courted by local and national Democratic politicians. By the early 1970s he had become a celebrity, with leading national Democratic figures attending his services. That rosy image only began to tarnish in the mid-1970s with a series of highly negative articles which were printed in the *San Francisco Examiner* and received national attention. Drawing on the testimony of ex-members, these articles inverted the public face of the Peoples Temple, accusing it of mistreating its members and being engaged in systematic fraud, extortion, coercion, beatings and psychological torture under the guidance of a megalomaniac leader. The entry into the public imagination of 'the cult', a sex scandal involving Jones himself and a number of departures (defections) by leading members led to rising paranoia within the Temple.[38] Jones perceived a conspiracy and took flight once again, moving the Peoples Temple to a substantial portion of jungle they had purchased in Guyana several years earlier: Jonestown was born.

Back in America a group of ex-members, calling themselves the Committee of Concerned Relatives, argued that the Temple's members were victims of brainwashing by the charismatic Jones. Tapping here into a stream of cultural consciousness that had emerged in response to the explosion of new religious movements in the early '70s, as the flower power generation matured in the shadow of the Vietnam War.[39] The 'anti-cult movement' viewed the new religions as uniquely dangerous, and Jonestown was soon to provide apparently definitive support for this sentiment. The Concerned Relatives were able to convince United States Congressman Leo Ryan to make an exploratory visit to Jonestown.[40] He arrived at Jonestown with a party of hostile press and a number of Concerned Relatives in November 1978. They were given a tour and then treated to a dinner and party in which the inhabitants seemed relaxed, happy and uncoerced.[41] Then one reporter was passed a note requesting that one of the residents be allowed to leave with the party. During the next twelve hours the requests grew to double figures, such that there were now insufficient places on the two aeroplanes to fit all the 'defectors'. As the group, with its new additions, got ready to depart, the congressman was attacked by a knife-wielding resident who was quickly disarmed, before the group headed out to the airstrip to await the arrival of the planes.

As the congressman, Concerned Relatives, ex-residents, and reporters waited on the strip, a tractor from Jonestown pulled up. A small group of armed men jumped out and began firing on the party just as they as they were beginning to board the plane. One of the defectors also pulled out a gun. By the time they all drove off, four were dead, including Congressman Ryan, and twelve were seriously wounded. At Jonestown, Jim Jones called everyone to the central pavilion. In an act that has now entered the common lexicon, en masse the nine hundred inhabitants of Jonestown 'drank the Kool-Aid' laced with potassium cyanide and sedatives. Men and women, black and white, old and young, including several hundred children and small babies, died foaming and convulsing. Their bodies were found bloated and rotting in the Guyana heat, littering the ground around the pavilion. Jones lay inside with a gunshot wound to the head surrounded by his closest advisors; he had been shot by his personal nurse before she turned the gun on herself.

Within the year journalists directly involved in the event had released books which consolidated the 'death cult' image of Peoples Temple.[42] The extreme disciplinary practices of the church were given great emphasis and the concept of brainwashing took centre stage. Jones was represented as a cynical nihilist whose eventual death by gunshot reveals that he had no real intention of joining the others in suicide.[43] In the account that formed in the immediate aftermath of the events, and broadly supported by the work written by the defectors who formed the Committee of Concerned Relatives, members stayed and in the end killed themselves out of a combination of direct coercion, Jones's charisma, and ideological programming. Later works, in particular Hall and Chidester, have to some extent challenged this vision, supported by survivors' oral histories.[44] Most surviving members of the Peoples Temple clearly held deep and genuine commitments to its mission, and continued to view their experiences within it in far from an exclusively negative light. As the oral histories make clear, if there was madness it was collectively shared.[45] Indeed, citizens of Jonestown appeared to have desired death; indeed, for one at least, death had been the issue all along:

> The death of self, the death of previous political or/and religious beliefs, the death of the previous style of dressing, the death of the pre-PT diet, the de facto death of the family of origin; the death of ego (everyone's excluding his); the death of desires for tobacco, sex, alcohol, money. It was all about dying all along the way, from beginning to end. . . . I see now that it ended just as it started.[46]

When Jones spoke in the pavilion on that fatal day, he declared their act a revolutionary suicide in the explicit mould of Newton. Newton's analysis of the racial politics and catastrophic trajectory of the United States formed a central pillar in the Jonestown signifying regime. The literature and world view of the Black Panthers, and the thematic of an order intrinsically threatened by black mobilisation, was a constant refrain in Jones's sermons to his largely black congregation. This is not, however, to say it was the only reference point. Jones drew from Christianity, atheism, faith healing, Marxist-Leninism, Maoism, civil rights, and Third Worldism: a heady semiotic mixture which attracted significant variety in its membership. The large body of members had often experienced genuine hardship and exclusion, with the radical socioeconomic promise of the church clearly a critical element of its appeal to most. The bulk of the leadership and later defecting members of the Concerned Relatives were, however, disproportionately from an affluent background. This breakdown also had racial and gendered dimensions, with the temple leadership almost exclusively white, young, and female.

The terror of fallout had been a persistent refrain within this heterogeneous signifying regime, particularly as Jones prepared his congregation for the move to

California.[47] Indeed, millenarian discourse rose to the surface of Jones's loosely integrated sea of content in distinct cycles, dictated by the shifting affective circumstances of the Temple.[48] The interaction between Jones's fluid world view and the increasingly hostile campaign resulted in a dynamic escalation. In this sense, Hall argues, the actions of the Concerned Relatives, who were well aware of the millenarian virtualities of the Peoples Temple, seems to have directly played a role in actualising it.[49] Anxieties about internal cohesion and external threats would recurrently drive visualisations of the apocalypse to the fore, increasingly taking the form of the imminent rise of a fascist state in America which would oversee a repeat of the genocidal racist concentration camps of World War II. Following the Temple's disintegrating status in San Francisco and the departure of a leading member, Grace Stoens, in 1976, Jones's axiomatic response had been another flight now to Guyana. The point here is that whilst a millenarian line was clearly always present in the Peoples Temple, it took the right conditions to fully capture the assemblage for its trajectory.[50] Reducing the act to a paradigmatically religious enactment of a transhistorical practice of redemptive sacrifice, however,[51] is to suggest that the affective mechanics of the Temple were secondary to its regime of signs.[52] In the event, it was the dynamics of desire which drew the Temple into a suicidal assemblage.

As a desiring-machine, the Peoples Temple was certainly highly distinctive. Jones placed himself at the despotic centre: the origin of all debts and the object of desire par excellence. He occupied a central role in the psychosexual lives of all members, and was referred to universally as Father. Jones used his supposed psychic powers to keep discipline, keeping copious files on every member, as well as letters of confession that members were required to write and deposit as leverage should they defect.[53] Combined with an apparently prodigious memory, this allowed Jones to pick out individual congregation members and discuss, at collective meetings, issues that reinforced the impression of omniscience. All women lusted after (or were obliged to pretend to lust after) him as a matter of collective principle, whilst declaiming that Jones was the paragon of sexual prowess. Indeed, his partners were expected to publically narrate tales of his stamina and virility. Men were expected to surrender their wives. Jones was both the sole legitimate receptacle and radically empty of desire. Sex, Jones claimed, was either an entirely communally focused act or a submission to capitalist commodification. He was the personification of a molar line, a desire for and of the community. As under fascism, this molar line relied on a distributed molecular resonance machine. Under Jones, the Peoples Temple saw itself as a radical embodiment of anti-Oedipal sexual relations. Jones surrounded himself with young women who, as his lovers, held authority over their husbands and the community.[54] The hierarchy of gender dominant in American society at large was thus displaced and inverted under the guidance of Jones the Father. Central to the circulation of desire within the temple was also a more generalised disruption of gender identities. Men were expected to 'confess' to homosexual tendencies, often through sexual engagement with Jones. This formalised process of confession took place in the public meetings that were regularly held, and used to discipline the members.[55]

Though individuals could and did marry in the Temple, they were always understood as members of a single indivisible postracial and postbiological family, within which children were collectively parented. Parents deemed too protective or possessive of their children were forced to send them for nights with other adults. This actively broke down and disrupted nuclear familial structures, and replaced them with a supple network of support, authority and pedagogy. The Peoples Temple as a desiring political assemblage was thus orientated vertically towards Jones as father figure, and horizontally outwards into a diffused molecular fabric of the Temple community. Despite the archaism of the diagram, Jones was not, therefore, inaccurate in framing the Peoples Temple as a revolution of desire. His alternative 'family' assumed a rejection of the normal social structures of American capitalism, via a radically novel assemblage of the molar and molecular. Communal living embodied the essence of the radical challenge to the bourgeois repression endemic in American society. In reforming a molecular fabric of family life, resonating upwards towards him as a cosmic father, Jones and his congregation saw themselves as building an entirely new diagram. There is no doubt, in this sense, that Jones was tapped into the milieu of critical psychoanalysis, including Reich and Laing, to which Deleuze and Guattari also belonged. The practical connotations of Deleuze and Guattari's model of the revolution precisely did not advocate the 'step by step transformation of society', but rather a called for 'microscopic attempts at creating communities'.[56] In this sense, the Peoples Temple may be read as a disastrous experiment in molecular revolution.

The radical ambition of its desiring-machine explains the enormous importance Jones placed upon particular individual's departure from the Temple and his apocalyptic responses to these departures. For Jones each departure threatened the viability of their alternative diagram and undermined its opposition to the oedipal dynamics of American capitalism. It also explains why Grace and Tim Stoens's campaign to regain custody of their son John represented such a radical threat to the Temple in Jones's eyes. The legal case to retrieve John was an attack on the institutional formations which made collective parenting possible. John thus quickly became the personification of the wider regime of opposition to Peoples Temple, as the 'living symbol of everything' in the alternative society, communal living and the struggle against bourgeois repression.[57] Jones explicitly saw failure in keeping John as the tip of an iceberg of potential cases that would inevitably erode and dissolve the Peoples Temple, as there were many children in the Temple with one parent vulnerable to a custody challenge.[58] The Concerned Relatives, in being organised around this legal campaign, for Jones showed the established regime acting against the very essence of Jonestown as an assemblage of desire. The battle for John's custody is central to understanding why Jones saw a collective flight of the temple for Guyana in 1977 as necessary, but also to his extreme response to the Stoens's (now Mills's)[59] consequent legal approach of the Guyanese authorities. The telegram released by Jones in response to the Guyanese court summons explicitly threatened mass suicide.

Jones saw the potential departure of John as the unravelling of the Temple desiring-machine. His response was to build a pure war machine on its lines.

Jonestown became host to an extreme militarisation. Following a further defection from the inner core, and her deposition to Congress asserting her fear that the promised mass suicide might actually happen, negative press exploded in America. Everyone could see what was on the horizon. The Six Day Siege in 1977 formed the prelude to what would become a practiced operation, wherein Jones would declare imminent and collective suicide the only response to an invasion by the CIA or the Guyanese army.[60] These were genuine rehearsals,[61] with participants not aware that they were mock events. Members would gather, drink, and wait to die. Appended by a tightening of intercommunal discipline, the Peoples Temple rehearsed its suicide until death became a practiced habit. Jones always claimed these suicides would leave a legacy, but he also claimed not to believe in a personal afterlife.[62] His only faith, as he put it, was in the revolution. We thus see in Jonestown the danger on the line of flight embodied.[63] To ensure its continuation, Jones built a revolutionary assemblage of desire which was indissociable from a wager on death.[64] He gathered the desiring-political leftovers 'washed ashore from the sixties shipwreck' and set them to flight.[65] Such a revolutionary passion could find outlet only in a headlong flight.[66] The danger haunting Deleuze and Guattari's political vision is precisely that which appears to be in operation here; when fidelity to death comes to be the secret of the revolution.

Millenarianism

The dystopian critical imaginary in circulation today has as much to do with Paul Virilio's resurgence in Anglophone literatures as it does with the work of Michel Foucault. For Virilio, Beck's vision of 'the very success of industrial and social modernity in managing risks [as] in fact generated new risks' fails to capture the extremity of our current situation.[67] For Virilio, Deleuze and Guattari's vision, far from allowing us a politics of deterritorialisation, is determinately transpolitical: an embrace of the efficiency of accidents. Virilio thus directly challenges their work as a futurist marriage of disastrousness and creativity. In this sense, he follows through on the eschatological implications of Deleuze and Guattari's thought: his own millenarian narrative defining our society as set on an inevitable path to self-abolition. This line haunts the horizon of Deleuze and Guattari's account, inasmuch as they contend that suicidal excess is not a departure from political life but its superabundant manifestation. For Paul Virilio this is not a vision of life at all, but simply the disastrous essence of technological speed ruled by a 'principle of indetermination'.[68] Virilio worries that such a vision can only offer a descent into suicidal war. Transpolitics is the panic consequent to embracing the accident, mistaking suicide for the revolution – just like Jim Jones.

Contemporary theorists of biopower are troubled by the idea of modern progress; they, with Deleuze,[69] worry what will append the imminent death of the man-form. The problematic which biopower poses, that of how to secure life itself as an infinitely recombinatory finite multiplicity, seems likely to lead to disastrous futures.[70] In his brief commentary on the emergence of *Societies of Control*, Deleuze pointed out that the disciplinary diagram's successful enclosures of the outside – as madness (in the asylum apparatus) or delinquency (in the prison apparatus) – is being displaced by a 'diagram of control' which functions by modulating rather than including-excluding, remote controlling, incorporating, means testing, data mining, turning us from individuals into 'dividuals' made up of discrete fluid codes which can be measured and controlled.[71] No longer seeing any need to fix the subject under binary striations, 'societies of control seek to define the individual through a series of different, modulated and overlapping states of risk'.[72] For contemporary Foucaultians such a vision of domination after the man-form is all too apt. Biopower's fantasy of machinic control over life itself leads to its accelerating securitisation; biopolitics is postpolitics. The danger presented by the life risks we don't know about inescapably becomes a justification for preemptive intervention, which seems to descend, inexorably, into incitement.[73] This goes beyond the idea that late modernity breeds insecurity in the form of resistance, or that contemporary (suicide) terrorism is idiomatic of biopolitical techniques of organisation and governance.[74] Rather, the implication is that our postpolitical condition literally enjoins us to skirt disaster through their project of nurturing contingent life understood as an infinitely recombinatory finite multiplicity. As Dillon puts it, liberalism's 'hypersecurity politics [are] fundamentally a politics of dangerous becoming'.[75]

Virilio's closely connected vision of a society set to its own transpolitical demolition assumes a conceptual association between deterritorialisation and suicide that resonates with Deleuze and Guattari's work. For Virilio, the central political problem facing us today is that of the disastrousness of accelerating technological innovation. It is our transcendent prioritisation of (technological) creation which has taken us to the liminal state we find ourselves in. One may therefore read Virilio's oeuvre, much like Badiou's, as a generalised critique of Deleuze and Guattari's naturalistic commitment to revolutionary life as deterritorialising desire. Virilio's millenarian narrative echoes Foucaultian anxiety in describing our society as one which is trending inexorably toward self-destruction. By embracing the panicked creativity of deterritorialisation, we have already replaced politics with transpolitical suicidalism. For Virilio, the modern project is defined by the pursuit of ever greater speeds of technological innovation or deterritorialisation.[76] Our lust for acceleration has simply rendered the accident the defining concept of our time.[77] The contemporary ascendency of the accident is both a symptom and the source of a malaise integral to the apotheosis of technological deterritorialisation.[78] Virilio's is an analysis of the increasingly 'suicidal features of life in society'.[79]

Politics, by contrast, has always been a question of sacrificial death for Virilio.[80] For Virilio, the polis is a locale in which mortality is regulated collectively, and multiple finite worlds can thus exist (as political spheres). The polis is defined as a shared field of temporality. 'It's not by accident that societies were organised by the death rites, the cult of ancestors etc.';[81] these are mechanisms for the organisation of 'citizen-trajects' by reference to the interruptions in flow, of which death is the most fundamental. It is the politician's task to organise social temporality vis-à-vis human mortality. Consciousness of death, in this way, is the organiser of the polis. The *polis*, as the only location for politics, was always legitimated and given its determinate form by reference to mortality of its citizens, with respect to which a common duration can be established. The polis is a death machine for ordering the circulation of its citizens. It is for this reason that, like Foucault and Baudrillard, Virilio sees the death penalty as the defining instrument of state politics. Virilio references the public cemetery or *Kerameikos* beyond the walls of Athens, where those who served were 'consecrated to an idealistic glory: the polis, the indivisible unity that owes its authority to the effacement of its Andres, its soldier-citizens, valorous yet identical and interchangeable'.[82] It demonstrates, for him, the theatrical engagement with mortality upon which Athenian public space was predicated, and by reference to which the trajective figure of the citizen was inscribed. The public cemetery, as a marker of politic citizenship in Athens, is an indicator of the 'funerary foundation' of all political societies.[83] A politics, for Virilio, is necessarily a (sacrificial) politics of the community collectively coded via its capacity to share consciousness of duration (mortality). We see here Virilio's intimacy with Baudrillard. Sacrificial political formations rooted on intensive collective consciousness of duration have been replaced today by the transpolitical logistics of absolute deterritorialisation which Virilio views as functionally identical to a generalised desire for death.[84] For Virilio, this project is currently reaching its 'negative horizon'.[85] Technological deterritorialisation is ushering in not a state of recombinatory revolutionary possibility but rather a finite world, which seems to Virilio increasingly likely to be final (for our species at least).

A theory of the accident underpins this claim. An accident is what happens unexpectedly, what 'crops up', yet 'reveals the substance'.[86] In contrast to the assumption that the 'accident is relative and contingent and the substance absolute and essential', we must recognise that no substance exists without 'its specific accident'.[87] The accident is not simply a temporary failure; it is programmed into all substances from the start. By turning our attention to the accident as integral to substance we reveal that which is hidden or beneath, yet simultaneously defines 'natural or man-made substances'.[88] All technological innovations entail a particular and specific accident, whether a mechanism of transport such as a car, ship, plane or train or the invention of the Internet. Invention is inseparable from its accident (car crash, plane crash, etc.) as 'indirect invention'.[89] The ever-proliferating innovation that marks modern society thus carries also the implication of a corresponding proliferating innovation of accidents.[90] Technological deterritorialisation does not simply increase the potentiality for specific disastrous events but as itself a global catastrophism. Virilio terms his recent work an *Accidentology*: a commentary on the ontological negatives of our contemporary emphasis on technological deterritorialisation. For Virilio it is the 'primary invention of the accident, of the disaster' which marks out military science; in this sense, the rise of the accident has an important link to the militarisation (colonisation by administrative logistics) of Western society and thought.[91] Military science is the celebration of the destructive accident of machine innovation. An embrace of the problem of creativity's integral disastrousness is definitively military. Virilio points out that it should be obvious that 'nothing can be gained without loss', but this does not mean we should encourage the apotheosis of that dynamic; indeed, doing so is to embrace a purely military or technologistical vision.[92] From this point of view, Deleuze and Guattari's naturalistic theory of the (revolutionary) event of deterritorialisation is uncomfortably close to promoting an apotheosis of the accident which is, for Virilio, already definitive of our society.

As the accident has colonised our society from top to bottom, Virilio argues, it cannot but render the political event obsolete. The global telecommunications revolution and the exponentially more connected and interactive world it constructs supports this process inasmuch as modern communications have supplied the accident with exponentially increased significance.[93] Instantaneous communication technologies transmit any accident into a global arena. This makes it possible, for the first time, for accidents to be experienced globally. Audiences all over the world were able to visually participate in the second plane crashing into the World Trade Center Towers *in real time*. This radically intensified the emotional and psychological impact of the event. Virilio argues that modern communications produce a 'great interiority', a global space which allows accidents to spark off unpredictable dynamic effects.[94] Informational instantaneity means that we are no longer able to distinguish between terrorist attacks, ecological calamities and technological catastrophes; all are flattened by the media-scape. 'Suicide bombing or accident? Information or disinformation? From now on, no one really knows'.[95] It is precisely the fact that political suicide, such as that which took place on 9/11, is significant because it instigates an uncontrollable deterritorialisation of affective content which means that, for Virilio, it cannot be seen as political. The fact that a strategy of the untimely defined the force of those suicides exemplifies, for Virilio, their transpoliticality. The apotheosis of the accident has, in the same gesture, obviated political interpretation of events like suicide bombings.

The rise of the accident is the chief characteristic of our current global condition of what Virilio terms impure war, defined by the strategisation of indeterminacy and disequilibrium by suicidal actors, against the equally suicidal logistics of population regulation. It becomes impossible to think of traditional modes of revolution or democratic politics in a condition in which any contingent event is enough to spark conflagrations if relayed on a loop through mass media. Such events thus aid in the replacement of political discourse by the strategy of accidents and their logistical management as unspecifiable futurity. Transpolitics is the utter corruption of the political by a logistics of contingent affect that is embraced on all sides. Virilio sees this as a direct extension from the revelation of humanity's limit in the possibility of nuclear self-destruction (pure war). This event made possible a consciousness of an accident that would be universal in its reach. From its origination, the milieu of the collective accident 'integrated us globally' only whilst promising the possibility of 'disintegrat[ing] us physically'.[96] What Virilio describes as the 'recent emergence of an end-of-world feeling' is thus more than simply the result of the exponential increase in catastrophic risks; we literally dwell in a globalised accidental milieu.[97] Globalisation gave birth to a world defined almost entirely by consciousness of its accidental status.[98] Inasmuch as the '*untimely*' nature of what crops up' now colonises our experience of political temporality, and 'replaces all events', accidentological strategies like suicide-bombings are substituted for political praxis.[99] This is the end of 'multiple times' marked by 'revolutionary events' and their replacement by a single 'revelationary' accidental time:[100] Our society has become an essentially disastrous one.[101]

A commitment to deterritorialisation such as Deleuze and Guattari's does nothing to repoliticise this condition. Indeed Virilio suggests that it simply celebrates the utter devastation of politicality today by promoting transpolitical strategies of excess (like suicide bombing). Deterritorialisation, far from being revolutionary, marks the categorical end of politics at the hands of accidentological transpolitics. To believe in deterritorialisation is simply to embrace catastrophe. Rather than celebrating deterritorialisation, for Virilio, we must build a reinvigorated mode of (eco)political critique that reveals the accident as 'the hidden face of technical and scientific progress'.[102] It is only through such a critique that we 'can bring about the progress of technical culture'. For Virilio, political critique is a question of 'collaboration or resistance' to technological deterritorialisation.[103] Drawing from Valery's postulate that 'consciousness only survives as awareness of accidents', Virilio argues that the failure to appreciate the challenge of 'the integral accident' marks a kind of deliberate descent into madness: The very opposite of philosophy, 'whereby the insane nature of our acts would not only stop consciously worrying us, but would thrill us and captivate us'.[104] This is clearly a direct critique of Deleuze and Guattari's naturalistic commitment to deterritorialisation. Virilio refuses to celebrate the panic-logistics of creation. He rejects any promise in unrestrained machinic acceleration. Rather we must 'make room in the realm of public information for fallibilism'.[105] This is the opposite of an analytic of risk which retains the myth of the linearity of progress and its assumption of the 'beneficial accident'.[106]

Rather than celebrate technological speed, we 'urgently need to sing the praises of inertia'.[107] Virilio's central injunction is to slow down, to inhibit deterritorialisation, precisely so that we can regain political speed. This is precisely a question of how we interpret death so as to become political. He argues that it is only a military vision that fully accepts death. The civilian sector develops 'an interpretation of death which differed from the military interpretation' precisely so that collective duration becomes possible. Politics is defined as a model of death which sees the necessity of interruption as a driver to collective organisation.[108] Believing we have evacuated the 'problem of death' with God, we embraced a transpolitical military logistics of the accident. The technological speed which defines modern society is thus the 'speed [rather than politics] of death'.[109] For Virilio it is the 'question of sedentariness and our relation to intensity is central' because 'that's where the question of politics lies, if politics has a future'.[110] Politics is the speed of living consciousness against death. Virilio demands our rejection of Deleuze and Guattari's naturalistic theory of revolutionary deterritorialisation – he suggests it is a technomilitaristic and thus fascistic nonpolitics.[111] It is simply insufficient for a politics to embrace the relationship between panic and creation. Only slowing down to speeds at which we can live allows a politics, in the form of a polis of communally experienced duration.

In question here is precisely the relationship between suicide and politics. For Virilio, suicide is the definitive transpolitical strategy. It seeks the purity of the machinic event as such, but rather than becoming-revolutionary, it achieves only the transpolitical apotheosis of accidents which already marks the purely logistical or technocratic societies we inhabit. Suicide's idiomatic relationship to modern accelerationary society is precisely the marker of its political deficiency. If, for Baudrillard, transpolitics had the capacity to implode the modern reality principle, for Virilio 'it's totally negative. It's the contamination of traditional political thought by military thought, period! There is nothing positive in my use of the term transpolitics. It's not post-politics, it's not the end of politics, it is its contamination. It's completely negative. Transpolitics means no more politics at all.'[112] The challenge Virilio presents to Deleuze and Guattari is that it is impossible think the politics of suicide in such a way that it is not a celebration of accidents, an embrace of the corruption of the political by a military logistics. This is why they must claim we can distinguish between political and accidental suicides: Whether they can provide enough rope to save us from disaster remains very much in question.

Dying well

A creative political life, for Deleuze and Guattari, is prone to catastrophe. Given creativity is integrally disastrous, how can we risk its unrestrained pursuit? Indeed, if every line of flight could end in Jonestown, why would we ever set out on them? Their response is distinctly cryptic: If you don't want to end up a fascist suicide, they tell us, you have to take precautions with death.

Here we see the naturalism of Deleuze and Guattari's vision clearly threatening to domesticate their political philosophy. If suicide is a failure due to overexcess, then surely a political life can only be located in slowing down as Virilio suggested. Deleuze and Guattari don't help themselves by discussing the dangers of deterritorialisation in biological terms as a cancer.[113] Their point seems clear: If the problem is a cancerous proliferation out of control, the preferential alternative is a healthy restratification, which allows the body to survive. This comes close to denying the association between the disastrousness of creativity and politics, in the suggestion that we can only be *so* creative. In this way, a fully revolutionary politics would too disastrous to ever be fully embraced. A resigned stoicism of the type Peter Hallward reads in Deleuze's work might find support here: able to observe creativity as disastrous, and as such to observe the political as occasionally suicidal, but unable to provide the grounds for a substantive politics of excess, or indeed, analysis of actual political suicide which does not reduce it to failure.[114] Even more worryingly, Deleuze and Guattari may be read otherwise to encourage us to embrace the transpolitical, instituting a revolutionary praxis that can only speculate that it will not end in horror. The politics of suicide in Deleuze and Guattari appears to suggest a suicide integral to their political philosophy.

Deleuze and Guattari, in developing their response to this charge in *A Thousand Plateaus*, imply that Virilio confuses the qualitative differences between speeds, and only therefore views all deterritorialisation as disastrous. In any machine, they argue, there is the potential to actualise a conservative trajectory, a revolutionary trajectory, or one that accelerates towards pure destruction.[115] For Virilio, one is either moving at metabolic speed or deterritorialising too fast. The tripartite distinction between qualities of speed or line in Deleuze and Guattari is a critical difference, because it indicates that it is possible to distinguish the panic of creation from the panic of pure destruction. It is in seeking to distinguish between the two that they introduce the curious concept of a revolutionary caution. Only a healthy caution, they argue, allows us to distinguish accidentological from evental politics. Such a caution is explicitly not a matter of slowing down to metabolic levels, since 'the faster of two elements or movements of deterritorialisation is not necessarily the most intense or most deterritorialized'.[116] Speed is not the issue. We cannot reach the new through acceleration alone. Rather, creation is defined by choices; specifically the refusal of some modalities of autodestruction whilst simultaneously embracing (counter-actualising) others. Making this distinction is, Deleuze and Guattari argue, never a matter of 'denouncing false desires';[117] rather, we need to distinguish '*within* desire between that which pertains to stratic proliferation, or else too-violent destratification'.[118] Deterritorialisation is defined as a work of pragmatic self-destruction.

Deleuze and Guattari spell this out as clearly as possible:

> This is how it should be done: Lodge yourself on a stratum, experiment with the opportunities it offers, find an adventurous place on it, find potential movements of deterritorialisation, possible lines of flight, experience them, produce flow conjunctions here and there, try out continuums of intensities segment by segment, have a small plot of new land at all times. It is through meticulous relation with the strata that one succeeds in freeing lines of flight, causing conjugated flows to pass and escape and bring forth continuous intensities . . . gently tip the assemblage, making it pass over.[119]

Becoming revolutionary is a 'long process of experimentation' with our assemblage in a wider field of social striation. In this sense, Deleuze and Guattari's turn to the concept of revolutionary caution implies the need for a patient dismantling of the self as a mortal milieu. This requires experiencing our death, but never doing so frenetically.[120] Having abandoned the concept of lack, which Badiou relies on to institute a generic restraint on revolutionary excess, Deleuze and Guattari have to ground revolutionary practice on a kind of pragmatics of play. One has to 'mimic the strata', and wear its masks, to identify openings for escape.[121] Since one is open to dissolution on any number of fronts, the trick is to choose which lines to disturb so as to be as experimental as possible. Such an immanent pragmatics of creation requires judgement. Creative existence here becomes the play of deterritorialisations: a matter of deciding between dissolutions on offer within the strata.[122] If one fails to take sufficient care in this experimentation, one risks throwing 'the strata into demented or suicidal collapse, which brings them down on us heavier than ever'.[123]

This is how Deleuze and Guattari seek to avoid simply 'parlay[ing] defeat into victory'.[124] Yet the problem remains here. Since creative politics is integrally a modality of suicide, it cannot be categorically distinguished from abolition pure and simple on such pragmatic lines. If each body has to make a judgement as to which kinds of death are worth dying, who can say they have succeeded or failed? Fallibility is constitutive of possibility here. In this sense, Deleuze and Guattari's thought raises, but cannot provide an answer to, the question of what it means to die well. For them, revolution is conducted on behalf of the play of innovation itself.[125] Virilio would no doubt see this as collaborating with technological catastrophe. Deleuze responded, in this context, that 'there is no need to fear or hope'; we should simply 'look for new weapons' for creative action as they become available in new technologies.[126] This simply confirmed that, for him, there could be no question of thinking against the death of man and avoiding disaster as a consequence.[127] We cannot have a creative politics without building machines that run to excess; suicide must remain the political possibility of health. By the same gesture, the potential for fascism starts to look disturbingly like the mandate of a machined nature.

Afterword: on machines

This book has traced the frayed limits of a philosophy which views self-destruction as a constitutive, if terrorising, feature of political life. This is a thought which runs against the grain of the major tradition in political philosophy, wherein political community is deemed to be an incremental collective achievement, the result of endless minor struggles, and temporary respite, in the face of an inevitable approaching individual defeat. Nowhere is this clearer than in the assumption that our consciousness of an integral lack provides the only means to save us from humanity's propensity to self-destruction on a catastrophic scale.[128] If creativity assumes proximity to suicide, danger cannot be forestalled by consciousness of tragedy without succumbing to other lines, not least those associated with the degenerative regime of consumer accumulation and its fissiparous securitisations, which also promise our abolition. Our head-on encounter with death appears to be inevitable.[129] If not through humility in the face of our finitude, then, how then can we navigate the hazards?

Deleuze and Guattari's *Capitalism and Schizophrenia* claims to be a political work only inasmuch as it is engaged in conceptual creation. It is perhaps inevitable that its excess of concepts has so regularly been taken to constitute a fundamental refutation of its value.[130] The creation of concepts is disturbing to meaning; this is the kernel of its political function. *Capitalism and Schizophrenia*'s startling conceptual plethora resists systematisation or final interpretation by nature and intent.[131] This follows from a distinctive conception of philosophy itself: 'Philosophy is not communicative, any more than it is contemplative and reflective: it is creative or even revolutionary, by nature'.[132] Conceptual excess is designed to insist upon experimentation and exploration on the part of the reader; to open up new territories or pathways for thinking, by offering tools to think anew and break open problematics across a wide spectrum.[133] It is in this sense that Deleuze and Guattari's text is a machine: the only criteria on which they wish their books to be judged is on what they can do. The operative question is never 'Is it true? But, does it work? What new thoughts does it make possible to think?'[134] This is to claim that a thought is only as worthwhile as those who read it, mutate it, and literally make it different. Deleuze expounded what might be termed a practice of perverse reading in this context. He sought to give the philosophers he read 'monstrous children' by revealing the textual grounds for radically subversive interpretations of their works.[135] This cannot be taken as an excuse for bad faith. Deleuze made clear that the authors must have borne the monster that is returned to them. But it is to claim that every faithful reading is one that explicitly seeks to do something with what is read, to redeploy concepts, and send them out into the world reborn. This is what it means, for Deleuze and Guattari, to be a friend to the concept.[136]

There is no doubt vulnerability, on Deleuze and Guattari's part, to Serge Leclaire's accusation that this book-machine functions like scripture, far too well for it to be trusted.[137] This is why, as Massumi and others have noted, we must resist the temptation to make it work too well:[138] Only reading deviations can make the machine work nonscripturally.[139] A faithful reading of the machine necessarily drifts and overemphasises some concepts over others. Such movements hope to set in play an overflow of the text into something entirely new.[140] Deleuze and Guattari's conception of the book as machine entails a profound recognition of the rupture that makes faithful readings possible. It assumes that a work can only be read as and through its successive redeployment and that without doubt this necessitates a certain betrayal.[141] An intervention into and beyond their work is the only way in which Deleuze and Guattari can be drawn on faithfully. It is according to such an understanding of the work that this book plugged the problem of politics and suicide into the book-machine, to see what it could do. One might say in the style of Badiou that this has been a work of fidelity to the text as a machine.[142] Thinking the relationship between politics and suicide is an exercise in reading *Capitalism and Schizophrenia*.

The intermingled menace and potential of machines is an understandable concern today. Machines deterritorialise; they exceed their mechanical constraints, reoperationalise their circuits, deviate from original functions and gather affects. They are all too easily weaponized. To brand reading as a machine process is to recognise its cutting edge. Deleuze and Guattari's work is often defined, in the literature, by the distance, both temporally and conceptually, between its two constitutive texts. *A Thousand Plateaus* is often read as a retreat from a dogmatic edge that is evident in *Anti-Oedipus*, by developing the problematic, indeed fascistic, character of deterritorialisation in some contexts.[143] What might appear to be a reductive position in *Anti-Oedipus* is certainly supplied with greater clarity in the later text. One of the central contentions of this work has been that whereas *A Thousand Plateaus* emphasised the dangers of deterritorialisation, in no way does it abandon the political philosophy articulated in *Anti-Oedipus*. The relationship between political creativity and suicide is that which is constitutively in play across both volumes.[144] In this sense, one might be tempted to suggest that reading *Capitalism and Schizophrenia* as a whole requires the thought that has been our central concern here. At stake here is not the spectre of an abandoned dogma haunting the text, but its commitment to productively wounding its readers.

The book is the original man-machine interface. To read faithfully is not to reapply another's thought, or act autonomously with respect to the material; it is to integrate pages into one's own circuitry, to plug in and deterritorialise. As a machine process, reading is always potentially revolutionary to the same degree it wounds us. Faithful practice requires we take flight. *Capitalism and Schizophrenia* is an itinerant text; it was built to insist the reader engages in ambulant creation. There are lessons here concerning the vitality in all man-machine interfaces. Creative experimentation, seeking new modes of subjectification though openness to becomings of all kinds is the only way we can face head-on the encounter with death.[145] To seek to preclude pathological repetitions, equilibrium traps or mass extinctions once and for all though a single defensive method or anchor can only be doomed to failure. To be an effective experimenter, to be a faithful reader, is a question of pragmatics: Machines have all manner of lines and intensities. There is never simply a question of application. Plugging in is how you work the machine.

Notes

1. As famously articulated in Michael Bakunin's claim that 'the passion for destructive is a creative passion too' (M. Bakunin, "Reaction in Germany from the Notebooks of a Frenchman" [as Jules Elysard] (essay) 1842, *The Anarchist Library*, https://archive.org/stream/al_Michail_Bakunin_The_Reaction_in_Germany_From_the_Notebooks_of_a_Frenchman_a4/Michail_Bakunin_The_Reaction_in_Germany_From_the_Notebooks_of_a_Frenchman_a4#page/n1/mode/2up).
2. H. P. Newton, *Revolutionary Suicide* (London: Wildwood House, 1974).
3. Ibid., p. 4.
4. Ibid.
5. Ibid.
6. Ibid., p. 5.
7. Ibid.
8. Bakunin denied involvement in the *Catechism of the Revolutionist*, having written a work with a very similar title, and a letter from Bakunin on 2 June 1870, now in the Bibliothèque Nationale, has him lambast Nechayev for writing a catechism of brigands damaging to the cause of liberty.
9. M. Bakunin, *Bakunin on Anarchism*, ed. S. Dolgoff (Montreal: Black Rose Books, 1980): 'To save France, the whole country must be turned into a desert. All houses blown up. All cities burnt to the ground. everything the bourgeoisie holds dear, capital, industry, commerce, in short, the whole land must be turned into one vast cemetery' (p. 412).
10. Ibid.
11. Ibid.
12. S. Nechayev, *Catechism of the Revolutionist* (London: Kropotkin's Lighthouse, 1971).
13. Ibid., p. 1.
14. The 'cold passion of revolutionary cause' displaces all warmth or sentiment. 'Day and night he must have only none thought, one aim – inexorable destruction. Striving

unfalteringly towards this aim, he must be ready to perish himself and to destroy with his own hands everything that hinders its realisation' (ibid., p. 6).
15. 'He is not a revolutionary if he is attached to anything in this world, if he can stop before the annihilation of any situation, relation or person belonging to this world' (ibid., pp. 11, 13).
16. Ibid.
17. For Guevara, willingness to die is definitive of the 'nobility' of guerrilla strategy that, looking beyond immediate tactical objective, goes on to decisively to achieve an ideal, to establish a new society, as is thus part of its distinctive 'fighting attitude'. Indeed 'the guerrilla combatant ought to risk his life whenever necessary and be ready to die without the least sign of doubt.' C. Guevara, *Guerrilla Warfare* (Lanham, MD: Rowman & Littlefield, 2002), p. 12.
18. Ibid., pp. 34, 82.
19. R. Debray, *Revolution in the Revolution. Armed Struggle and Political Struggle in Latin America* (London: Penguin Books, 1967), p. 57.
20. Ibid., p. 24.
21. Indeed 'to risk all means that, having risen in the mountains, the fighters must wage a war to death, a war that does not admit of truces, retreats, or compromises' (ibid., p. 58).
22. Mao saw 'China [a]s littered all over with dry firewood which will soon be kindled into a conflagration. The proverb "a single spark can start a prairie fire" appropriately describes how the current situation will develop. We need only to look at the development of the Workers' strike, peasants uprisings, soldiers' mutinies and students' strikes in many places to see that it will undoubtedly not take long for these "sparks" to become "a prairie fire".' See M. Tse-tung, *A Single Spark Can Start a Prairie Fire* (Peking: Foreign Language Press, 1953), p. 10.
23. Ibid., p. 173.
24. M. Tse-tung, *The Red Guard's Handbook*, trans. Stewart Fraser (Nashville, TN: George Peabody, 1967), pp. 181, 185.
25. 'All men must die, but death can vary in its significance. The ancient Chinese writer Szuma Chien said, "though death befalls all men alike, it may be heavier than Mount Tai or lighter than a feather." To die for the people is heavier than mount Tai, but to work for the exploiters and oppressors is lighter than a feather'. Tse-tung 1967, p. 174.
26. Newton 1974, p. 50.
27. Ibid., p. 6.
28. Newton argues that 'a revolutionary death is the reality and victory the dream. Because the revolutionary lives so dangerously, his survival is a miracle' (ibid., p. 6).
29. Newton 1974, p. 7.
30. Ibid.
31. Ibid.
32. Ibid., p. 6.
33. Ibid., p. 7: 'Is the government of the United States suicidal? I think so.'
34. V.S. Naipaul saw 'an idealism that had already gone wrong, that had already lost its way and been twisted out of shape in the promiscuous chaos of the sixties'. V.S. Naipaul, *Journey to Nowhere: A New World Tragedy* (New York: Simon & Schuster, 1980), p. 297.
35. Jean Clancy: 'How we as human beings can, with the best of intentions proceed along such a path and end in total catastrophe ... I mean, I don't believe the Peoples temple was that unique'. (quoted in L. Fondakowski, *Stories from Jonestown*, Minneapolis: University of Minnesota Press, 2013, p. 169).
36. Whose faith healing and social activism in the early 1950s was a key influence on Jones, see C.E. Lincoln and L. Mamiya, "Daddy Jones and the Father Divine," in *Peoples Temple and Black Religion in America*, ed. R. Moore, A.B. Pinn, and M.R. Sawyer (Bloomington: Indiana University Press, 2004).

37. See Hall, John R. *Gone from the promised land: Jonestown in American cultural history*. Transaction Publishers, 1987.
38. The most important of these was the defection of Grace Stoens, whose son John remained in the Temple with Jim Jones and her husband Tim. It was an open belief in the church that John was in fact Jim Jones's son, and he was treated as the heir to the throne. Grace Jones decided, around this time, that she wanted custody over John, and was about to go through the courts (a case she, as biological mother, would have won).
39. C. Krause, *Guyana Massacre* (New York: Berkley, 1978), p. 119.
40. Ryan also had a direct, though not close, personal link to someone with family in the Temple.
41. Jones was another matter; paranoid and seemingly unwell, he responded poorly and evasively to questioning.
42. M. Kilduff and R. Javers. *The Suicide Cult: The Inside Story of the Peoples Temple Sect and the Massacre in Guyana* (New York: Bantam Books, 1978); Krause 1978.
43. J. Mills, *Six Years with God: Life inside the Reverend Jim Jones Peoples Temple* (New York: A&W, 1979), p. 318.
44. Such as E. Feinsod, *Awake in a Nightmare: Jonestown, the Only Eyewitness Account* (New York: W.W. Norton, 1981). Personal accounts that move beyond the group of ex-members associated with the concerned relatives – who showed themselves to be willing to embellish their accounts to fit the death cult narrative – show a much broader range of experiences and feelings about the Peoples Temple amongst the members of the Temple.
45. Barring of course, the presence of children involved. A single dissenter to the act was debated by Jones before being shouted down (she would eventually participate in the mass suicide), and then member after member took the stand to declare their assent to the act.
46. L. Johnson in Fondakowski 2013, p. 182.
47. Claimed by Jones to be a safer geographical zone. Jones during this period also spent a considerable period in Brazil, apparently because the southern hemisphere would escape most devastation. D. Chidester, *Salvation and Suicide: An Interpretation of Jim Jones, the Peoples Temple, and Jonestown* (Bloomington: Indiana University Press, 1991), p. 109.
48. The move to Ukiah in the Redwood Valley clearly had other core motivations behind it for Jones, specifically as a response to the rise in local hostility and media attention, but also the departure, under the accusation of insufficient radicalism, of a number of key young people.
49. See J.R. Hall, *Gone from the Promised Land: Jonestown in American Cultural History* (New Brunswick, NJ: Transaction, 1987). As Hall notes, the sense of a 'crushing embrace' by powerful enemies drove Jones to accelerate the disciplinary dynamics within Jonestown, which alienated more members, ironically realising the Concerned Relatives' worst fears. Despite mapping the affective dynamics of this clash, even Hall privileges unified semiosis over the assemblage of desire here, principally, the search for immortality. Hall thus reads the Jonestown suicides as the fulfilment of a universal pattern of theological response, in contexts of conflict between persecuted religious minorities and extant political orders. That suicide, however, may be attributed to the religious strand, is explicitly stated by Hall: 'Jones followers could create a kind of immortality that is not really a possibility for political revolutionaries. They could abandon apocalyptic hell by the act of mass suicide' (p. 229), shut out the opponents of the temple, and realise the '"promised land" so common in religious mythology'. The mass suicide was thus the result of a religious regime of signs, which allowed them to '[seek] immortality in death' (p. 303). It was only the combination of modern methods with an 'ancient theology' which made mass suicide possible and meaningful, as the final expression of a division of the sacred community from the profane world, through a prophetic vision of the Promised Land (p. 74; see also Chidester 1991, p. 166). This

established the priority of a religious regime of signs organised around a religious concept of 'exodus' for Hall.
50. 'I'd just as soon bring it to a gallant, glorious, screaming end, a screeching stop in one glorious moment of triumph' (Chidester 1991, p. 128).
51. The two principal texts on the subject, Chidester (1991) and Hall (1987), assume that the Jonestown suicide must be understood though exploring how the Peoples Temples mixed religious with political content. For Hall,

> the key to understanding mass suicide at Jonestown lies in recurrent dynamics of conflict between religious communities claiming autonomy and external political orders. In the general case a demand to submit to the external order forces a choice within the community between the sacred and evil. The choice brings religious conviction to a question of honour and is the seedbed of martyrdom. (p. 296)

For Chidester, who is primarily a scholar of religion, the Peoples Temple organised bodies in space and time according to a universal pattern present in religious movements. In mapping the way in which Jones gave spatial and temporal significance to the Peoples Temple, Chidester argues that we can see in their suicidal actions a search for redemption or salvation from dehumanisation. In the face of perceived exclusion from the human, the Jonestown mass suicide must be understood as an attempt to declaim their humanity. This process, Chidester argues, is a common feature of religious sacrifice, which as noted at the outset includes several strands of meaning, of seeking to transform the status of an oppressed community. Chidester recognises that 'every religious worldview inevitably has a political dimension in its concern for meaning and exercise of power within human social relations' (1991, p. 166), but what gave the Jonestown massacre meaning was a religious dynamic, affirming religion as a means to achieve and instantiate the salvation of the human (p. 169). Clearly Chidester reserves the ontological primacy for the religious dimension of the suicidal act. Jonestown's act of revolutionary mass suicide was, for Chidester, an attempt to achieve a revolution of meaning against dehumanisation: to declare the humanity of the community in the face of exclusion. Just as in biopolitical readings of suicide bombings discussed in chapter 4, the Jonestown mass suicide becomes part of an abstract sacrificial will to the affirmation of human dignity. For Chidester, then, mass suicide is a fundamentally religious response to a sense of excommunication from the human: 'As proud Black Socialists, they could achieve a fully human death, by avoiding a subhuman death, through a single superhuman act' (p. 159).
52. Just as took place with the old Believers, for whom the rise and fall of moderate leaderships was much more important in the dynamics of mass suicides that the far from universal fact of excommunication. T. Robbins, "Religious Mass Suicide before Jonestown: The Russian Old Believers," *Sociology of Religion* 47, no. 1 (1986): 1–20. This argument may be found in both Hall (1987) and Chidester (1991).
53. Confessing to all number of crimes, but often past child molesting (Feinsod 1981, p. 95).
54. 'Empowered by him, empowered by god, empowered by sex, empowered by thrills, empowered by ideology, whatever it is. Empowered. And they took it on. If there ever was an example when power corrupts absolutely, this was it. We don't think of young women leading the death march, brutalizing others under their control, but they did. They did it with an incredible sense of control and power, They did it with love in their hearts' (Katsaris quoted in Fondakowski 2013, p. 135).
55. Homosexual confession was particularly important for men in the inner circle – apparently playing an important role in Tim Stoens's critical defection to the Concerned Relatives in 1977.
56. F. Guattari, *Chaosophy* (Los Angeles: Semiotext(e), 2009), p. 223.

57. Feinsod 1981, p. 106.
58. Hall 1987.
59. The Stoenses took the new surname, Mills, after leaving the Temple.
60. Throughout this period Jones was seen very irregularly, and claimed that he was exploring avenues for a further flight to Russia.
61. Odell Rhodes:

> it would always come around to what we were going to do when they attacked us. sometimes we'd talk fighting, and then he'd remind us we couldn't fight the Guyanese, and then other pop, would bring up various alternatives, but he'd keep shaking his head and ruling them all out . . . he was trying to make people understand how serious it was – to let them know we were all in this together, and we damn well better be prepared to see it though all the way to the end – whatever it was. He wanted people to say they were willing to die. There was a whole lot of talk about whether people were willing to die for their beliefs or not and he was always telling people there were a whole lot of things worse than dying for your beliefs. He said living against your beliefs was living in hell – and, if you were dead, well – at least you were free. I don't know if I agreed with all that exactly, but to me it was real simple. shit I spent eight fucking years in the army ready to die for a country that hadn't done balls for me. I was damn well ready to die for Jonestown – it that's what it came down to. (quoted in Feinsod 1981, p. 135)

62. Thus his "ambivalence" about the concept of immortality. See Chidester 1991, p. 124.
63. As Jones put it: 'We can't go Back' (Fondakowski 2013, p. 238).
64. As Harris and Watermen note, unlike the Black Panthers, who fought on the streets of Oakland, Watts, Harlem, Detroit and Chicago to try and bring a better life for those who lived there, the Peoples Temple turned inwards. D. Harris and A. Johnson Waterman, "To Die for the Peoples Temple: Religion and Revolution after Black Power," in *Peoples Temple and Black Religion in America*, ed. R. Moore et al. (Bloomington: Indiana University Press, 2004), p. 118.
65. As Naipaul argues, soon after, ecological and mystical fancies would come to offer a much more risk-free alternative to political action. See Naipaul 1980, pp. 297, 266.
66. Of which the Weathermen and Symbionese Liberation Army were simply other examples.
67. Collier, S. J. and A. Lakoff (2009). *On Vital Systems Security*. Paper presented at the University of Helsinki Collegium, Helsinki, Finland, June 2008. The New School International Affairs Working Paper 2009–01. February 2009. p3–3. See U. Beck, *Risk Society: Towards a New Modernity* (London: Sage, 1992); U. Beck, *World Risk Society* (Cambridge: Polity, 1999).
68. The transpolitics of impure war (P. Virilio and S. Lotringer, *Pure War: Twenty-Five Years Later*, Los Angeles: Semiotext(e), 2007, p. 7).
69. G. Deleuze, *Foucault* (Paris: Continuum, 1999).
70. Reid and Dillon potentially to lead to disastrous futures (J. Reid and M. Dillon, *The Liberal Way of War: Killing to Make Life Live*, London: Routledge, 2009).
71. G. Deleuze, "Postscript on the Societies of Control," *October* 59 (1992): 3–7.
72. Newman in M. Poster and D. Savat, *Deleuze and New Technology* (Edinburgh: Edinburgh University Press, 2009), p. 107.
73. 'The logic which underwrites this is rather simple. With it understood that the most effective way to confront the problem of emergence is to deal with it on your terms, then the "best option is to help make it proliferate more." Indeed, perhaps the only feasible way one can fight an unspecified threat is to "actively contribute to producing it"' (B. Evans, "Terror in All Eventuality," *Theory & Event* 13, no. 3 [2010]: 11). C. Aradau and R. Van Munster, "Governing Terrorism and the (Non-)Politics of Risk," *Political Science Publications, Sydannsk University* 11 (2005).
74. Reid and Dillon, 2009, p. 131.

75. M. Dillon, "Governing Terror: The State of Emergency of Biopolitical Emergence," *International Political Sociology* 1, no. 1 (2007): 7–28, 24.
76. Virilio and Lotringer 2007, p. 152.
77. Ibid., p. 3.
78. P. Virilio, *The University of Disaster* (Cambridge: Polity, 2010), p. 8.
79. P. Virilio, *City of Panic* (Oxford: Berg, 2005), p. 8.
80. As it is for Baudrillard (J. Baudrillard and I. H. Grant, *Symbolic Exchange and Death*, London: Sage, 1993).
81. Virilio and Lotringer 2007, p. 139.
82. P. Virilio, *Negative Horizon* (New York: Continuum, 2005), p. 176.
83. Ibid., p. 178.
84. P. Virilio, *A Landscape of Events* (Cambridge, MA: MIT Press, 2000), p. 63.
85. Virilio 2005.
86. Virilio and Lotringer 2007, p. 5.
87. Ibid., p. 70.
88. Virilio 2000, p. 56; Virilio and Lotringer 2007, p. 10.
89. Virilio and Lotringer 2007, p. 5.
90. Ibid., p. 11.
91. Virilio 2000, p. 54.
92. Virilio and Lotringer 2007, p. 93.
93. Ibid., p. 33.
94. Ibid., p. 51.
95. Ibid., p. 19.
96. Ibid., pp. 51, 47.
97. As we speed up, our phenomenological experience of the world is bereft of its spatial referents; territorial (political) distance is literally dephenomenalized. The accident in Time is the other side of the spatial collapse which has followed the acceleration of society. Society now exists in the pure time of a radical instantaneity. The global village is in fact a totalitarianism of the moment (ibid., p. 222).
98. Ibid., p. 222. In globalisation, therefore, the 'euthanasia of humanity is at issue' (p. 37).
99. Ibid., p. 230; Virilio 2010, p. 4.
100. Virilio and Lotringer 2007, p. 50.
101. Ibid., p. 223.
102. Virilio 2000, p. 53.
103. P. Virilio, *The Politics of the Very Worst: An Interview with Philippe Petit* (New York: Semiotext(e), 1999), p. 33.
104. Virilio and Lotringer 2007, p. 7.
105. A 'Museum of Accidents' is necessary to unmask industries' other face. The accident museum aims to make us aware of the integral accident it is 'a museum to what crops up impromptu'.
106. Virilio 2000, p. 56. The arrogance of risk leads it to extremist feats. In this way, for Virilio, technologies of risk replace the ideologies of totalitarian regimes, both in their historical role and in the havoc they cause. Risk-technologies are animated by a kind of fascist 'will to power' because they 'ignore the accident' (Virilio 2010, p. 128).
107. Virilio 2010, p. 66.
108. Virilio and Lotringer 2007, p. 138.
109. P. Virilio and S. Lotringer, *Pure War* (New York: Semiotext, 1997), p. 136; also quoted in Redhead 2004, p. 117.
110. Virilio and Lotringer 2007, p. 152.
111. Theirs is, after all, a machinic vision of life.
112. Virilio and Lotringer 2007, p. 153.
113. 'Cancerous tissue: each instant, each second, a cell becomes cancerous, mad, proliferates and loses its configuration, takes over everything; the organism must resubmit it to its rule or restratify it, not only for its survival, but also to make possible an

escape' (G. Deleuze and F. Guattari, *A Thousand Plateaus*, London: Continuum, 2004b, p. 180).
114. Peter Hallward, *Out of This World: Deleuze and the Philosophy of Creation* (London: Verso, 2006).
115. I am indebted to Crogan on this point. See Patrick Crogan, "Theory of State: Deleuze, Guattari and Virilio on the State, Technology and Speed," *Angelaki: Journal of the Theoretical Humanities* 4, no. 2 (1999): 144.
116. Deleuze and Guattari 2004b, p. 193.
117. Ibid., p. 183.
118. Ibid.
119. Ibid., pp. 178–179.
120. Ibid., p. 179.
121. Ibid., p. 178.
122. This is Foucault's point regarding 'working on ones suicide' (see J. Miller, *The Passion of Michel Foucault*, New York: Simon & Schuster, 1993, p. 351).
123. Deleuze and Guattari 2004b, p. 178.
124. B. Noys, *Malign Velocities: Acceleration and Capitalism* (London: Zero Books, 2014), pp. 70, 74.
125. Guattari 2009, p. 108.
126. Deleuze 1992, p. 4.
127. Here Deleuze and Guattari's claim echoes with Foucault's injunction to 'work on one's suicide throughout one's life'. It also seems clear that caution's distance from Badiou's understanding of revolutionary humility is slight; the difference is simply that Deleuze and Guattari see only the counter-revolutionary impulse in the turn to lack (slow down). Caution remains revolutionary only inasmuch as it categorically refuses the order of lack.
128. See M.J. Rees, *Our Final Century* (London: Heinemann, 2003).
129. F. Guattari, *The Three Ecologies* (London: Continuum, 2008), p. 44.
130. Manfred Frank (2001), for example, was so mystified by their style that he accused them developing a discourse the only purpose of which is to 'lock out the reader' (p. 1271). Frank reads only a 'delirious chatter running through dozens of pages, causing all connections to sink into a swamp of retractions and unredeemed preinterpretations' (p. 1267). M. Frank, "The World as Will and Representation: Deleuze and Guattari's Critique of Capitalism as Schizo-analysis and Schizo-discourse," in *Deleuze and Guattari: Critical Assessments of Leading Philosophers*, ed. G. Genosko (London: Routledge, 2001).
131. See B. Massumi, *A User's Guide to* Capitalism and Schizophrenia: *Deviations from Deleuze and Guattari* (Cambridge, MA: MIT Press, 1992).
132. 'In that it is ceaselessly creating new concepts. The only condition is that these should have a necessity, as well as a strangeness, and they have both to the extent they respond to real problems. Concepts are what stops thought being mere opinion, a view, an exchange of views, gossip' (Deleuze, G., Ed. (1995). *Negotiations*. New York, Colombia University Press. p. 136).
133. See Deleuze and Guattari 2004b; interview with Guattari in C.J. Stivale, *The Two-Fold Thought of Deleuze and Guattari: Intersections and Animations* (New York: Guilford Press, 1998). As against totalisation 'al la Hegel', see G. Deleuze and F. Guattari, *Anti-Oedipus* (London: Continuum, 2004a), p. xiv. As Massumi points out, the work 'does not pretend to have the final word' (1992, p. 7).
134. Massumi 1992, p. 8; also quoted in E. Holland, *Deleuze and Guattari's* Anti-Oedipus: *Introduction to Schizoanalysis* (London: Routledge, 1999), p. xii.
135. S. Zizek, *Organs without Bodies: On Deleuze and Consequences* (London: Routledge, 2004); I. Buchanan, ed., *A Deleuzean Century?* (Durham, NC: Duke University Press, 1999).

136. G. Deleuze, F. Guattari et al., *What Is Philosophy?* (London: Verso, 1994). Accusations that Deleuze and Guattari's 'non representational and non anthropological' concepts are little more than a mask, or trick that 'confers a kind of immunity' from criticism on their work, therefore fail to recognise the expressively creative functionality of their conceptual machinism (C. L. Miller, "The Postidentitarian Predicament in the Footnotes of *A Thousand Plateaus*: Nomadology, Anthropology and Authority," in *Deleuze and Guattari: Critical Assessments of the Leading Philosophers*, ed. G. Genosko, Routledge: 2001, p. 1119). Far from simply a meaningless semiotic anarchism, the conceptual plethora this serves a rigorous theoretical, if explicitly destructive, function (see Frank 2001, p. 1276).
137. Leclaire quoted in Guattari, 2009:

> The machine of the book . . . puts [their] readers, if they are somewhat perceptive, in a situation that leaves them only the prospect of being absorbed, digested, tied up and quashed in the admirable operationality of this machine . . . [which is] . . . perfectly totalising, absorbing, liable to integrate and absorb all the questions one might be tempted to raise. (p. 77)

138. Buchanan 1999, p. 2; see Deleuze in Guattari, 2009, p. 79.
139. Massumi 1992, p. 8.
140. See Buchanan (1999), who has cogently pointed out that to read faithfully 'one must take to heart Deleuze and Guattari's axiom that philosophy progresses only by succession. Deleuze's work must be treated as an arrow that has hit its target and now waits to be fired once more from a newly strung bow' (p. 2).
141. As Buchanan (1999) puts it, 'to be Deleuzean one must abandon Deleuze' (p. 2). See Kaufman (2004) for an excellent discussion of this Deleuzean paradox vis-à-vis Zizek and Badiou. E. Kaufman, "Betraying Well," *Criticism* 46, no. 4 (2004): 651–659.
142. Reading *Capitalism and Schizophrenia* is perhaps paradigmatically antiscriptural.
143. See this point in Stivale 1998, p. 29. As Holland (1999) suggests, this may be precisely why 'the second volume of *Capitalism and Schizophrenia* has proven more durable or popular than the first.'
144. Here this book is in disagreement with Brent Adkins, who argues that death 'becomes something not worth talking about' in *A Thousand Plateaus*. Whilst certainly far less explicitly discussed than in *Anti-Oedipus*, which has psychoanalysis as its central referent; the concept of the 'suicidal line of flight' in the later text is seen here as the direct extension of the death-problematic developed in the former. B. Adkins, *Death and Desire in Hegel, Heidegger and Deleuze* (Edinburgh: Edinburgh University Press, 2007), p. 195.
145. Guattari 2008, p. 44.

Index

Anti-Oedipus 23–4, 26–7, 67–9, 103–4, 108, 110, 179
Arendt, Hannah 4, 6, 138
acceleration, accelerate 23, 28, 63, 78, 84, 102, 172, 175, 177
accident 103, 171, 172, 173, 174, 175, 176
Agamben, Giorgio 11, 136–9, 141, 143, 144

Badiou, Alain 4, 10, 32–42, 67, 70, 72, 73, 74, 77, 80, 81, 110, 112, 172, 177, 179
Baudrillard, Jean 4, 11, 107–15, 149, 173, 176
Bataille, Georges 8, 9, 106, 110, 138
Benjamin, Walter, 65, 109
biopolitics 135–7, 139–41, 143, 150–1, 172; body 137; diagram, contemporary 149, 151; government 136–7, 142–3; liberal 146, 151; modes 135–6, 140–1
biopower 134–43, 149–52, 171; contemporary 140, 150; regimes of 136, 138
Bouazizi, Mohammed 1, 10, 57–9, 61, 62, 66
Bolt, Neville 62, 63

capitalism 21–2, 27, 34, 103, 105–7, 109, 115, 150
Capitalism and Schizophrenia (Deleuze and Guattari) 9, 20–1, 73
capitalist society 106–7 catastrophe 2, 9, 17, 22, 37, 38, 39, 44, 69, 82, 83, 84, 85, 100, 142, 174, 175, 176, 178
Canetti, Elias 133
cherry blossom 29–32
Clastres, Pierre 102–5, 115
Clausewitz 22, 83
Cold War 11, 82–5, 114
community, political 137, 178

conflict 15, 63, 81
contingent events 149, 174
counter-actualisation 70, 73, 81
creativity 11, 20, 22, 40, 76, 99, 112, 132, 148–9, 171, 173, 176, 178; political 9, 180
critique, political 139, 175
cult, and revolution 163–80

Davison, Emily Wilding 101
death 7–11, 15–19, 25–6, 37, 39–44, 64–76, 81, 99–116, 130–43, 145–8, 150–2, 163–6, 168, 171–3, 175–8; camps 137–8; coding 105, 108, 111; drive 38, 69; event of 114, 116; events and 70; impulse 40; individual 77, 141; instinct 18, 106, 110, 131; life through 17; living 137, 165; model of 66–9, 76, 146, 150, 175; reclaiming 134, 140; sacrificial 172; sentence 131, 134; spaces 137, 140; symbolic 108, 112–13
death-in-life 138
debts 104–5, 108, 130–1, 169
decoded flows 103, 111
decoding 21, 81, 103–5, 107, 109; death 106
Derrida, Jacques 65
despot 32, 105–6, 130–1, 133
despotic regime 21, 130, 133
despotic state 22, 130
desire 3, 9, 11, 15, 18–24, 26, 28–30, 33, 36, 37, 39, 41, 42, 59–61, 66–70, 77–82, 99, 101–7, 110–12, 115, 126, 127, 129, 130, 131, 144, 148, 150, 151, 168–73, 177
desiring-machine 21, 25, 67, 69, 80, 169, 170
deterrence, nuclear 83–4

deterritorialisation 20–1, 23, 26–7, 36, 39, 73–4, 76, 78–81, 102–3, 130, 132, 171–2, 174–5, 177, 179; relative 20–1; technological 172–3, 175
Devji, Faisal, 144, 145, 146
disaster 35, 37, 82, 83, 172, 173, 176, 178

evental contingency 143, 148
experimentation 20, 27, 177, 178, 180
excess 7–9, 18, 32, 33, 34, 35, 36, 37, 39, 64–6, 74, 77, 97, 99, 102, 110, 146, 147, 151, 152, 171, 175–8
excessive 1, 7, 8, 22, 34, 35, 36, 37, 41, 44, 110
Esposito 131

fascism 10, 18, 22–6, 28, 31, 35–6, 40, 42–4, 128, 169, 178
fascists 18, 23, 32, 41–2, 84
Feldman, Allen 101
fidelity 34–5, 37, 39, 44, 73, 81, 112, 171, 179
Fierke, Karin 58, 59, 61–3
Fitzgerald, Scott 75
Figner, Vera 100
finitude 7, 35, 37–8, 40, 66, 71, 81, 142, 145, 148, 151, 166, 178; human 37, 40, 141–4, 146
force-feeding 99–101
Freud 18, 68
Foucault, Michel 4, 11, 131, 134, 135, 136, 138, 141, 142, 143, 147, 148, 149, 150, 151, 171, 173

Girard, Rene 64–5
Guantanamo Bay 99–100, 102, 114

Hagakure 16, 42, 43
Hardt and Negri 140, 141
Hegel, G. W. F. 4–6, 8, 19
Heidegger, Martin 4, 6–8, 17, 19
holy terror 128
Hobbes, Thomas, 4–7
human bomb 11, 84, 126–52
humanity 68, 107, 137, 145
human life, liberalism's logistics of 145
human subject 68
hunger, politics of 11, 100
hunger strikers 65, 100–2, 113–15
hunger strikes 9–11, 62, 64, 66, 99–116

immanent mortal risks 143–4
immanent necropolitics 144–5

immolations 26, 59–60
immortality 109
inscription, of body 101–2, 104, 108
Islamism, political 36

Japan 16, 23, 29, 31, 32, 40, 41, 42
Japanese suicide state 32
Jones, Jim 166–7, 171
Jonestown 166–8, 170–1, 176

Khan, Mohammad Siddique 141, 144, 146

Lacan 19, 38, 111
lack, lacking 3, 7, 8, 16, 19, 20, 33, 34, 35, 37, 39, 40, 41, 42, 43, 59, 61, 68, 81, 99, 107, 108, 115, 134, 144, 151, 177, 178
labour 65, 72, 109
language, minor 132
Land, Nick 27, 68
last glass 99
liberalism 137, 140–4, 146–7, 152, 172
line of flight 4, 22, 24, 25, 26, 27, 28, 30, 31, 34, 36, 42, 70, 76, 77, 79, 80, 102, 133, 171, 176
liberal life 144, 146
liberal suicides 134
life taking death hostage 109
The Logic of Sense (Deleuze) 72, 73
long live death 25, 30

machine 18–26, 29–32, 39, 40, 42, 43, 44, 67–9, 75, 78, 82–5, 103, 104, 107, 111, 112, 115, 129, 130, 147, 166, 169, 170, 173, 177–80
machinic 68, 69, 172, 175, 176
Mauss and Hubert, 60, 64
martial death 16, 31
martyrdom 2, 126, 128, 129, 130, 138
mass suicides 9–10
Meiji regime 15–16, 30, 42–3
Metzger, Gustav 84
Mishima, Yukio 10, 40–4
microfascisms 24
molecularity 21–2, 24, 26
molecular resonance machine 30–1
molar 20–5, 27–30, 32, 41, 44, 60, 62, 75, 77, 78, 79, 82, 169, 170
molarity 21, 23, 26, 41, 77
monotheism 130
morbidity 143, 145
mortality 7, 19, 37, 39, 66, 68, 72, 81, 106, 108, 134, 141–7, 151, 172–3

monotheism 130
Muslims 144, 146
mythic violence of law 65

National Socialism 24–6, 28
National Socialist movement 23, 27–8, 32
naturalistic theory 174–5
Nazi regime 25, 27–8
Nazism 23–5, 27–8, 30, 35
necropolitics 138–9
Newton, Huey 163, 164, 165, 166, 168

obscure subject 36
order-word 131–4, 141
Ohnuki-Tierney, Emiko 17, 29, 30

Palestinian suicide bombings 138
Palach, Jan 10, 11, 57, 76–85
Peoples Temple 166–71
philosophy 10–11, 17–19, 43, 70, 74–5, 175, 178; political 18, 37, 176, 178–9
pluripotency 142–4, 146–7
politicality 8, 62, 147, 175
political life 7, 11, 44, 73, 81, 84, 137, 139, 171, 176, 178; creative 176
politics 7–11, 18–20, 22–3, 33, 35–7, 39–41, 61–2, 74–6, 81–4, 101–2, 130–1, 136–9, 149–52, 171–3, 175–6; action 74–5, 102; antisovereign 149, 166; consequences 57–8; creative 81–2, 178; of death 136–9, 141; evental 114, 177; events 9, 34, 38, 74, 174; function 78, 108, 111, 178; global administrative life 136; intelligibility 139, 141, 144; liberal 143, 146, 152; of life 136–7, 139, 146; nonsovereign 9, 62, 134, 163; practice 100, 139–40; pure 149, 151; of self-burning 61, 63; sovereign death 136; spaces 8, 62, 64, 66; subject 33, 59, 61–2, 64–6, 145; suicide 116, 147, 174, 176; suicide and 9–11, 44, 84, 178–9; terrorism 128; theology 130, 135, 137, 139, 144; theorisation 9, 11, 130, 136; theory 7, 9; thought 9, 163; trials 77; violence 65, 128; vital 43, 149, 151
populations 32, 78, 80, 134–7, 139, 142–4, 151
positivity 114–15, 148, 151
power 8–9, 40, 61, 63, 70, 72, 77–8, 101, 103, 109–10, 113–14, 131–2, 134–7, 139–42, 147–50; global 115–16; political 136; zero-death 136

Prague Spring 76–83
primitive regimes 22, 103–5, 111, 115
primitive societies 103–5, 108, 111
psychoanalysis 18, 110

reforms 29, 76, 78–80
resilient life 147
resistance, political 61, 150
reterritorialisation 20–1, 81, 103, 114, 132
revolution 33, 38–9, 109; agency 151; caution 177; deterritorialisation 26, 112, 175; events 20, 33, 38–9, 44, 175; flight 36, 44; life 81, 172; nationalisms 25, 27; politics 10–11, 19–20, 32, 34, 38–40, 109, 134, 150, 163, 166, 176; project 33; subjects 33, 35, 37; suicide 163, 165–6, 168
risk suicide 73

sacrifice, political 60, 64
sacrificial rites 60, 63–4
Sands, Bobby 62, 66, 101–2
Schizophrenia 9, 20, 23, 27, 33, 70, 73, 152, 179–80
Schmitt, Carl, 28, 130, 136
self-annihilation 62, 64–5
self-burnings 9, 57, 59, 63–4
self-destruction 8–9, 15, 43, 62, 64, 150, 172, 178; political 58, 84
self-immolation 59–60, 63, 74
self-incinerations 10–11, 57–8, 63
self-sacrifice 11, 60–2, 113, 139; political 61
September 11th 113–16
Seery, John 4, 6, 135, 136
slave life 138
social life 60, 64, 104, 106, 108, 111
social movement 23–4, 29–30
social order 22, 27, 62, 64–5, 101–2, 105–6, 108, 164
Societies of Control 171, 172
sovereign necropolitics 140, 144
sovereign order 62–3, 66, 131
sovereign politics 144
sovereign power 131, 134, 137, 141
sovereign semiosis 62, 64–6
sovereignty 61–3, 65, 131, 134–8, 163, 166; of law 64–5; political 8, 137
state assemblage 30
state totalitarianism 23–5
stoic 70, 97, 143, 146
stoicism 16, 70, 176
subjectivity, fractured 19

subjectivization 68
suffragettes, hunger-striking 100–1
suicidal flight 99, 141; war machine's 31
suicidalism 24–6, 30, 115
suicide 8–11, 15–17, 23–6, 39–41, 44, 68, 71–4, 76–7, 81–5, 113–16, 127–31, 150–2, 163–6, 171–2, 176–80; bombers 127, 139–41, 145–7, 152; bombings 9–11, 59, 64, 126–30, 135–6, 138–41, 144–7, 174–5; collective 9, 11, 15, 84, 171; commitment 126, 164; committing 15; death 9, 64; desiring-political 24; excess 32, 171; fascist 10, 176; line of flight 23, 25–8, 30; missions 25, 128; politics of 11, 77, 81, 108–9, 131, 136, 147, 176; reactionary 163, 165; state 10, 15, 17, 22–3, 30–2; state concept 17, 26, 29; violence 128, 140, 144, 164; war machine 18, 26
superego 41
symbolic exchange 109, 111–15
Symbolic Exchange and Death 112, 115
Svitak, Ivan 80, 82, 83

Tanweer, Shehzad 145–6
terrorism 8, 11, 33, 35, 38–9, 41, 83, 103, 112–15, 126–52, 168, 172; political 128
thanatopolitical spaces 137
A Thousand Plateaus 22, 23, 68–9, 74
totalitarianisms 18, 24–6, 32, 35, 41–2, 136

transpolitical suicidalism 172
tragedy 8, 80, 127, 178
tragic 4, 5, 6, 7, 18, 31, 40, 44, 75, 80, 81, 140, 141
transpolitics 171, 174, 176
truth 8, 23–4, 34–8, 80–2, 142; event 34–7; processes 34–5, 37, 74
Thich Quang Duc 10, 57, 63

unlimited finity 147, 150–2
unconscious 19, 20, 24, 70, 104, 110, 112
Urstaat model 132, 134
Universal History 11, 21, 22, 103, 105, 106, 109, 112, 149, 150, 151, 152

violence 7–8, 63–5, 102, 112–14, 127, 164; disorder 64; divine 65–6, 109
Virilio, Paul 10–11, 23, 26, 32, 171

war machine 18, 22, 24–6, 30–2, 40, 42, 44, 83; aesthetic 30–1; suicidal state 83
War on Terror 11, 114–15, 152
Warsaw Pact 76, 79–81, 84
women 167, 169
work of art 72, 74–5

zero-death system 114–15
Zizek, Slavoj 31, 32, 33, 37–40